Teaching Writing in Globalization

Cultural Studies/Pedagogy/Activism

Series Editors

Rachel Riedner, The George Washington University
Randi Kristensen, The George Washington University
Kevin Mahoney, Kutztown University

Advisory Board

Paul Apostolidis, Whitman College; Byron Hawk, George Mason University; Susan Jarratt, University of California, Irvine; Robert McRuer, The George Washington University; Dan Moshenberg, The George Washington University; Pegeen Reichert Powell, Columbia College; Dan Smith, University of South Carolina; Susan Wells, Temple University

The Lexington Press book series Cultural Studies/Pedagogy/Activism offers books that engage questions in contemporary cultural studies, critical pedagogy, and activism. Books in the series will be of interest to interdisciplinary audiences in cultural studies, feminism, political theory, political economy, rhetoric and composition, postcolonial theory, transnational studies, literature, philosophy, sociology, Latino Studies, and many more.

Titles in Series:

Cultural Studies and the Corporate University, by Rachel Riedner and Kevin Mahoney

Democracies to Come: Rhetorical Action, Neoliberalism, and Communities of Resistance, by Rachel Riedner and Kevin Mahoney

Gramsci, Language, and Translation, edited by Peter Ives and Rocco Lacorte

Rhetorics for Community Action: Public Writing and Writing Publics, by Phyllis Mentzell Ryder

Circulating Communities: The Tactics and Strategies of Community Publishing, edited by Paula Mathieu, Steve Parks, and Tiffany Rousculp

Teaching Writing in Globalization

Remapping Disciplinary Work

Edited by Darin Payne and Daphne Desser

LEXINGTON BOOKS
Lanham • Boulder • New York • Toronto • Plymouth, UK

Published by Lexington Books
A wholly owned subsidiary of The Rowman & Littlefield Publishing Group, Inc.
4501 Forbes Boulevard, Suite 200, Lanham, Maryland 20706
http://www.lexingtonbooks.com

Estover Road, Plymouth PL6 7PY, United Kingdom

British Library Cataloguing in Publication Information Available

Library of Congress Cataloging-in-Publication Data

Teaching writing in globalization : remapping disciplinary work / edited by Darin Payne
and Daphne Desser.
    pages cm. — (Cultural studies/pedagogy/activism)
  ISBN 978-0-7391-6796-0 (cloth : alk. paper) — ISBN 978-0-7391-7244-5 (ebook)
  1. English language—Rhetoric—Study and teaching. 2. Academic writing—Study and
teaching. 3. Education and globalization. I. Payne, Darin, 1967– II. Desser, Daphne,
1965–
  PE1404.T39944 2012
  808'.042071—dc23

                                                                          2011044703

Contents

Foreword

This is not a neutral review of meanings. It is an exploration of the vocabulary of a crucial area of social and cultural discussion, which has been inherited within precise historical and social conditions and which has to be made conscious and critical – subject to change as well as to continuity – if the millions of people in whom it is active are to see it as active: not a tradition to be learned, nor a consensus to be accepted, nor a set of meanings which, because it is "our language," has a natural authority; but as a shaping and reshaping, in real circumstances and from profoundly different and important points of view: a vocabulary to use, to find our own ways in, to change as we find it necessary to change it, as we go on making our own language and history. (Williams 24)[1]

This passage is from *Keywords*, Raymond Williams's exploration of "indicative" words that show us where cultural activity is taking place. In his comprehensive review of significant words that are used to shape culture and society, Williams focuses on the social usefulness and vitality of language, the way we actively use language to create, and the literate practices through which we live our lives. For Williams, language is not just a tradition to be inherited but a vibrant social activity. Rather, it is an active "shaping and reshaping" of the available meanings of economic, political, and cultural activity, which we make and use to assert, feel for, put forth, gesture to, or conjure meaning.

For Desser and Payne, globalization is exactly the kind of pivotal and contested keyword that Williams describes. *Teaching Writing in Globalization* shares Williams's focus on our capacity to shape and reshape the vocabulary we have available, to use it to articulate profoundly different points of view, and to actively create our own history and meanings: agency. Its "significance and difficulty" (Williams 15) reveal the major role globalization plays in public discourse as well as in academic disciplines. On the one hand, it is an economic and political policy and practice invested with, and often overdetermined by,

vii

powerful interests. Globalization is used to stand in for the exercise of economic, political, and cultural power across geographical borders, and as such it appears as common sense. On the other hand, *Teaching Writing in Globalization* emphasizes that applying our critical capacities to the policies and practices of globalization opens up possibilities for critique, resistance, and/or negotiation of its various features as they evolve. Desser and Payne, and their contributors, interrogate the role of globalization in our research and teaching in order to find the openings for active participation in shaping its meanings by those of us whose daily life has been impacted by global decisions we are meant to accept, not challenge or shape.

Essays in the anthology, moreover, take into account the complex operations of globalized power at work in economic, political, cultural, biopolitical, disciplinary, and rhetorical forms and mixtures. Rather than a hasty overview of globalization that quickly moves to heroic moments of agency and resistance, the collected essays are attentive to dense conjunctures of sovereign power, political economy, and the fraught and contested ideologies that organize social institutions and practices. Each author critically and assiduously accounts for the local and global circumstances in which people act, speak, communicate, negotiate, and struggle, from Washington, DC, to New Zealand, IMF/World Bank protests to WPA work. From the specific contingencies of these different situations, they propose possibilities for critique, resistance, negotiation, and agency within specific material and rhetorical circumstances.

We are excited to offer this work as part of the Cultural Studies/Pedagogy/Activism series, as an invitation to scholars and activists in globalization, rhetoric, and cultural studies, and more, to challenge, refine, and expand the operations and meanings of globalization in each of our specific locations. The essays in *Teaching Writing in Globalization* break new ground in cultural and rhetoric studies to demonstrate how, in fraught and complex contexts of globalization, people create knowledge and teach themselves. They provide a necessary and welcome opening into the multiple contexts in which we actively (re)write and (re)read ourselves in and beyond globalization.

Rachel Riedner
Randi Gray Kristensen

Note

1. Williams, Raymond. Keywords: A Vocabulary of Culture and Society. New York: Oxford University Press, 1976.

Acknowledgments

This project took longer to complete than we initially imagined, in large part because of the unfolding and expanding economic crisis that emerged in the United States and beyond not long after we began. At the precise moment we began seeking publishers, presses began shrinking, shuttering, even folding, as states began to withhold funding to universities in ever-increasing numbers and amounts. So we felt fortunate to have found a home for this book in this particular series, one that is promoting smart and valuable projects and adding significantly to knowledge about globalization, education, culture, and politics.

The editors of this series, Rachel and Randi, not only offered us an opportunity to have it in print; they made it considerably stronger by sharpening its focus, by providing careful, timely feedback on each and every chapter, and by encouraging us and collaborating with us at multiple stages. To them, I offer my sincerest thanks and my recognition of the hard work that editing a series such as this entails. I also wish to thank our contributors, who were exceptionally patient amidst the various twists and turns that stretched the timeline of this project beyond initial expectations. Not only were the writers patient, but they revised their drafts with intellect, grace, and humility as the book emerged in its final form. Their willingness to accommodate slight shifts in audience and purpose, not to mention new information relevant to globalization and education that was unfolding during drafting stages, is reflective of their strength as scholars and as colleagues in the field. I wish I could take classes from each of them.

Finally, I wish to acknowledge the critical insights, the perseverance, and the even-tempered nature of my co-editor and colleague, Daphne, without whom this book would surely still just be an idea that we talked about one day over lunch—in gentle tradewinds and under a warm Hawaiian sun—between classes.

—DP

ix

Mahalo to Darin, Zoe, and Henry Payne, Rachel Riedner, Randi Kristensen, Phyllis Ryder, our talented contributors, and the University of Hawai'i 'ohana.
—DD

Pedagogy of the Globalized:
Education as a Practice of Intervention

Darin Payne

Like many other disciplines in the academy, Composition and Rhetoric (hereafter "comp/rhet") has begun to grapple with the implications of globalization on our disciplinary work. What began as a trickle with a few notable articles and inquiries—usually designed to draw the field's attention to what globalization even is and to indicate why it matters to our ongoing teaching, research, and service (Lu; Horner and Trimbur; Hesford; Canagarajah; Lauer)—has evolved into a steady stream of conference papers, articles, books, blog posts, and daily conversations. Such disciplinary attention has been defined as an emergent paradigm shift[1] and explicitly named as one: Wendy Hesford's use of the phrase "the global turn" to mark this moment in our field is being adopted and circulated with relative ease. In short, the floodgates are opening.

The global turn in the humanities more generally has brought with it a wide range of academic responses that run a gamut from adaptation and accommodation to critique and resistance. Where scholars and teachers lie on that admittedly reductive spectrum often depends upon how they define globalization. For some, it is a social, economic, cultural, and political shift that is so massive in scope and scale that our primary job as academics seems simply to figure out how to adapt to it. For example, as Marcelo M. Suarez-Orozco and Desiree Baolian Qin-Hilliard state in their book, *Globalization, Culture, and Education in the New Millenium*, "Globalization is generating changes of a magnitude comparable to the emergence of agriculture ten thousand years ago or the industrial revolution two hundred years ago. It will demand fundamental rethinking of the aims and processes of education" (14). Those aims and processes, in their formulation, need to be revised to "fit" the following dominant features of globali-

zation: (1) postnational forms of production and distribution of goods and services, (2) information, communication, and media technologies that facilitate
exchange and instantaneously connect people across vast geographies and place
a premium on knowledge-intensive work, (3) growing levels of world-wide mi-
gration, and (4) the resultant cultural transformations and exchanges that challenge traditional values and norms in sending and receiving countries (14). What
is noteworthy about the imperative to fit into the unfolding processes of globalization is that they are defined, implicitly at least, as a set of objective phenomena beyond our control. (I would also as a rhetorician note the ways in which, in
the above formulation, they are discursively constructed as objective phenomena.) They exist; we adapt. Results of this view include curricular remappings
that seek to equip students as "global citizens" who are at ease with transnational
structures of employment, residency, and commerce, who are capable of intercultural relations, and who are literate in globally networked digital communications.

A different way of conceiving of globalization is to recognize its processes
and products as inherently social arbitraries,[2] as malleable and open to contestation, as subjective rather than objective. To see globalization this way is to open
up possibilities for intervention—for critique, resistance, and/or negotiation of
its various features as they evolve. Those who seek to rethink education on these
grounds are also invested in producing "global citizens"; however, their global
citizens would be marked not simply by their ease or competence within the new
world order, but also by a critical awareness about that order and by their ability
to have a hand in shaping it. Education seen this way is, as Paulo Freire might
have called it, a practice of freedom. Indeed scholars in comp/rhet will readily
recognize the allusion in this essay's title to Freire's *Pedagogy of the Oppressed*,
one of our field's most influential texts and a touchstone for comp/rhet's extensive efforts to develop "liberatory," "radical," and "critical" pedagogies. While
those terms are too often conflated, they indicate overlapping related projects in
the field to actively investigate, challenge, and reform the social, economic, cultural, and political structures that shape our students' lives. Many of us studying
and teaching the arts of communication these days have been informed by, and
are committed to, these traditions to the extent that our seemingly mundane
practices of teaching writing are in effect efforts to produce discursive agents of
social change.

To be sure, many writing teachers would no doubt identify with the earlier
referenced model of pedagogical *adaptation*, seeing in globalization new communicative mediums and genres to be learned by students for their successful
integration into globalized professional contexts. For such teachers, student
agency is not to be found only in critical analyses of structural oppression nor in
challenges to systems of power; it is to be found in upward mobility via mastery
of appropriate literate practices. This should come as little surprise, given that
writing instruction has long been semi-complicit in maintaining the university's

historic role in producing literate workers for an industrialized economy. And as that economy shifts—from national and Fordist models of production and consumption to transnational, post-Fordist models of information work—so too must writing instruction shift within the framework of the university-as-workforce-supplier. This is not to suggest that such writing teachers feel ethically obligated to satisfying the needs of the managerial class; it *is* to say that many, if not most, feel ethically obligated to helping students acquire the jobs being offered by the managerial class. And to be fair, many writing teachers do their best to teach students both the skills they need in professional contexts as well as the capacities for negotiating and reforming those contexts.

Still, at the heart of the current workforce supply model—as opposed to the previous century's supply model based on industrial capitalism—is an accommodation not just to a global economy but also to the neoliberal ideology upon which much of that economy is based. Neoliberalism is not just a set of financial policies and practices favoring free markets, privatization, and deregulation; it is a language and philosophy that is rapidly transforming the social imaginaries of citizens across the globe—and often not for the better. The critiques of neoliberalism are far and wide, beyond the scope of this book; they are, nonetheless, a significant part of the context within which our work is situated and to which it contributes. For those of us presently invested in structural or systemic reforms, or education as a practice of freedom, the teaching of writing (and by extension the institutional work facilitating writing instruction) must address the transformations occurring under globalization, particularly those inflected by and constitutive of a neoliberal ideology. While that may sound like critiquing neoliberalism is our central project, it is not. We are instead working from the premise that globalization does not have to equal neoliberalism, that there are alternative models for organizing social, economic, cultural, and political relations in a moment characterized by growing global connections, communications, and movements. Moreover, we are working from the premise that all our disciplinary activities as academics—be they scholarly, pedagogical, or administrative—can be engaged by that agenda and, in keeping with comp/rhet theory and practice, that such activities are mutually enriching and often inclusive. Also in keeping with theories and practices central to comp/rhet, we believe that such work is not limited to critique, but that critique is, as Thomas P. Miller has argued, a "prelude to action" (32). In short, comp/rhet's pedagogical agenda is usually geared toward students' critical production at least as much as their critical reception of texts that have social purposes.[3]

Given those premises, our efforts to remap disciplinary work are efforts at intervention. Globalization is here to stay, but it has not arrived fully formed, nor does it exist outside of human activity. It is evolving, and we want to have a hand in its evolution. We use the term "remap" to guide this project because the mapping metaphor is particularly apt for globalization as both the subject and context of our work. We cannot think about revisions to our disciplinary activities in this moment without also thinking about the places of those activities. Moreover, postmodern geographers have revealed how mapping is an activity that constitutes reality, that reflects but also creates spaces and the relations within and among them. In remapping our disciplinary work, we are moving beyond "reforming" or "reconfiguring" it in an abstract, decontextualized sense to also considering its place in higher education and, in turn, the place of higher education in globalization. An early article in the growing literature of globalization and writing instruction—Min-Zhan Lu's "An Essay on the Work of Composition: Composing English against the Order of Fast Capitalism"—is indicative of such remapping: it is a call for those of us in the field to become more effectively cognizant of the outcomes of our curricula on other parts of our world, which is a world now ordered by global capital to systematically privilege standardized American English. Lu asks us to reimagine alternatives, inviting us to see the ways in which those reimaginings can eventually impact and change the systematic educational and everyday functions of English and, more ideally, world englishes across the globe.

The intellectual content at the heart of Lu's essay has implications for institutional reforms by writing program administrators (WPAs), for pedagogical reforms by teachers, and for new avenues of research by scholars in comp/rhet and literacy studies. That tripartite overlap among the primary domains of academic life is not merely coincidental, nor is it representative of the work of a small minority of holistic scholar-teacher-administrators in comp/rhet; it is rather a normative approach to our disciplinary work, one that is a product of comp/rhet's relatively short institutional history, its present instantiation originating mainly with open admissions policies of the 1970s and the emerging economic need to staff vast sections of basic writing courses. Many scholars see neoliberalism originating in this same time period, gaining tremendous momentum in the 1980s and 1990s—running roughly parallel in growth to the U.S. rise in comp/rhet graduate programs, scholarly journals, and institutional fixity. Comp/rhet's very existence as a mechanism in higher education's transition to providing workers for the global economy is at least in some (perhaps ironic) respects one reason behind its particular brand of layered academic work, in which theory, pedagogy, and institutional administration are interwoven routinely as a matter of course.

Thus comp/rhet's historic role in the university makes it, on the one hand, complicit in the policies, practices, and logics of a global economy informed by neoliberalism. As Sharon Crowley and Marc Bousquet have each separately demonstrated, the ways in which writing instruction is usually institutionally deployed in the United States reflects those logics and that context at work: as universities (land-grant state institutions as well as private and for-profit schools) have increasingly become marketized, they have relied on labor casualization, developing a system of writing instruction that is a model of corporate efficiency. (Bousquet has framed this condition within his "excrement theory" of capital accumulation and waste, noting that the production of PhD holders in English studies ultimately serves a process of cheap labor that eventually has to be expelled from the system to maintain its efficiency.)

On the other hand, comp/rhet's role in the university has also had the effect of making its members more cognizant of these contours of disciplinary and academic functions within the economy. As a result, or at least as a corollary, our disciplinary history is also one of struggle against the very system we belong and contribute to. (Crowley's and Bousquet's works are equally indicative of that, too.) For all our field's structural and systemic complicity vis-à-vis its raison d'être, it is nonetheless a field in which teaching, scholarship, and programmatic work are regularly constituted by institutional critiques, challenges to economic efficiency, and negotiations of (and sometimes outright resistance to) corporate ideologies and practices. Comp/rhet is a discipline whose intellectual traditions lie in the making of citizens capable of participating in democratic deliberations, capable of expressing themselves against the grain of oppressive social scripts, and capable of revising normative discourses of identity and identification. From the 1970s onward, comp/rhet's dominant schools of thought—manifested across all its disciplinary work—have been comprised of challenges to the status quo: the expressivists of the 1970s offered a direct rebuttal to the current-traditional paradigm that previously had demanded students adopt the discursive norms of the institution; the social constructivists of the 1980s revealed that those norms were neither universal nor innate but instead historically privileged and cultivated; in the 1990s, under the influence of (and sometimes in concert with) cultural studies, identity politics became central to our work, resulting in programmatic, pedagogical, and scholarly conceptions of writing and writing instruction that grappled with representations and negotiations of race, class, gender, and sexual orientation. There have of course been myriad other schools of thought that have inflected the work of comp/rhet, not the least of which has been the Freirian agendas referenced earlier, which have been sustained for three decades amidst other developments. But across the majority of trends, the questions have been similar: how do we assist the marginalized, the oppressed, the underprivileged? How do we challenge and reform systems of domination and oppression? How do we, as discourse workers, undo the debilitating effects of macro- and micro-political policies and practices emanating from the centers of power in society?

Having arrived at "the global turn" in our field, it is precisely that set of historical questions, coupled with comp/rhet's particular role in the academy, that makes its disciplinary contributions valuable to others wishing to intervene in the evolution of globalization. Academics in cultural studies, women's studies, anthropology, economics, political science, and other fields may see in comp/rhet a model of integrated contradictory engagement that is not just critical or theoretical, but also programmatic and pedagogical, often in the same instance. If it is true that we are already a part of globalization's policies, practices, and logics in the multifaceted disciplinary work we do, then it is also true that we can affect its development by working at the very nexus of research, teaching, and administration where those policies, practices, and logics can be reshaped. While critique is vital to this kind of work, it must extend beyond disciplinary journals and lecture notes; it must also be routinized in classroom exercises, departmental and university service projects, and programmatic activities like curricular design, textbook creation and adoption, assessment, and budgeting. For those of us in comp/rhet, this is the everyday. We regularly inhabit and produce what Henri Lefebvre has termed "contradictory spaces," concretizing the university's potentiality as a site of dialectic, one in which, as Chandra Mohanty has argued, hegemonic and counter-hegemonic struggles can play out.

Indeed the contributors to this collection exemplify a critical remapping of disciplinary work as both a response to and an intervention into processes and products of globalization, at least insofar as they relate to writing and writing instruction in higher education today. In the chapters that follow, the authors offer ways of reforming our disciplinary work, from new developments in rhetorical theory to specific classroom practices to program management. In each case, what is at stake is both ideology and practice; there is always an effort to understand (and to help students understand) the ways in which our lives within globalization can contribute to its evolution and become challenges to its oppressive, destructive forms. This book is not targeted, then, toward those who are uncritical of globalization or of the neoliberal ideologies so central to its current formation. Nor is it targeted toward those who conceive of themselves as "anti-globalization." The book overall tends to subscribe to Douglas Kellner's assertion that we have moved beyond simple pro and con positions relative to a process of global restructuring that is far too complex, multifaceted, and contradictory to be reductively characterized as "good" or "bad." Kellner does provide a useful alternative framework that many scholars here are either explicitly or implicitly, wittingly or unwittingly, working within—namely "top down" and "bottom up" forms of globalization. The former references the policies and practices emanating from centers of power and designed to further positions of extant privilege and control; consider as examples the roles played by the World Bank (WB), the World Trade Organization (WTO), and the International Monetary Fund (IMF)—all entities that function to manage capital for transnational elites while reforming entire nation states' fiscal policies in ways that create new markets for consumption, cheap labor for production, and expanded control by the wealthy of material resources. "Bottom-up" globalization, on the other hand, references the kinds of social activities that seek to connect and empower marginalized and/or oppressed groups from around the globe in shared struggles against various forms of domination, including those mentioned above. The Zapatistas, students against sweatshops, protests against the WTO, and the World Social Forum are all examples of globalization from below, reliant as those movements are on internetworked communications, global mobility, and cross-cultural interactions characteristic of globalization. They are also reliant on global discourses of human rights that tend to invoke allegedly self-evident, universalizing ideals analogous at least in form to neoliberalism's discourses of global markets.

As much as some of the participants in those movements might label themselves as anti-globalization, they are more precisely staking out binary positions against a narrow definition of globalization, one that is built upon neoliberal economic policy, practice, and ideology and seeks to colonize and marketize the world according to logics of late capitalism, the outcomes of which can be increased poverty, environmental degradation, and political disempowerment for whole regions, despite contrary promises of economic prosperity and political freedoms offered by neoliberal apologists (of which there are many). Consider, as one example of that particular brand of globalization, Bolivia's water wars of a decade ago. Thirty years prior, right next door in Brazil, Freire was outlining problem-posing education as a means of helping peasant students understand how their lives are subjugated by a ruling class and, importantly, how they might work to create local changes, how they might organize and agitate for, say, clean drinking water in specific communities. All well and good, but by 2000, the relations of production and consumption had shifted, as evidenced in Bolivia: San Francisco's Bechtel Corporation is part of a transnational consortium that had gained ownership over that country's drinking water. Bechtel's acquisition of such a fundamental local resource was the outcome of neoliberalizing loan terms dictated by the WB, which insisted on privatization when Bolivia sought loans to rebuild their water systems (Shiva). When local citizens protested the immediate and massive rate hikes that occurred within weeks of transnational privatization, they suffered police brutality (including tear gas and rubber bullets, leading to numerous casualties and five deaths) in a series of skirmishes that eventually led to the undoing of the contract (which had been set to last an astonishing forty years). The turning point in the water wars, it could be argued, was the global media coverage of teenager Victor Hugo Daza being shot in the face, and thus killed, by state police. In such a moment, bottom-up and top-down forms of globalization were in play at the levels of media production and distribution, corporate ownership, government control, social activism, and police suppression.

Bolivia's struggles for clean drinking water not only demonstrate the ways in which pedagogies (in this case, Freirian) must be revised for the dialectics of globalization; they also exemplify why an inherent critique of neoliberalism must infuse that revision if such pedagogies are to be effectively liberatory. Moreover, critical revisions of pedagogy must occur in concert with a broader revision of institutional and scholarly academic work attuned to the top-down, bottom-up struggles that define globalization. It is toward those ends and within that framework that the contributors to this book see in globalization possibili-

ties for critical agency and intervention, for disciplinary work that doesn't merely meet the world as it is being defined and structured by others but participates
in the structuring. This book will be of use, then, to those who have moved beyond the pro and con positions relative to reductive characterizations of globalization by offering ways of conceiving of academic activities that are responsive
rather than adaptive, interventionist rather than acquiescent, and holistic rather
than compartmental in productively bridging various facets of disciplinary work.
For those in comp/rhet, the latter point will seem obvious, as it has long been
normative to how we conceive of our work; for those outside of comp/rhet, this
may add further value to this volume by demonstrating ways to fuse pedagogy,
administration, and scholarship for complementary ethical ends.

The first chapter, for example, is an effort to revise a longstanding theoretical construct in comp/rhet—namely "the rhetorical situation"—to reflect shifting
realities of global contexts for communication and political action. The authors,
U.S. comp/rhet scholar Sharon Stevens and New Zealand Māori scholar Lachlan
Paterson, collaborate across cultures, nationalities, and knowledge bases to
describe the *globalized rhetorical situation*, examining how the cross-national
diffusion of rhetoric impacts the actual arguments made in an increasingly
global public sphere. As a case study, Stevens and Paterson focus on how the
Māori rights rhetoric of the 1970s borrowed from U.S. black civil rights
rhetoric. Notably the authors also examine how the specificity of Māori
experience (which is itself multivocal) uniquely inflects Māori arguments. The
resultant rhetoric can be read as a practice of bottom-up globalization
appropriate for indigenous peoples seeking to reclaim power and self-
determination in colonial, postcolonial, and neo-colonial contexts.

More than just a theoretical proposition, though, the essay works to reimagine educational approaches and outcomes for writing instruction, offering a
bridge between theory and practice that scholars and teachers alike can build
upon. For apprenticing rhetors and rhetoricians, what this chapter provides is not
a simple understanding of how to adapt to an emergent world order: as the
authors themselves note, they are working to revise and rethink common classroom practices related to the construct of the rhetorical situation, ones that usually seek "to emphasize the assimilation of writers to audience expectations, or at
least to emphasize the effectiveness of rhetoric that reinforces audience
knowledge and values" (18). Sounding both critical and activist in their agenda,
Stevens and Paterson argue that their case study demonstrates that in the context
of globalization, "there may be times when effective rhetoric radically resists
audience expectations and even resists audience self-identifications. Given
differences in power, such rhetorical strategies may be risky, but they may also
offer increased potential to alter power relations" (18). Given the ubiquity of
composition curricula and textbooks that are reliant upon taxonomies from
classical rhetoric (particularly the various substrata of *invention*, within which
the rhetorical situation is normally placed), what Stevens and Paterson offer is

thus a significant point of entry for potential reforms, not just in disciplinary journals but also in textbook content and pedagogical practice. Add to that the fact that writing programs in most universities are centrally managed by comp/rhet scholars (the WPAs of most English departments) who select textbooks and establish curricula, and it becomes easier to understand how institutional work around this one key disciplinary term can be holistic, critical, and interventionist in its response to the unfolding conditions of globalization.

Eileen E. Schell would undoubtedly agree, given the academic project she theorizes and describes in her chapter, "Think Global, Eat Local: Teaching Alternative Agrarian Literacy in a Globalized Age." Schell works, along with her students, to explicate "the global food industrial complex" in order to better understand the political economies of today's food production, distribution, and consumption. As a site of research and as a process that can be intervened in (through rhetorical engagement, through consumer choice, and through collective action), global agribusiness is more than thematic content for a standard composition course. Certainly it can be conceived of in those ways, and Schell acknowledges that; but as she demonstrates, it is more substantively a focal point for the development of literacies appropriate to globalization, literacies that are indeed informed by and productive of critical agency. Shell writes, "a focus on the issue of food provides a space for fostering the critical consciousness and critical literacy needed to assess and attend to the problematic effects and unequal power relations inherent in globalization given the environmental, political, and social consequences of industrialized, globalized food production."

Like Stevens and Paterson before her, Schell moves with ease and clarity among theory and practice. In outlining her chapter, she explains: "To understand how a focus on food literacy might work in a composition classroom, I offer a brief analysis of the problematic of global food and literacy. [. . . The] latter half of the essay will bring conversations about global and local food politics into the writing classroom through a brief discussion of the sophomore-level critical research and writing course (WRT 205) that I teach at Syracuse University" (43). In the context of both the classroom and the scholarly volume, then, Schell is attempting to foster ways of seeing, of knowing, and of acting in the current era. She is engaging her students and her colleagues in the field as local and global agents invested in and informed by the political economies of food. Disciplinary projects like these demonstrate the value of academic work as a productive force in history (rather than as a disinterested observer of that history): they extend and reform the work of comp/rhet so that it responds directly and explicitly to processes of globalization—most notably to those processes in which a dialectic can be fostered and the political, economic, social, and cultural relations that dominate can be challenged. Such work need not be about food, of course. Yet Schell's precise focus on food is neither an accident nor a personal idiosyncrasy: food's entanglement within a globalized complex of production, distribution, and consumption (one increasingly shaped by neoliberal ideologies, foreign and domestic policies, trade agreements, and corporate ownership) makes it a material site of academic intervention par excellence.

Such intervention is a welcome counterpoint to the more hegemonic institutional functions of comp/rhet's disciplinary work referenced earlier in this essay. It is worth recognizing that the engagements with globalization described thus far are also struggles within the contradictory space that is academia. The scholar, teacher, or administrator who works to embrace and extend the kinds of projects outlined by Schell or by Stevens and Paterson does so within and against institutional contexts historically constructed by the very forces of globalization that those authors deem destructive and oppressive.

Still, even the maintenance and management of those contexts can become practices of critique, intervention, and reform. Bruce Horner demonstrates this amply in his chapter following Schell's, wherein he examines the institutional role of WPAs as "brokers" of commodities in the increasingly global(ized) marketplace of course credits, instructors, students, and student writing. Horner notes the concrete ways in which administrative work, like pedagogical work, is being transformed into a practice of commodity exchange under global capitalism, and he attempts to redefine the role of the WPA as an informed, resistant broker in response. He writes that increases in the speed and scope of the flow of capital and labor associated with the current globalizing of communication technologies and the market economy (along with the concomitant privatization and commodification of all aspects of education, including knowledge work in English) mandates that WPAs take into account the global context in which their brokering is conducted in order to resist those effects of globalizing that threaten the value of the work of writing and its learning and teaching. Horner examines WPA discourses revolving around the concept of "programmatic coherence" and the continued exploitation of composition labor "to show how dominant approaches to addressing these challenges in strictly local institutional terms prevents substantive resistance to the forces that largely account for these challenges in the first place" (58).

The forces outlined by Horner include local institutional ones, to be sure: students in classrooms, colleagues in departments, and administrators in schools and colleges. But they also include (and are put into effective relief against) broader hierarchical relations of power that determine the relations of production of writing and of writing instruction. Those relations are evolving in a global market economy in which literacy skill sets are being defined as commodities that, in order to be exchanged, need to be standardized. They also need to be movable and interchangeable in ways similar to other commodities; hence the steady rise in WPA conversations about contingent labor pools, teacher training, and "articulation agreements" within state, national, and even international educational systems. If we accept Horner's characterization of writing program administration as brokering, it becomes difficult to *not* see our disciplinary work as little more than a product of—and for—global capitalist relations of production, distribution, and consumption. If there is a dialectic play to be found and agency to be enacted, at least part of their constitution lies in the discourses producing and produced by WPAs. Horner's chapter serves, then, as a metadiscursive analysis aimed at changing how, and about what, administrators talk and write amidst globalization. At the same time, it serves as both a theoretical and practical guide for revising the administrative landscape that both arises from and shapes the teaching of writing.

The anxieties expressed by Horner—about the increasing corporatization of the university and the function of WPA discourses—belong categorically to the discourses of globalization analyzed by Donna Strickland and Rebecca Dingo, who argue in their chapter that conditions of global capitalism have helped to produce most college writing students as anxious consumers and many college writing teachers as equally anxious contingent labor. Both groups are stakeholders in the new economy, as are the WPAs who mediate them, a triadic relationship described by Strickland and Dingo that in many ways is a direct complement to Horner's characterization of the WPA as broker. The "anxious rhetorics" that circulate amidst these authors' select triad need to be interrupted and reframed, according to Strickland and Dingo, who see them as elements of a closed "Mobius strip" of discourse that prevents critical engagement with the evolution of globalization.

While Strickland and Dingo might agree with Kellner that many of us have moved beyond "anti" and "pro" sentiments regarding globalization in our academic arguments, they also reveal through rhetorical analyses the affective impact of discourses that do indeed regularly reduce understandings of globalization in our everyday work. Drawing on Raymond Williams, they write that if "structures of feeling" shape and sustain an economic system, "then the dominant globalized economics of neoliberalism are shaped by feelings of anxiety," and they are "sustained by defensive mechanisms and morale boosting," each of which tends to tout globalization in binary terms as either the problem or the solution to socioeconomic ills (80). Hence the authors' desire to reframe such affect-driven discourses, to open them up in ways that allow for shared and negotiated structures of feeling that are linked across local and global networks. Like Horner, the authors see possibilities for change in discursive action, in the rhetorical grounds that administrators and other disciplinary members construct for their arguments amidst the conditions of late capitalism and at the intersections of the various strands of disciplinary activity.

The critical and activist work in "reframing" disciplinary activity is similarly performed, but targeted more specifically on teaching, in the chapter that follows Dingo and Strickland's: working from Kellner's dialectic framework, Hill Taylor, Jr. outlines ways to reframe liberatory pedagogies to account for the top-down and bottom-up manifestations of globalization. He describes and theorizes a localized literacy project in the D.C. area, one in which first-year African American students engage in "urbanism as a social practice," mapping and articulating spaces and communities that challenge and change those that emerge primarily from top-down globalizing processes and their dominant social scripts. Taylor invokes those processes' dialectical alternative to define a pedagogy that reflects the ways in which marginalized individuals and social movements resist globalization and/or use its institutions and instruments to further democratization and social justice. In addition to relying on Kellner's framework to describe possibilities for globalization from below, Taylor aligns his work with that of Michael Hardt and Antonio Negri, whose well-known books *Empire* and *Multitude* comprise an optimistic project in granting local social actors collective agency in the face of imperial global power. Taylor attempts to offer his students critical tools to deconstruct and redefine everyday practices and identities—in and on the students' own terms. This is ultimately an effort to suture the local and the global in service of a liberatory pedagogy.

Taylor's focus on the play among the local and the global is an effective complement to his focus on the play among globalization practices from above and from below. This is not to suggest that Taylor constructs globalization from below as purely local and globalization from above as purely global; the dynamics are much more complex, as his project demonstrates. The local/global dynamic becomes a conceptual and material "way in" to the problematic of globalization. Indeed, to varying degrees of explicitness, all of the contributors to this volume exploit the local and global dynamic, making productive use of its concrete possibilities and abstract propositions. While Stevens and Paterson demonstrate the ways in which Māori rhetoric is ultimately a "glocal" construct (a term I borrow from Roland Robertson to apply to their chapter), so too do Schell, Horner, Dingo, and Strickland demonstrate that the relational activities between local actors and global forces are opportunities for interruption, contestation, negotiation, and struggle—in short, for dialectic.

Similarly, in the chapter following Taylor's, Daphne Desser critically examines dialectical tensions among competing rhetorics situated within and constitutive of specific forms of globalization from above and below. Writing from Hawai'i, a "glocality" shaped by global capitalism, Western colonialism, and indigenous struggles, Desser analyzes the rhetorical situation that occurred when a transnational financial institution's attempts to engage in "business as usual" were subverted by activists who employed rhetorical strategies and argumentative content embodying epistemologies distinctly different than those most often considered normative in neoliberal discourses. More specifically, Desser summarizes the clash that occurred between the Asian Development Bank (ADB), which hosted a significant conference in Hawai'i in 2001, and local indigenous protest groups, who organized a peaceful, multifaceted public response designed to interrupt and challenge the normalcy (and normativity) of the proceedings.

Through her analysis of this particular moment in this particular place, Desser demonstrates the need for writing instructors to be more critically aware of the globalized rhetorical contexts within which their work is occurring. Within the case of Hawai'i, she argues that in order to teach writing responsibly in that locale, the dynamic clash in rhetorics, values, and epistemologies illustrated by the protests of the ADB must be brought to the students' attention, not as a sidenote or supplement to instruction, but as a means to help them "situate themselves, their rhetorical positions, their arguments and their writing within this complex context." For readers outside of Hawai'i, Desser's essay, as she puts it, "can serve as one exemplum among many of how educators can productively and proactively engage in globalization's history and, to be sure, its future—by focusing critical, analytic, and rhetorical work on the local and the global contexts in which they occur and to which they contribute" (114). Desser's work as a scholar and teacher thus becomes a project in interrupting, complicating, and revising the dominant rhetorics and epistemologies produced in globalization, in part as a response to its history and in part as a contribution to its continued development.

Following Desser's chapter, but extending her explorations into the complexities of local and global relations, dialectical rhetorical exchanges, and formal education, is an overview by Chris Anson of the varieties of inter- and transnational writing instruction rapidly becoming commonplace in this current historical moment. Similarly critical of and responsive to (rather than acquiescent and adaptive to) evolutions of higher education under the presently dominant form of globalization, Anson describes a number of initiatives mediated and structured by conditions of late capitalism. He observes, for example, that such educational programs can become powerful vehicles for the continued hegemony of the English language and American Internet genres across the globe, echoing in his critique work by scholars both in this collection and beyond. At the same time, nonetheless, Anson also observes that educational formations have the contradictory potential to facilitate dialectic exchanges—of knowledges, cultures, languages, and identities. The emergent and growing linkages he describes between teachers and students in new initiatives transcend borders and limitations of time and geographic space. As such, they can help shape students as global citizens by routinely locating them (and *re*locating them) as border crossers who can be guided (and whose experiences can be structured) by an "exploration of dominance," one that may help to produce "intercultural attitudes leading to the exchange of ideas, information, and interpersonal actions between persons of different groups or nations" (147). In short, Anson, like the other contributors to this volume, writes from the premise that disciplinary work around writing instruction in globalization—be it by teachers, scholars, administrators, or students—simply cannot be passive or accommodationist; it must instead be attentive to both the productive and destructive possibilities inherent in its material and discursive conditions, and it must be active in shaping those conditions as much as working within them.

Anson's chapter is a fitting final chapter of the book, then, for the ways that it is both critical and optimistic. It is also fitting as a broad overview of overlapping established and emergent forms of inter- and transnational education, for it provides material exempla for readers to examine as simultaneously local and global, as inflected and informed by dominant forces and traditions as well as by their counterparts. And because it is more broad than specific, readers can take more of a bird's-eye view on the emerging shape of educational trends in globalization and apply to them the very methods, perspectives, themes, and foci consistent across the contributions to this book. Indeed such consistency makes this volume both a collection of diverse intellectual engagements as well as a coherent argument developed and extended with a cohesion normally found in monographs. Just as the relations among the local and the global are a consistent theme running throughout the contributions of this book, so is the argument in favor of seeing disciplinary work as a necessary fusion of activities that are simultaneously critical and activist, pedagogical and administrative, scholarly and institutional. Working at those junctures and from such multifaceted positions, the contributors to this collection all demonstrate the dialectic realities and potentialities of both education and globalization as unfinished projects—all of which readers can draw upon in examining and reforming their own disciplinary work.

Readers of, and contributors to, this collection are thus beginning a more complex, more challenging, and ultimately more rewarding "fundamental rethinking" of education than the example referenced at the start of this chapter. Rather than simply adapting to the changes that are upon us (a tempting enough prospect given the overwhelming scope and feel of those changes), we can instead find in our daily activities and discourses opportunities for more ethically engaged responses. We can have a hand in shaping historical outcomes. And perhaps most importantly, we can produce (among ourselves and our students) a mode of civic engagement and responsibility that will far outlast and outweigh any scholarly critiques of top-down globalization, neoliberalism, corpra-colonialism, or transnational capitalism that we might offer one another.

As a final note, it is worth acknowledging here that this book's thematic, methodological, and critical coherence sketched in these last few paragraphs is, to be sure, a rhetorical construct typical of western academic discourse. Yes, that consistency is there, and it does reinforce and strengthen the arguments of the collection as a whole. It demonstrates what some teachers of writing might call a "manageable focus." Yet this is not the only way to map globalization and disciplinary work; nor is it the only way to summarize these very contributions in this specific volume, which offer diverse arguments about, and operational definitions of, globalization. Readers will undoubtedly find different emphases and construct different meanings in the chapters that follow. That can only increase the value of this book. The scholarship represented here, much of it by leading figures in the field of comp/rhet, should be open to interpretation, negotiation, and reconfiguration—not unlike the processes and products of globalization.

Notes

1. See Payne in Borrowman, Brown, and Miller, eds. *Renewing Rhetoric's Relations to Composition.*

2. In using the term "arbitrary," I am following Pierre Bourdieu's sense of the term, discussed in *Distinction* and elsewhere to reference a social construction as opposed to a natural or autonomous existence.

3. For more on this binary, see Hesford's essay, "Global Turns and Cautions in Rhetoric and Composition Studies."

Works Cited

Bourdieu, Pierre. *Distinction.* Trans. Richard Nice. Cambridge, MA: Harvard UP, 1984.

Bousquet, Marc. *How the University Works: Higher Education and the Low-Wage Nation.* NYU Press, 2008.

Canagarajah, A. Suresh. "The Place of World Englishes in Composition: Pluralization Continued." *College Composition and Communication* 47,4 (2006): 586-619.

Crowley, Sharon. *Composition in the University: Historical and Polemical Essays.* Pittsburgh: U of Pittsburgh P, 1998.

Freire, Paulo. *Pedagogy of the Oppressed.* New York: Continuum, 2007.

Kellner, Douglas. "Theorizing Globalization." *Sociological Theory* 20,3 (2002): 285-305.

Lauer, Janice. "Rhetoric: The Cornerstone of a Graduate Program." *Renewing Rhetoric's Relation to Composition: Essays in Honor of Theresa Jarnagin Enos.* Ed. Shane Borrowman, Thomas P. Miller, and Stuart C. Brown. Taylor and Francis Press. 2009. 104-16.

Lefebvre, Henri. *The Production of Space.* Trans. Donald Nicholson-Smith. Oxford: Basil Blackwell Ltd., 1991.

Lu, Min Zhan. "An Essay on the Work of Composition: Composing English against the Order of Fast Capitalism." *College Composition and Communication* 56.1 (2004): 16-50.

Hesford, Wendy. "Global Turns and Cautions in Rhetoric and Composition Studies." *PMLA* 121,3 (May 2006): 787-801.

Horner, Bruce, and John Trimbur. "English Only and U.S. College Composition." *College Composition and Communication* 53 (2002): 594–630.

Miller, Thomas P. *The Formation of College English: Rhetoric and Belles Lettres in the British Cultural Provinces.* Pittsburgh: U of Pittsburgh P, 1997

Mohanty, Chandra Talpade. *Feminism without Borders: Decolonizing Theory, Practicing Solidarity.* Durham and London: Duke University Press, 2003.

Payne, Darin. "Globalization, New(er) Rhetoric, and the Necessary Centrality of Both to Graduate Studies in Composition." *Renewing Rhetoric's Relation to Composition: Essays in Honor of Theresa Jarnagin Enos.* Ed. Shane Borrowman, Thomas P. Miller, and Stuart C. Brown. Taylor and Francis Press, 2009. 117-36.

Shiva, Vandana. *Water Wars: Privatization, Pollution, and Profit.* Cambridge, MA: South End Press, 2002.

Suarez-Orozco, Marcelo and Desiree Qin-Hilliard, eds. *Globalization: Culture and Education in the New Millennium.* Berkeley: University of California P, 2004.

Nga Tamatoa and the Rhetoric of Brown Power: Re-Situating Collective Rhetorics in Global Colonialism

Sharon McKenzie Stevens and Lachlan Paterson

In the 1960s, New Zealand had the best race relations in the world. So went the popular story, a story reinforced through comparison with strained race relations, protest, and conflict in other nations, including the United States. In consequence, many Kiwis were shocked when, at the end of the decade, Māori activists and their Pākehā[1] supporters mobilized around claims that the New Zealand government had violated the 1840 Treaty of Waitangi, unjustly alienating Māori land and eroding iwi (tribal)[2] authority guaranteed by Te Tiriti o Waitangi, the Te Reo (Māori language) version of the treaty. When activists began grieving at national Waitangi Day celebrations, much of the mainstream Pākehā audience felt confused, challenged, "scared and irritated" (Sharp 11), while many Māori felt embarrassed by behavior they thought was inappropriate.[3]

At its outset, then, the Māori rights movement made public a counter-statement to orthodox perceptions of racial harmony. As a Nga Tamatoa activist put it in 1971, "the Pakeha can't lie any more, can't talk for Maori as well and say those lies like our Race Relations are Second to None in the World" (MOOHR 5). This discrepancy between mainstream and radical interpretations of New Zealand race relations led to different definitions of the exigence presented by Waitangi day.

Despite disapproving and uncomprehending audience judgments, however, the hard-to-assimilate rhetorical shock presented by protest, by the public display of heterodoxy, served as an important step in the transformation of New Zealand society. Confrontation, defined as a "strategic clash of perspectives, value priorities, beliefs, attitudes, and symbols," creates "a dialectical struggle between frames of reference," as Robert Heath explains in his study of U.S. black radicalism (168). The dialectic set in motion by confrontation supports consciousness-raising and, ultimately, the transformation of relationships between activists and their audiences.

This type of confrontation, which refuses to give priority to rhetor-audience identification, challenges several common emphases, if not exactly tenets, in common pedagogical and analytical approaches to *the rhetorical situation*. Our chapter argues this point by examining how the eventual, though partial, effectiveness of Māori activists' shocking tactics might offer a new perspective on composition instruction. Our argument supports the work of Elizabeth Ervin, who argues that radical activists may deliberately use situationally inappropriate rhetorical strategies to challenge the status quo. Our complementary perspective is that Māori activists' radical rhetoric is invented out of radical redefinitions of their situation, and these redefinitions then change the criteria for judging what is appropriate. Despite now common dialectical arguments about whether rhetorical situations are discovered or invented (cf. Bitzer; Vatz; Biesecker), it remains common for composition scholars, especially when guiding students, to emphasize the assimilation of writers to audience expectations, or at least to emphasize the effectiveness of rhetoric that reinforces audience knowledge and values. In fact, teaching often invokes audiences to justify judgments about what makes writing good. Yet, as the influence of Māori Waitangi Day protests indicates, there may be times when effective rhetoric radically resists audience expectations and even resists audience self-identifications. Given differences in power, such rhetorical strategies may be risky, but they may also offer increased potential to alter power relations.

Our second major claim is that Māori activist rhetoric also suggests the shortfall of analyses that over-emphasize local aspects of rhetorical situations. It is not uncommon for situation-conscious assignment design to incline toward closed—and often local—parameters to make writing real and relevant for students. Erika Lindemann's influential *A Rhetoric for Writing Teachers*, for example, illustrates what a well-designed rhetorical problem might look like with an assignment asking students to analyze their university's advertisements (218-19). Though Lindemann recognizes open assignments might have a place, she does not discuss them at length. We wish to reverse this emphasis by arguing that Māori activists underscored the incompleteness of settled and local problem definition by relocating stories about New Zealand race relations in a global colonial context. While basing their claims on the national Te Tiriti, activists identified with other oppressed peoples worldwide, routinely referring to the U.S. black struggle for civil rights, the Vietnam War, South African Apartheid, and the general colonization of black people. The activists' example suggests that rhetors construct their exigence by selecting found aspects of the material and discursive world to link together interpretively within a system of relationships, and these relationships, especially in a time of increasing globalization, might have both global and local features. Defining these relationships is itself a complex task that should not be excised from invention, as Māori rights activists demonstrated over time by shifting the nature of their identifications with other colonized peoples.

The Māori activist example thereby complicates understandings of *the rhetorical situation* by showing the possibility of a strategic misfit between audience and rhetor interpretations of exigencies and by highlighting how complex connections between local and global sources can feed into that misfit. Nonetheless, many common teaching and learning strategies based on simplified understandings of particular situations remain effective for teaching pragmatic and individualized agency in discrete, short-term cases. Our third and final point is that the Māori example indicates the limits of these approaches when the goal is to construct collective agency as an alternative to hegemonic forms of power. In these circumstances, one particularly effective rhetorical strategy is to construct a new collective identity. Since identities, as we argue below, are themselves constituted out of a system of relationships, creating a new identity requires refiguring rhetorical situations.

In the remainder of this chapter, we support these three points through historical narrative and rhetorical analysis that take as their fulcrum Māori borrowing from U.S. black separatist rhetoric during 1971, a year when Māori radicalism became especially public. First, however, we support our basic definition of *the rhetorical situation* as a constructed system that articulates the material to the discursive, the global to the local. With this definition in place, we turn to our case, offering a brief history of New Zealand race relations from first settlement until 1971 to highlight how material aspects of this system, such as the movement of people through globalization, impacts rhetorical constructions, such as the development of new collective identities and the local interpretation of grievances. We then turn to a detailed rhetorical analysis of a few extant print sources for the activist rhetoric of Nga Tamatoa, a radical organization that took center stage in 1971 through Treaty protests. Then, we briefly indicate how this radical period has set the stage for further material and discursive changes that have continued to articulate local and global rhetorics while crafting a new, specifically indigenous identity for Māori. Finally, we step back from this narrative organization to highlight how features of the Māori activist example illustrate the three major claims we have noted in this introduction. In particular, we emphasize how each of these claims not only redefines *the rhetorical situation* but also works to redefine common pedagogical practices.

The Rhetorical Situation in a Global System

We wish to begin our redefinition by considering the impact of globalization on how social actors interpret their everyday experiences, and even their own identities. By globalization, we refer to the increasing density of connections between economies, political systems, and cultures in a system of linkages, identifications, and exchanges. This systems approach is advanced by anthropologist George Marcus in a discussion of how "ethnographic subjects of study"—such as ethnic identities—are embedded "within contexts of a world system, historical political economies of colonialism, market regimes, state formation, and nation-building" (97). Through historic colonizing processes, for example, new national and ethnic identities have developed in response to systems of economic exchange, population mobility, and education (Anderson). More recently, technological developments and the increasing density of information exchanges have also had an impact on how social actors understand their situation and their place within it (Melucci; Pieterse).

As new, systemic social relations emerge through globalizing processes, therefore, contemporary actors experience their lives from within "a situation of shifting, complementary, and contradictory meanings" (Ong 2). When speakers and writers act rhetorically, they do so while embedded in this global, relational system, and they address audiences who are also embedded in relationships with multiple others. The density of these relationships can make history appear overdetermined. At the heart of rhetorical practice, however, is the remembrance that situations can change, that the future is contingent, and that agency—though it may require ongoing struggle (Hauser and mcclellan 44-45)—is a real possibility. This point is underlined in the work of anthropologist Aihwa Ong, for example, when she describes how aspects of Malaysian identities are changing in response to globalization. Ong argues that globalization processes cannot predetermine the direction of cultural change, and that local forms of resistance interact dialectically with those processes, leading to the development of multiple, often contradictory, forms of power relations. This dialectic struggle over culture, Ong asserts, extends as far as "the experience of reality itself" (3). Globalizing processes may tend toward establishing the hegemony of, for example, neoliberal capitalism, or, in the New Zealand case, British colonial culture. These possible hegemonies, however, are not given as reality, but must instead be constituted from the many possible relationships available within the world system. Because this system can expand indefinitely, actors within it must make selections and demarcate some material and discursive relationships as more important than others.

Through this demarcating process, any given representation of the world system can become, potentially, an activist one, because that representation will itself then become a part of the associations and exchanges of the system (Marcus 96). Textual links to both local and global referents, in other words, have the potential to be interested, selective, and strategic; this sort of reflexive textual construction actively participates in building the world it describes. If activists change any points within a system, including re-defining their own identities, those changes ripple outwards, potentially persuading others to enter into a new set of relationships. In fact, the exigence for rhetoric can be understood as differences between audience and rhetor perceptions, including differences between how they experience and interpret their everyday life.

This systems approach thereby provides a way to reinterpret *the rhetorical situation*. In his foundational definition of this as any "complex" of referents and relations that present an "exigence" that can be removed, in whole or in part, by discourse (6), Lloyd Bitzer emphasizes relationships and change in a way useful for analyses of social movement rhetorics in globalized contexts. Yet Bitzer's insistence that situations are found—a "natural context" (5)—and his emphasis on constraints do not anticipate radical rhetoric that disregards audience beliefs and values. Nonetheless, the extreme constructivist counter-statement that "situations obtain their character from the rhetoric which surrounds them or creates them" (Vatz 159) is also faulty because it ignores how rhetorical acts participate in relationships that have developed over time. A systemic definition of *the rhetorical situation*, then, must be based in something that more fully accounts not only for global systems but also for their *histories*, with all the stability and change those histories imply.

In short, a systems approach makes clear that only dialectic explains fully how actors come to understand their reality (Ong). In her critique of Bitzer's article, Barbara Biesecker perceptively argues that, by setting up a dialectical opposition to Bitzer, Vatz enables a deconstruction that refuses to take any components of rhetorical situations for granted, including speakers or writing subjects, audiences, and their contexts. As a new model, Biesecker defines *the rhetorical situation* as "an event that makes possible the production of identities and social relations" (126), and she emphasizes the in-process qualities of these identities and relations to help scholars "rethink rhetoric as radical possibility" (127). Biesecker thereby indicates that exigence does not exist as a discrete, natural entity; audiences do not serve as preconstituted constraints on rhetoric.

A theoretical emphasis on change and deconstructive play, however, can easily under-represent the resistance activists experience in the public arena, and this is why empirical and especially historical studies of rhetoric are necessary. By examining the radical rhetoric of Māori activists, we wish to emphasize the importance of incremental change over time and the significance of building rhetorical strength through the construction of collective identities. This emphasis on incremental change has precedent in the work of Carolyn D. Rude, who develops a picture of an "extended rhetorical situation" that acknowledges an "increasing complexity of the rhetorical exigence, the audience, and compet-ing arguments on this worldwide stage" (285). In a global system, the construction of identities out of local and global interests and issues can provide a basis for coalition-building.

In fact, the reflexive development of new collective identities is at once 1) an indication that social change is already occurring (Gusfield), 2) an inducement to sustain long-term action (Friedman and McAdam 157), and 3) a direct means for contesting the systemic relations of the broader society (Gusfield; Melucci). Alberto Melucci, a leading contributor to the field of new social movement studies, argues that, as social control takes on new forms, so does resistance. Cultural action that targets everyday experience and meaning becomes increasingly significant. Within a global system, developing resistant collective identities contests the meaning of reality, challenges the production of information, and otherwise introduces (or makes more overt) conflict within the cultural sphere. This has the potential to destabilize power relations, setting in motion an ongoing process of identity-formation, of becoming.

This act of collective identification and culture-based social action is profoundly rhetorical. As sociologist Michael Billig argues, movement identities, like all others, are relational, dialogic, and developed through rhetorical negotiation. In their current overview of communications-based rhetorical scholarship, Gerard Hauser and erin daina mcclellan similarly highlight rhetoric's constitutive role in social action: "At the center of all resistance movements lie rhetorical resources and forces that express opposition, agitate for change, inspire and signal cohesion, and project visions of a transformed social order" (24). Within a systems context, all these rhetorical resources are linked to each other in a series of relationships, so that forms of control and resistance arise together, as do collective identities and the social relations in which those identities act. In New Zealand's case, cultural politics have developed as a rhetorical response to such globalizing processes as colonization, population mobility, and the international exchange of information and images. Māori activists have made meaning, and have re-made their own identities, by integrating their understanding of a global system, and especially of a colonial system, into their version of reality, their understanding of their rhetorical situation, and their interpretation of the exigence presented by Waitangi Day.

In the next section of our article, we offer a short history of race relations throughout New Zealand's colonial period up until 1971, when radical activism drew mainstream attention. We do this to illustrate how Māori identities form and reform within a system of relations, especially changing in response to two globalizing processes: 1) colonization and 2) increasingly dense forms of transnational communication. We also indicate the impacts of local history on Māori experiences within New Zealand society to show why Māori, in spite of changing global relations, have consistently understood the exigence for rhetoric in terms of land rights and self-governance. The upcoming section, then, provides context for our subsequent analysis of how radical Māori rhetoric links together local and global referents to create a unique rhetorical situation.

Māori-Pākehā Relations and Identity Formation in Aotearoa/New Zealand[4]

Prior to colonization, "Māori" did not exist, at least not as a recognized collective. The Polynesians who would later be called Māori arrived in New Zealand, possibly as early as 1100 CE. As they adapted to a new, larger, colder environment, they developed a distinctive indigenous culture. Although culturally and linguistically homogenous, they were divided politically into iwi and hapū and did not share any concept of Māori-ness. This emerged later, as tāngata māori (normal human beings) made contact with pākehā (others), who came in increasing numbers after Cook visited the islands in 1769. This contact quickly led to a system of exchange. From Pākehā—sealers, whalers, beachcombers, missionaries and traders—Māori gained venereal disease, alcohol, tobacco, muskets, iron tools, new animals and plants, Christianity and literacy.

These exchanges would eventually lead to colonization, creating a rift between Māori and Pākehā understandings of their relationship to one another. Contact was heaviest in the north, although in the late 1830s, a private English company established a colonial settlement further south in the Cook Strait region. This settlement, combined with concerns about Pākehā lawlessness and about French and U.S. designs on New Zealand, led the British Crown and Māori chiefs to sign the Treaty of Waitangi in 1840. In the English version of the Treaty, Māori ceded sovereignty to the Crown in return for the security of Māori land and resource ownership. New Zealand's colonization was supposed to be different from Australia's and North America's: the Crown had agreed to safeguard Māori interests. However, Te Tiriti, the Te Reo version, gave rights of "government" to the Crown while Queen Victoria guaranteed Māori tino rangatiratanga, their tribal independence.[5] This tension between Crown sovereignty and Māori rights, a tension inscribed by two rhetorical acts purportedly united through translation (the two versions of the treaty), has informed race relations in New Zealand ever since.

Additionally, colonization immediately led to changing immigration patterns that further increased tensions and ultimately led to land disputes that even today remain central to Māori grievances. Around 1858, Māori and Pākehā populations reached parity; by 1900 Māori made up only about five percent of New Zealand's citizens. New Zealand's independence from Britain has been a gradual process, but by 1856 new settlers gained self-government, and in 1865 they took responsibility for governing Māori also. The Treaty guaranteed Māori ownership of the land, but during the next one hundred fifty years, the government sought to alienate it for Pākehā settlement. This was achieved first through government purchases both good and bad, then through war and confiscation, then through the establishment of the Native Land Court. This court sought to convert Māori communal tenure to blocks of land, which could be easily acquired by unscrupulous land sharks. By 1900, little Māori land remained.

Māori iwi reacted to colonization with various strategies: armed resistance, passive resistance, separation, or cautious cooperation. At times, Māori pooled their resources to form pan-iwi alliances; at other times, iwi concerns were paramount. Syncretic religious movements, mixing Old Testament liberation theology with Māori spirituality, gave hope to many Māori as Pākehā gained their lands and destroyed their economic, social, and political standing. While for Pākehā the Treaty of Waitangi was a historical curio with no legal standing, Māori, in their enduring struggle for justice, argued that the Crown had made a covenant to protect Māori interests. In the late 1960s and early 1970s, activists would point to these acts of resistance as precedents for collective action.

The vast majority of Pākehā, however, overlooked this early resistance, and the physical separation of Māori and Pākehā enabled the development of a myth of racial harmony that would remain largely intact until disrupted by radical activism. Throughout the late nineteenth and early twentieth century, Māori continued to live rurally and largely in poverty, while most Pākehā lived in towns. The myth of racial harmony was further reinforced by global comparisons: Pākehā did not treat "their Māoris" like the blacks of Australia, South Africa, or the southern United States.[6] Dwindling numbers of Māori made it easy for Pākehā to further marginalize Māori or even nostalgically locate them in the past, as a "dying race."[7] For many years, survival and rebuilding left little energy for resistance to the strident government policy of assimilating Māori into Pākehā society.

The Second World War and its aftermath, however, led to significant changes in how Māori related to the rest of New Zealand society, and these changes in turn led to new Māori understandings of their own identity. During the war, New Zealand's role as loyal daughter within the British Empire saw large numbers of young men leave to fight overseas. Many Māori enthusiastically supported New Zealand's participation in the war and sacrificed their sons in the Māori Battalion as the "price of citizenship" within the nation state. During this same period, and especially into the post-war boom years, Māori migrated in large numbers to the cities, confronting urban Pākehā in numbers for the first time. While Pākehā and Māori mixed in some domains, urbanization led to racial discrimination, with Māori being relegated to low-skill jobs and poor housing, while also experiencing dislocation from their iwi and hapū with an accompanying loss of their language and culture. From 1960, the government attempted a policy of "integration," creating a composite national culture out of the best of Māori and Pākehā ways of life.

Cultural marginalization, coupled with increased awareness through education, angered urban Māori youth but also raised their consciousness and provided a shared feeling of Māori-ness in the face of the dominant white culture. Radical groups, such as Nga Tamatoa (young braves), assailed the view that New Zealand had the best race relations in the world, protesting at 1971 and subsequent national Waitangi Day celebrations. In the next section we analyze the performative rhetoric of the 1971 protests together with three textual examples published that same year, when the radical element of Māori activism was most visible. Within this section, we draw most heavily on an interview that provides one of the more lengthy (if not the lengthiest) written records of Nga Tamatoa's 1971 rhetoric, with the added benefit that, as a transcribed interview, it represents not the carefully crafted framing of publications that might be revised multiple times, but rather the everyday understanding of Nga Tamatoa's spokespersons.

The Radical Rhetoric of Brown Power

Although groups of Māori had long complained about colonization, it was Nga Tamatoa's February 6, 1971, protests at Waitangi Day celebrations that created sustained national attention to Māori grievances (Greenland 94-95). Though spokespersons for Nga Tamatoa were divided on whether or not the treaty should be rejected or simply be made into a basis of future reform (Greenland 95), the symbolism of protests favored a revolutionary interpretation. Protesters disrupted celebrations by performing haka (war challenges) and by breaking into ceremonial enclosures in funeral dress (Johnson 1-2). They thereby inverted the symbolism of putative racial harmony and cast the treaty as a grievance, suggesting that New Zealand's legal foundation is a travesty and that the treaty cannot provide a basis for future race relations. The shock occasioned by this performative rhetoric helped place radicalism at center stage.

Why was the radical form of activist rhetoric developed, and why was it so influential during precisely this historic moment? The answers to these questions depend on the articulation of local history with global influence, and with how changing relationships between Māori and other members of both the national and global society provided both the exigence and the resources to develop an activist collective identity.

On a national level, as previously discussed, urbanization reorganized Māori society, so that Māori identity became increasingly more significant than identifications with iwi or hapū, even at times stretching to a broader identification with urbanized Polynesians (Johnson 7-9). These new identifications were further supported by a breakdown in intergenerational cultural transmission. In "The Resurrection of Maori Identity,"[8] Nga Tamatoa argued that not only had "the land of his ancestors … been taken away" from the Māori, but "his native tongue has just about been torn out of his mouth." Echoing nineteenth-century sentiments that Māori were a dying race, but placing this dying squarely in a cultural rather than an ancestral context, Nga Tamatoa continued: "The Maori is quickly realising that very soon, unless severe measures are taken, his identity as a Maori will be as extinct as the Moa. ... The Maori doesn't want to be a brown skinned New Zealander" (1). This theme was rearticulated, and linked explicitly to the government's policy of integration, in Nga Tamatoa's May 1971 "The Fly," a self-published two-page newsletter. Here, Nga Tamatoa argued that young Māori required a "substitute identity" because their parents, in the name of integration or assimilation, failed to pass on the Māori culture and language; at the same time, Pākehā continued to reject young Māori, leaving them between cultures without a unique identity (2).

The loss of a traditional cultural identity, however, does not explain the substitute development of an activist identity. Other responses were available. Many young Māori formed apolitical gangs (Nga Tamatoa "The Fly"). Yet several global influences led to the concurrent development of an explicitly politicized identity. Urbanization supported not only gang development but also new forms of education. In Otara, Hillary College focused on politicizing Māori through exposure to world movement leaders such as Gandhi, and Tamatoa members held up Paulo Freire as a model for an anti-assimilationist education (Johnson 9). The Vietnam War also contributed. Many Māori served in the war, while news media widely reported on U.S. student-led war protests. Further, Tamatoa activists were radicalized on the streets through their participation in anti-apartheid protests, which became particularly intense when Māori players were dropped from rugby teams selected to play in South Africa and when all-white Springbok teams toured within New Zealand. The national obsession with rugby magnified these protests' impact. This combination of formal and street routes to an activist education led to the development of a protest culture that was explicitly informed by global events.

A final global influence was engagement with the ideas of U.S. black activists such as Stokely Carmichael (Johnson 20). Even the names of some gangs indicated global influences, such as Black Power and the Panthers, and these same influences led other Māori to develop more politicized identities. Within Nga Tamatoa, a radical faction advocated the principles of both Black Power and its Māori variation, Brown Power (Johnson 45). This revolutionary faction stressed blackness to create a polar opposite from white Pākehā identity and to suggest unity with blacks worldwide (Greenland 98-99). Rejecting the government's policy of integration, leaders routinely drew upon the separatist rhetoric of Malcolm X, Stokely Carmichael, and other radical leaders of U.S. blacks to the extent that, at times, the Māori activism of the late sixties and early seventies is referred to as the brown power movement after its adoption of this phrase as a slogan (Greenland 92, 101).

One aspect of revolutionary Tamatoa members' vision that resonated strongly with Malcolm X's rhetoric was the argument that they should fight for their rights. That Nga Tamatoa understood violence as a defense against ongoing oppression was evident in an interview published by MOOHR (Māori Organization on Human Rights), an organization that sympathized with Nga Tamatoa in spite of having different tactics and an organizational frame that accommodated working-class Pākehā interests. In this interview, a Tamatoa member claimed, "Well, if the Pākehā disagrees and just won't have our government, we stick up for our rights. Y'know—like: Get Off Our Land. You've no right" (2). When the MOOHR interviewer raised the possibility of forceful opposition, the Tamatoa members clarified, "Oh, if they move troops in, we might have to fight. When the Pākehā picks up the gun to fight us, that's when it starts. When the Pākehā makes a move to prevent us from doing things and they pick up the gun, well that's the finish. We'll pick up the gun too" (2-3). This acceptance of defensive violence resonates with the Black Power language that frightened so many middle class whites in the United States despite black arguments that "retaliatory violence was ... a justified response to continued incidents of terrorism and police brutality" (Van Deburg 19).

Yet while this support of defensive violence suggests rhetorical identifications with Black Power, the Tamatoa interviewees also explicitly justified their platform in terms that resonate with local history. These local influences included both historic land alienation and precedents such as the Māori King movement, which from the 1850s similarly asserted an independent Māori state[9]: "Yeah, well our ancestors had to do it [pick up the gun] before, see. They never knew we lost" (3). In this way, the rhetoric of Nga Tamatoa's radical members—and of Māori activists more generally—used both global influence and the particularity of Māori experience as resources for rejecting hegemonic white understandings of the Treaty of Waitangi.

Nga Tamatoa goals and grievances similarly made both local and global connections by advocating separatism, following the global example, while simultaneously articulating particular separatist desires that reflected the history of New Zealand race relations. In the MOOHR interview, for example, members of Nga Tamatoa advocated rejecting the Dutch name New Zealand in favor of Aotearoa, developing separate Māori laws and a separate judicial system based on appealing to offenders as opposed to violence (imprisonment) and fines, creating an alternative education system, bolstering an alternative economy based on communal sharing of goods and labor, and, most importantly, securing Māori land ownership (MOOHR 1-5). As this separatist program suggested, Nga Tamatoa's basic framing of Māori grievances through references to the treaty and colonial settler history were local (national) in detail, but the frame nonetheless fit seamlessly with Malcolm X's emphasis on how white colonization links together black communities worldwide (Van Deburg 4).

Indeed, while the rhetoric of brown power and Māori separatism marked the particularly strong identification of Māori with U.S. black activists, Māori activists also identified with other non-white oppressed and colonized groups abroad, including Vietnamese, Native Americans, African Americans, and black South Africans. During the MOOHR interview, after the questioner mentioned a range of international groups, a Tamatoa member elaborated on Māori relations with others across the globe by saying:

> It's only recently since I've begun to interpret the Pākehā—ah-uh-what's the word—yea, the IMPERIALISM of the British, y'know they went around to bring civilisation to all the dark people of the different lands. Well, that was really racist. Because they thought they were the superior race, they thought their culture was good for the Māori. (5)

In this excerpt, the speaker moved beyond particular identifications to adopt a frame based in an encompassing experience of global racism. In fact, the speaker's reach for the word "imperialism" indicated a nascent shift from simply identifying with the experiences and borrowing the rhetoric and tactics of others across the globe toward articulating a new, systemic framework for understanding oppression as a shared experience of colonization. Ultimately, this rearticulation of oppression as a linked global phenomenon developed alongside the rhetoric of brown power, leading to an indigenous people's frame articulated most strongly by reformist members of Tamatoa.

Even in 1971, the height of Māori activism, challenges to separatist rhetoric were evident. While Nga Tamatoa made headlines with the extreme versions of its claims, its members faced the challenge of sustaining their interpretation of their rhetorical situation in the face of audience backlash, underscoring that there are substantial risks to adopting tactics that radically challenge audience understanding. Activists' concern not to alienate their audience was evident during the September MOOHR interview. At times Tamatoa members openly denounced white racism but at times they instead stepped around this claim, first by carefully justifying the interpretation, then by ensuring the adjective "racist" modified acts, not people, and, finally, by immediately substituting the term "race-dominant" for the more emotionally charged epithet "racist" (3).[10] Nonetheless, Tamatoa members faced widespread criticism for framing grievances in terms of white racism and for their radical tactics. This criticism was even leveled at activists by other Māori, especially those of older generations. After 1971, divisions within Māori society plus the government's movement toward biculturalism ultimately increased the legitimacy of reform-oriented activists at the expense of revolutionaries.

From Black Separatism to Indigenous Rights

Despite their inability to fully persuade most of their audience and to meet goals suggested by their separatist rhetoric, radical activists did effectively put Māori grievances on the national agenda. In response, the Labour government of 1972-75 moved to appease Māori concerns. Prime Minister Norman Kirk critiqued the previous integration policy:

We are not one people; we are one nation. The idea of one people grew out of the days when fashionable folk talked about integration. So far as the majority and the minority are concerned, integration is precisely what cats do to mice. They integrate them. The majority swallows up the minority; makes it sacrifice its culture and traditions and often its belongings to conform to the traditions and culture of the majority. (Qtd. in NZ Parliament 2690-91)

As Kirk realized, integration was quite similar to assimilation. From this time, the government policy turned to biculturalism and multiculturalism.

These government policies have had the ironic effect of weakening overarching ethnic identifications in favor of iwi and hapū identifications, though both sets of identities continue to be important to many Māori. For Māori, cultural identity has always been strongly tied to their ancestral lands, and young radical Māori were able to engage with their elders over the 1975 Land March on Parliament, soon followed by occupations of disputed land at Bastion Point and Raglan. However, land issues, especially when several iwi have competing claims, tend to push Māori concerns towards their tribal rural roots and away from the urban milieu that most Māori find themselves in. This iwi-centrism advanced further in 1985 when Māori were granted the right to take historical claims to the Waitangi Tribunal, a quasi-judicial state agency which advises government on how to compensate breeches of Māori Treaty rights. Māori have vigorously claimed cultural grievances and historic land alienation, resulting in a number of multi-million dollar settlements.

Throughout this period, reform-oriented activists also began to develop arguments in favor of biculturalism that meshed with the new government policy, though always seeking to push reforms one step further. An example of this developing rhetoric is Linda Tuhiwai Smith's 1999 *Decolonizing Methodologies: Research and Indigenous Peoples.* In the 1970s, Smith served as a reform leader in Nga Tamatoa (Johnson 26). As Nga Tamatoa members grew older, they moved into different protest groups and followed other avenues for political action. As Professor of Education at the University of Auckland, Smith researches indigenous education, and she has also helped to develop wānanga (tribal universities). In *Decolonizing Methodologies,* Smith writes explicitly from "the vantage point of the colonized" with a primary audience of other indigenous peoples (1). Notably, this globally-oriented indigenous identity is her primary *ethos*, even though her examples recognize more unique identities. For example, she presents her views not only by discussing unique Māori experiences, values, and forms of knowledge, but she also regularly bases her claims on the unique experiences of particular iwi and hapū. Smith seeks a global audience, but explicitly excludes non-indigenous researchers as a significant component of that audience (17). This approach is less a call for separatism than it is an assertion that indigenous culture is a solid foundation for a research program that has no need to rely on European methodologies. Smith's desire for an indigenous people's movement (Smith 7) rather than a brown power movement served as one part of a general frame transformation,[11] which Hauraki Greenland has called a move from negritude to ethnicity, from blackness to indigeneity, from straightforward identification with the overseas rhetoric of Black Power to a more locally and unique understanding of ethnicity and culture.

Nonetheless, traces of the rhetoric of black and brown power have also remained a major rhetorical resource for activist Māori writing. For example, Andrew Eruera Vercoe takes "power" as a key word in his 1998 *Educating Jake: Pathways to Empowerment*. Over and over Vercoe uses the word "power" to support Māori developing their own strategies for addressing their social problems and to emphasize what Māori culture offers to this development. In a particularly telling move, Vercoe at one point suggests an elision of "power" with "mana." The cultural importance of the latter term draws attention to Vercoe's choice to introduce it as a subordinate elaboration on his primary concept of Māori power (11).[12] In sum, Vercoe's explicitly anti-assimilationist message of Māori autonomy shows the continued viability of a re-accented rhetoric of brown power that was first developed in the late 1960s/early 1970s.

The separation of reformist and revolutionary goals, and of the rhetorical movements of indigenous peoples and brown power, should not be overemphasized, as overlapping memberships in MOOHR, Nga Tamatoa, and other Māori organizations brought these perspectives in constant dialogue with each other. Even in the marked divisions of the early 1970s, before legal and social change signaled the clear ascendancy of biculturalism, the prevalence of face-to-face protest actions such as the 1975 Māori Land March or the 1977 Bastion Point occupation ensured constant dialogical exchange. While marked by internal differences, these shared actions nonetheless enabled a collective renegotiation of Māori identity (Greenland 96-97).

One inflection of this renegotiation indicates an overlap between separatist goals and a rhetoric based more deeply on indigenous Māori experience than on global identifications. In *Maori Sovereignty*, which was published in sections during the early 1980s, Donna Awatere, a radical who maintained her membership in Nga Tamatoa longer than most others, articulates a continued separatist vision (Johnson 73). Yet, even as Awatere makes Māori sovereignty her superordinate concern ("It is sovereignty or nothing" [32], she writes), and even as she makes indigenous Māori experience her primary means of developing her argument, she does not reject global connections between colonized black persons. Echoing Sojourner Truth's famous mid-nineteenth century speech to the Women's Convention in Ohio, Awatere asks her primarily feminist audience, "Aren't I a woman?" Like Truth and other U.S. black feminists since her, Awatere continues to explain that the "200,000 Maori girls and women ... in *our* [i.e. Māori] country" should have a primary say in deciding the priorities of New Zealand feminists (43, emphasis in the original). In this way, Awatere articulates a unique rhetoric of Māori sovereignty in solidarity with other blacks internationally, echoing their arguments as support for her primary claim to Māori rangatiratanga. As with so many other Māori who were radicalized in the late 1960s and the 1970s, Awatere's rhetoric integrally relies on global rhetorical resources, on an understanding of identities formed through colonization and population shifts, and on systemically connecting these to unique aspects of Māori culture and local history, dramatically interpreted through a history of treaty grievances.

Pedagogical Uptakes from Collective Action

In this section, we return explicitly to the claims of our introduction and highlight how the above history of Māori activism leads to a reconstructed understanding of *the rhetorical situation*, defined as an interested set of associations, relations, and exchanges selected from the larger global system and articulated with the local. Following our exemplification of each point, we suggest, in brief, a pedagogical implication.

1. Introducing new forms of rhetoric involves crafting new sets of relationships and therefore requires the active construction of a rhetorical situation. All components of this situation are up for grabs, including the identities of rhetors and audiences, as Biesecker argues. Yet whether audiences will accept how they are identified and whether they will find a rhetorical act persuasive depends on their own understanding of the relationships brought together within that rhetorical act.

Prior to 1971, public responses to the recurrent exigence of Waitangi Day remembrances focused on celebration. To mobilize a protest, activists needed to connect this 1840 treaty, which had previously been understood simply as the founding of a nation, to other historic events, such as ongoing acts of land alienation. When Nga Tamatoa began to protest at treaty celebrations in 1971, the resulting rhetorical shock to mainstream Pākehā indicated a mismatch between Pākehā and activist understandings of the treaty and, additionally, the existence of disparate understandings of the audience themselves. Did the audience consist of white racists? Despite initial incomprehension from the audience, over time activism led to incrementally better conditions for Māori and a shift in Pākehā opinion. In particular, the New Zealand government grew to accept Māori claims that there has been historical injustice and that there still are contemporary power imbalances, and the government has subsequently responded to many land grievances and increased its recognition of Māori language and culture.

By underscoring the importance of constructed relationships to rhetorical situations, this example suggests that judgments of appropriate rhetoric are also constructed and, further, these judgments are not always controlled by the audience, even in originally unequal power relations. This calls into question standard practices of assessing student work according to a given rhetorical situation that is known best by the teacher. An alternative approach would be for teachers and students to explore together rhetorical influences that students bring to assignments instead of privileging teacher understandings. This would reverse overemphases on the importance of pre-established discourse communities, emphases that Victor Villanueva and others have critiqued as assimilationist. Yet it should be recognized that a major source of resistance to anti-normative rhetoric is that it not only produces new arguments; it also often repositions audiences in ways they resist. If composition teaching is to allow radical rhetoric and "radical possibility" (Biesecker 127), instruction on *the rhetorical situation* should include discussion of the benefits, as well as the drawbacks, of confronting audiences' self-understanding. While social movement rhetoric should not be held up as a better or even alternative model for students to emulate, which would simply replicate assimilation in a new way, classroom discussion of social movement rhetorics can provide students with a more complex understanding of the rhetorical choices available to them. Such choices should not be romanticized, as successful audience confrontation often entails a long-term commitment to "becoming" on the part of both rhetors and audiences engaged in a process of changing relations.

2. Because rhetorical situations are made by linking together aspects of a system into a series of relationships, effective rhetoric can readily shift between local and global relations, or point to both at once.

The rhetoric of "brown power" required Māori to build new relationships between themselves and with blacks from the U.S., South Africa, and other nations worldwide. While the basic structure of this slogan indicates these global identifications, the switch from "black" to "brown" emphasizes local features of the rhetorical situation. Similarly, the indigenous people's movement also relies on both global and local relationships to situate rhetoric that acts to change the world system. Through the rhetoric of indigeneity, Māori activists are able to build common cause worldwide while still acting through distinctive features of Māori, iwi, and hapū culture and society. This combination of global and local identifications illustrates a play of differences that allows both heterogeneity and coalition-building.

Many classrooms emphasize local features of rhetorical situations, often at the expense of global ones. Designing assignments for narrowly-understood situations can certainly help students focus and make classroom writing seem more directly analogous to writing situations with clearly-defined tasks serving routine purposes. Additionally, when responding to a specific and readily-imagined situation, student writing may become more concrete and purposeful.

In order to create this specific situation, however, the teacher must select the most important relationships, letting students avoid the task of sorting through complex systems to decide the most relevant connections themselves. The price of such simplification is that students have less practice imagining how they might exercise rhetorical agency in an increasingly globalized world. An alternative is to invite students into the process of defining the exigencies for assignments.

3. Because the construction of a rhetorical situation articulates rhetor identities in a system of relationships, the development of collective identities can be a key strategy for social movements seeking the reconstruction of those relationships.

Nga Tamatoa's identity was resisted not only by mainstream Pākehā but often, and sometimes more strongly, by older, more conservative Māori who believed Tamatoa had departed from traditional and valued aspects of Māori culture. Nonetheless, Nga Tamatoa members argued that their activist identity played an important role in highlighting, first, the breakdown of Māori culture and, second, the continued oppression of Māori by Pākehā. This identity thereby called for a restructuring of relationships within Māori society and between Māori and Pākehā. As Aroha Harris stated, "In an acknowledgement that understanding ourselves is an access to understanding each other, Pakeha were challenged to learn about themselves–their own culture, identity and history" (89). Because it created a politicized identity, Nga Tomatoa could not easily be ignored, and any response to the activists, even critical responses, needed to engage Nga Tamatoa's understanding of social relations and their embodiment of a new way of being Māori.

This focus on collective rhetors, while supported by the collaborative emphases of some composition pedagogies, is still typically subordinated to individual work within writing instruction, and it is especially undermined by the individual assessment academic institutions often make routine. This individualism ignores the importance of collective identity construction as a key rhetorical strategy in a global system; an emphasis on the collective instead suggests the value of pedagogies that articulate student work in shared projects developed over time through dialogue.

Conclusion

For decades, composition teachers, writing handbooks, and theorists have found *the rhetorical situation* a useful concept for contextualizing and locating writing. In particular, defined rhetorical situations are used to guide student invention by providing clear constraints on the rhetoric deemed appropriate for particular audiences. Despite the usefulness of the concept, the critiques of

Biesecker, Ervin, Rude, and others increasingly note limits to early understandings of *the rhetorical situation* as an easily identifiable (natural) and discrete (ephemeral) context. One of the particular challenges to understanding this "context" is the increasingly global relations in which we are all embedded and how this system changes strategies for exercising rhetorical agency.

In this chapter, we have used the example of Māori activists, especially Nga Tamatoa activists, to exemplify some of the ways that globalization can change theoretical understandings of *the rhetorical situation.* 1970s activists' rhetorical strategies included the construction of collective identities, the combination of global and local elements within their rhetorical situation, and a readiness to contradict their audience's understanding of that situation. These strategies suggest that radical rhetorics can articulate alternative views of the present—they can even articulate alternative world systems. In so doing, these strategies also suggest that all components of rhetorical situations—audience, rhetors, referents, and the relationships between them—are potentially changeable, in a process of social movement.

Notes

1. Pākehā, meaning "other," refers to white descendants of European colonists.
2. Māori tribal groups are known as iwi, which are made up of smaller kin groups, hapū.
3. See, for example, Aroha Harris (89); David Slack (77-78); Andrew Sharp (11, 41); Pat Snedden (40-41). *New Zealand Herald* reports on protests also indicate reactions including hostility, confusion, shame, and support ("Noisy"; "Support"; "Protesters").
4. New Zealand historians have reached a general consensus about the factual claims in this section. James Belich's recent two-volume history of New Zealand is an invaluable general source. For a general popular history, see Michael King. Ranginui Walker offers a valuable overall Māori history. Claudia Orange provides an account of the Treaty of Waitangi and its subsequent influence.
5. The English version guaranteed "the full, exclusive, and undisturbed possession of their Lands and Estates, Forests, Fisheries, and other property"; the Māori version upheld "the tino Rangatiratanga [full chiefdomship] of their lands, settlements, and all valued things."
6. American sociologist, David P. Ausubel, who researched New Zealand society in the late 1950s, notes that Pākehā New Zealanders consistently compared unfavorable the race relations of the United States with their own.
7. Isaac Featherston, an early colonial politician, is credited with this remark, which was subsequently used through the nineteenth century.
8. This article, written in March 1971, was intended for publication in the New Zealand Listener. Rejected from that forum, Nga Tamatoa circulated the article as photocopies.
9. In an interesting parallel, the King Movement looked to Haiti as an exemplar of power wrested by blacks from whites (Paterson).

10. "If they withhold our language from the schools, it really means that they force their language on us—well, y'know, that's a racist act, it's being race-dominant" (MOOHR 2).

11. Building on the work of Ervin Goffman, David Snow et al. first apply the term "frame transformation" to social movements. For a review of social movement framing theory, see Robert Benford and David Snow.

12. Vercoe writes, "The people who are going to make the difference are already there working at the flax roots. That's where our power lies and that's the way it's always been—this is what my people need to realise. An āriki's mana comes from his people—it's always been that way" (11).

Works Cited

Anderson, Benedict. *Imagined Communities*. 2nd ed. London: Verso, 1991.

Ausubel, David P. *The Fern and the Tiki: An American View of New Zealand: National Character, Social Attitudes and Race Relations*. Sydney: Angus & Robertson, 1960.

Awatere, Donna. *Maori Sovereignty*. Auckland, New Zealand: Broadsheet, 1984.

Belich, James. *Making Peoples: A History of the New Zealanders from Polynesian Settlement to the End of the Nineteenth Century*. Honolulu: University of Hawai'i Press, 1996.

——. *Paradise Reforged: A History of the New Zealanders From the 1880s to the Year 2000*. Honolulu: University of Hawai'i Press, 2001.

Benford, Robert D., and David A. Snow. "Framing Processes and Social Movements: An Overview and Assessment." *Annual Review of Sociology* 26 (2000): 611-39.

Biesecker, Barbara A. "Rethinking the Rhetorical Situation from within the Thematic of Differánce." *Philosophy and Rhetoric* 22,2 (1989): 110-30.

Billig, Michael. "Rhetorical Psychology, Ideological Thinking, and Imagining Nationhood." *Social Movements and Culture*. Eds. Hank Johnston and Bert Klandermans. Minneapolis: University of Minnesota Press, 1995. 64-81.

Bitzer, Lloyd F. "The Rhetorical Situation." *Philosophy and Rhetoric* 1 (1968): 1-14.

Ervin, Elizabeth. "Rhetorical Situations and the Straits of Inappropriateness: Teaching Feminist Activism." *Rhetoric Review* 25 (2006): 316-33.

Friedman, Debra, and Doug McAdam. "Collective Identity and Activism: Networks, Choices, and the Life of a Social Movement." *Frontiers in Social Movement Theory*. Eds. Aldon D. Morris and Carol McClurg Mueller. New Haven, CT: Yale University Press, 1992. 156-73.

Goffman, Ervin. *Frame Analysis*. New York: Harper and Row, 1974.

Greenland, Hauraki. "Maori Ethnicity as Ideology." *Nga Take: Ethnic Relations and Racism in Aotearoa/New Zealand*. Eds. Paul Spoonley, David Pearson, and Cluny Macpherson. Palmerston North, New Zealand: Dunmore Press, 1991.

Gusfield, Joseph R. "The Reflexivity of Social Movements: From Ideology to Identity." *New Social Movements: From Ideology to Identity*. Eds. Enrique Laraña, Hank Johnston, and Joseph R. Gusfield. Philadelphia: Temple University Press, 1994. 58-78.

Harris, Aroha. *Hīkoi: Forty Years of Māori Protest*. Wellington: Huia Publishers, 2004.

Hauser, Gerard, and erin daina mcclellan. "Vernacular Rhetoric and Social Movements: Performances of Resistance in the Rhetoric of the Everyday." *Active Voices: Composing a Rhetoric of Social Movements*. Eds. Sharon

McKenzie Stevens and Patricia Malesh. Albany, NY: State University of New York Press, 2009. 23-46.

Heath, Robert L. "Dialectical Confrontation: A Strategy of Black Radicalism." *Central States Speech Journal* 24 (1973): 168-77.

Johnson, Lin. "Nga Tamatoa: Just a 'Raggle-Taggle Band' of Trouble Makers?" *Bachelor of Arts with Honours*. Massey University, 2005.

King, Michael. *The Penguin History of New Zealand*. Auckland, New Zealand: Penguin Books, 2003.

Lindemann, Erika. *A Rhetoric for Writing Teachers*. 4th ed. New York: Oxford University Press, 2001.

Maori Organisation on Human Rights (MOOHR). "MOOHR Interviews Two Members of Nga Tamatoa Tuatoru." Interview. *MOOHR Newsletter* September 1971: 1-7.

Marcus, George. "Ethnography in/of the World System: The Emergence of Multi-Sited Ethnography." *Annual Review of Anthropology* 24 (1995): 95-117.

Melucci, Alberto. "The Process of Collective Identity." *Social Movements and Culture*. Eds. Hank Johnston and Bert Klandermans. Minneapolis: University of Minnesota Press, 1995. 41-63.

New Zealand Parliament. *Parliamentary Debates*. Vol. 391. 1974.

Nga Tamatoa Council. "The Fly." 1971. 3.

———. "The Resurrection of Maori Identity." 1971. 2.

"Noisy Protesters Disrupt Waitangi Event." *New Zealand Herald* 8 Feb. 1971: 3.

Ong, Aihwa. *Spirits of Resistance and Capitalist Discipline: Factory Women in Malaysia*. Albany, NY: State University of New York Press, 1987.

Orange, Claudia. *The Treaty of Waitangi*. Wellington, New Zealand: Bridget Williams Books, 1992.

Paterson, Lachlan. *Colonial Discourses: Niupepa Māori 1855-1863*. Dunedin: Otago University Press, 2006.

Pieterse, Jan Nederveen. *Globalization and Culture: Global Mélange*. Oxford: Rowman & Littlefield, 2004.

"Protesters at Waitangi." *New Zealand Herald* 8 Feb. 1971: 6.

Rude, Carolyn D. "Toward an Expanded Concept of Rhetorical Delivery: The Uses of Reports in Public Policy Debates." *Technical Communication Quarterly* 13,3 (2004): 271-88.

Sharp, Andrew. *Justice and the Maori: Maori Claims in New Zealand Political Argument in the 1980s*. Auckland: Oxford University Press, 1991.

Slack, David. *Bullshit, Backlash and Bleeding Hearts: A Confused Person's Guide to the Great Race Row*. Auckland: Penguin, 2004.

Smith, Linda Tuhiwai. *Decolonizing Methodologies: Research and Indigenous Peoples*. London: Zed Books; Dunedin: University of Otago Press, 1999.

Snedden, Pat. *Pākehā and the Treaty: Why It's Our Treaty Too*. Auckland: Random House, 2005.

Snow, David A., et al. "Frame Alignment Processes, Micromobilization, and Movement Participation." *American Sociological Review* 51 (1986): 464-81.

"Support by Some, Shame Felt by Others." *New Zealand Herald* 8 Feb. 1971: 3.

Van Deburg, William L. *New Day in Babylon: The Black Power Movement and American Culture, 1965-1975.* Chicago: University of Chicago Press, 1992.

Vatz, Richard E. "The Myth of the Rhetorical Situation." *Philosophy and Rhetoric* 6,3 (1973): 154-61.

Vercoe, Andrew Eruera. *Educating Jake: Pathways to Empowerment.* Auckland, New Zealand: HarperCollins, 1998.

Villanueva, Victor. "The Politics of Literacy across the Curriculum." *WAC for the New Millennium: Strategies for Continuing Writing-Across-the-Curriculum Programs.* Eds. Susan H. McLeod, et al. Urbana, IL: NCTE, 2001. 165-78.

Walker, Ranginui. *Ka Whawhai Tonu Matou: Struggle without End.* Auckland, New Zealand: Penguin Books, 2004.

Think Global, Eat Local: Teaching Alternative Agrarian Literacy in a Globalized Age

Eileen E. Schell

The food business is far and away the most important business in the world. Everything else is a luxury. Food is what you need to sustain life every day. Food is fuel. You can't run a tractor without fuel and you can't run a human being without it either. Food is the absolute beginning. (Dwayne Andreas, former CEO of Archer Daniels Midland, qtd in Cockburn and St. Clair)

To solve the world hunger crisis, it's necessary to do more than send emergency food aid to countries facing famine. Leaders must address the globalized system of agricultural production and trade that favors large corporate agriculture and export oriented crops while discriminating against small-scale farmers and agriculture oriented to local needs. As a result of official inaction, more than thirty million people die of malnutrition and starvation every year, while large industrial farms export ever more strawberries and cut flowers to affluent consumers. Excessive meat production, again largely for the affluent, requires massive amounts of feed grains that might otherwise sustain poor families. Giant agribusiness, chemical and restaurant companies like Cargill, Monsanto and McDonalds dominate the world's food chain, building a global dependence on unhealthy and genetically dangerous products. These companies are racing to secure patents on every plant and living organism and their intensive advertising seeks to persuade the world's consumers to eat more and more sweets, snacks, burgers, and soft drinks. (The Global Policy Forum, "Hunger and the Globalized System of Trade and Food Production.")

Globalization, one of the "buzzwords of the decade," as noted by Douglas

Kellner in "Globalization and the Postmodern Turn," has been debated by "[j]ournalists, politicians, business executives, academics, and others [who] are using the word to signify that something profound is happening, that the world is changing, that a new world economic, political, and cultural order is emerging." As Kellner points out, the term *globalization* has a range of meanings adapted for different purposes and contexts, which makes it "difficult to ascertain what is at stake in the globalization problematic, what function the term serves, and what effects it has for contemporary theory and politics." In the mission statements of our colleges and universities we frequently hear proclamations about the need to prepare students to live and work in an information-rich, global economy. Implied in this pro-globalization rhetoric is the idea of students developing the cultural sensitivity and savvy to be successful navigators and consumers of the global market economy. At the same time that such statements appear with increasing frequency and force in our college and university mission statements, the critical consciousness and critical literacy needed to assess and attend to the problematic effects and unequal power relations inherent in globalization are often not addressed. Many of us in higher education, and I include myself in this number, are suspicious of the heady embrace of "globalization" discourses proffered by our institutions. In the words of Kellner, we may see globalization as potentially "bringing about the devastating destruction of local traditions, the continued subordination of poorer nations and regions by richer ones, environmental destruction, and a homogenization of culture and everyday life." Yet "globalization," as Kellner says, is a "theoretical construct that is itself contested and open for various meanings and inflections"; it can be seen as a multivalent process that "describe[s] highly complex and multidimensional processes in the economy, polity, culture, and everyday life." In other words, globalization can function rhetorically to describe a range of processes with possibilities and consequences that are dependent on the material, cultural, social, political, and emotional effects of globalization.

Trying to define and grapple with the rhetorics of globalization is a challenge that began for me as a scholar in 1999 as I began to connect the scholarly work I had been doing for almost a decade on contingent academic labor issues to the struggles of the November 30, 1999, World Trade Organization Protests in Seattle, popularly known as the "Battle for Seattle." In three essays I drafted and published on the labor organizing strategies of contingent faculty members, I focused on how contingent faculty and their supporters were building strategic alliances and coalitions across borders in the Americas (United States, Canada, and Mexico). Through this coalition, advocates organized an international week of solidarity and action—Campus Equity Week— meant to call attention to the working conditions of contingent faculty. Like the protestors involved in the "Battle for Seattle," contingent faculty and their supporters were using a variety of strategies to address their working conditions—allying with workers in other sectors of the university service economy (cafeteria, physical plant, and janitorial staff) and with other contingent workers across national borders, lobbying the legislature, speaking with reporters, writing op-eds for local newspapers, conducting teach-ins, staging street protests, and enacting skits and guerrilla theater in visible places on college campuses.

As I organized events related to Campus Equity Week with colleagues on my local campus in 2001, 2003, and 2005, I became acquainted with undergraduate students from the Student Coalition on Organized Labor (SCOOL) who were organizing to address the ethical and moral challenge posed by sweatshops manufacturing U.S. university sports apparel in Mexico and Asia. Student activists on campus successfully worked over the span of several months to persuade the Syracuse University administration to join the independent labor rights monitoring organization known as the Workers Rights Consortium (WRC). As the student activists persuaded the university to join the WRC, they urged all of us on campus to take action against the unethical and often brutal conditions of globalized sweatshops.

Inspired by the student activists' courageous work and example, I designed a unit on gender, globalization, and sweatshop labor in 2002 as a topic of inquiry in my first-year writing course at Syracuse University; I describe this course in detail in a chapter for the collection *Teaching Rhetorica*. My goal was to present globalization, in Kellner's terms, as a "problematic" for students to consider and sweatshop labor as a specific site of analysis connected to questions of consumption, development, ethics, economics, human rights, and international trade policies. The work I began with students on sweatshop labor also sparked me to consider the larger debates over labor and public policy being addressed with increasing frequency around the global food industrial complex. This was an issue I felt strongly about as a member of a third generation family farm from eastern Washington state—a farm family that saw their livelihood and future in farming cease in 2001 after eighty-three years of operation, in part, due to globalization and corporate consolidation in the apple industry.

My interest in taking up food politics as a topic of inquiry in my writing courses also coincided with the growing reach of the local food movement. The local food—or what some have called the "real food"—movement and its public intellectuals Michael Pollan (*The Omnivore's Dilemma, In Defense of Food*), Marion Nestle (*Food Politics*), Barbara Kingsolver (*Animal, Vegetable, Miracle*), and Vandana Shiva (*Stolen Harvest*) among others have fostered a widescale public debate about the consequences of the industrialized and globalized food system. They have called our attention to growth and consolidation of multinational agribusiness corporations, the inequities of so-called "free trade," the creation of genetically modified organisms or "Frankenfoods, " increasing food insecurity among many nations and communities, and the growing obesity epidemic and diet-related health concerns in the developed and developing world.

The local food movement takes as a central tenet the challenge of "food literacy," knowing what "real food" is versus manufactured food-like substances and knowing how local food—food grown locally or regionally—can provide environmental, health, and community benefits over the globalized and industrialized food system, which I will describe in more detail in a later section of this essay. The local food movement is gaining purchase on college campuses that have joined in the sustainable or "green" campus movement. Many campuses have signed "green" charters to reduce greenhouse gas emissions and have pledged to become carbon neutral within particular time spans. In doing so, they have pledged to reduce their carbon footprint in part by purchasing local or regional food for campus dining facilities since food transport accounts for a large portion of greenhouse gas emissions nationally and globally. As the editors of *Sustainability on Campus: Stories and Strategies for Change* argue: "Campuses across the United States alone represent an enormous investment in buildings and land, and therefore how we maintain and build our physical plant, engage in buying practices, dispose of waste, and consumer energy is critically important to the environmental health of the broader society" (Bartlett and Chase 5).

Some organizations and groups on college campuses cultivate their own gardens, participate in community gardening and urban farm projects, and sponsor farmer's markets on campuses. Many college campuses have taken local food efforts a step further and introduced "food literacy" education into their college dining plans, providing students with literature and fact sheets about local and regional food sources and ways to eat locally and seasonally. And, as I will demonstrate in this essay, some academic departments and disciplines have introduced "food literacy" as a major component of their academic curricula and introductory courses.

In our own field of Rhetoric and Composition, attention to addressing global vs. local food and food literacy issues is on the rise in both scholarly and pedagogical venues. With ecocomposition, sustainability, place-based writing, and globalization becoming increasingly strong research and teaching interests among rhetoric and writing professionals, work in this area is on the rise. For instance, *College English* published a special issue on food writing in 2008.[1] An in-progress edited collection on the rhetoric of food writing *Foodsumptions: Fun, Games, and the Politics of What We Eat* is currently being edited by Risa Gorelick and Lisa DeTora. Jeff and Jenny Rice are editing a special issue of the journal *Pre/Text* of "articles that push the connection between critical theory and food." Rachel Riedner, co-editor of the Lexington book series in which this collection appears, is researching and writing about the "survival economies" of women growing food in community gardens in Cape Town, South Africa. My own work in the co-authored volume *Rural Literacies* (Donehower and Hogg, 2007) and also a new co-edited volume *Reclaiming Rural Literacies*, currently under review at Southern Illinois University Press, offers three essays addressing agricultural literacies. A focus on food has appeared in popular composition textbooks and readers. For instance, the composition reader *Global Issues, Local Arguments* edited by June Johnson contains a cluster of readings on "Feeding

Global Populations" that addresses global food issues: the Green Revolution, global food trade and policy-making, and the politics of world hunger (Johnson 404-5).

As this work demonstrates, scholars and teachers of writing have a growing stake in examining "food" and also the global food industrial complex. For one, our courses reach most of the students in our college and universities. In addition, many large writing programs are situated in land-grant institutions where students majoring in agriculture, agricultural economics, environmental science, food science or nutrition, and rural sociology make up a considerable portion of the student population. However, no matter where one teaches, "food" is an important issue to raise as it poses questions of globalization, environmental health, personal and societal health, consumer choices, social justice, and contemporary politics. Second, a focus on the global food industrial complex fits in well with the focus in many introductory composition courses on critical analysis, critical research, and argument. With the significant public attention given to issues of the global food industrial complex in public essays, editorials, book length studies, and documentaries, there is plenty of written material for students to assess, analyze, and debate (see Berry, Hanson, Kingsolver, Lappe, Nestle, Pollan, Schlosser, Spurlock). Third, a focus on food politics complements efforts in our field to address the environment and ecocomposition (Dobrin and Weisser), place-based education (Brooke), and sustainability (Owens). Derek Owens argues in *Composition and Sustainability* that "sustainable culture cannot exist unless sustainability features prominently throughout the curriculum" (28). Owens argues that students should have a basic understanding of sustainable agriculture and forestry before graduation. Fourth, a focus on the issue of food provides a space for fostering the critical consciousness and critical literacy needed to assess and attend to the problematic effects and unequal power relations inherent in globalization given the environmental, political, and social consequences of industrialized, globalized food production.

To understand how a focus on food literacy might work in a composition classroom, I offer a brief analysis of the problematic of global food and literacy. Finally, the latter half of the essay will bring conversations about global and local food politics into the writing classroom through a brief discussion of the sophomore-level critical research and writing course (WRT 205) that I teach at Syracuse University.

The Problematic of Global Food and Literacy

Although food is one of the most highly trafficked global commodities and local food movements are on the rise, as noted earlier, many United States citizens are still largely "agriculturally illiterate," unaware of how our food supply is grown, harvested, transported, processed, distributed, and sold. Whereas the majority of food in the developed and developing world was once grown on small family-owned farms, since World War II most food in developed nations, especially the United States, is grown on increasingly large and distant farms in the United States or imported from other countries, traveling an average of 1,200 miles or more to our tables ("Global Warming"). Moreover, food is distributed by a handful of global food corporations that exert a sizable influence over domestic and international agricultural policies. In short, the global food industrial complex has transformed how we consume and relate to food.

In our daily lives in the United States, we are encouraged by large transnational food corporations, by corporate grocery chains, and by a lack of critical literacy education on food and farming issues to adopt a stance toward food based on neoliberal literacy. Neoliberal literacy, according to Jacqueline Edmondson, is a discourse of neoliberalism that "reads rural life through a language that constitutes mass production, efficiency, and more recently, neoliberal principles. This discourse values agribusiness, market-based logic, and fast capitalism" (15). Neoliberal literacy emphasizes the realization of the principles of the market economy—maximizing profits and efficiency, exploiting resources and labor, expanding operations, and providing consumers with copious choices while increasingly divorcing them from understanding the means of production. A neoliberal literacy teaches those of us in the developed world to believe that food must be cheap, fast, and accessible, and we shouldn't have to think about how it is produced and at what cost other than choosing what we want in the grocery store or at our favorite restaurants. The actual environmental and human costs of food production—due to agricultural methods, consolidation and integration, environmental impacts, labor issues, and trade relations—are far removed from most Americans' imagination and daily thinking, the subject of op-eds, special interest books, or documentaries read or viewed by a small minority of the population. Thus, neoliberal literacy, at its core, keeps the majority of the consuming public "illiterate" about how food is grown and at what environmental and societal costs.

I do not have the space here to devote to a detailed discussion of the transformation of the food system from a local, regional, and national system to a global system—an issue I address at length in a chapter of my co-authored book *Rural Literacies*. What I do wish to indicate, though, is that the global food industry has spotlighted the problem of power and control: "Decisions about how our food is grown and by whom are made behind closed doors. Trade and agricultural ministers have allowed multinational corporations to gain unprecedented power and control over our food system. As a result, America's reliance on imported foods has increased" ("The Global"). Meanwhile, consumers are "largely left in the dark about the negative impacts of cheap imports within the domestic food system" ("The Global"). Furthermore the move toward so-called "free trade" means that the United States and many other industrialized nations have become dependent on a global food economy where export crops are featured prominently. The environmental consequences of global food are worth noting, especially in a time of diminishing fossil fuel resources. Helena Norberg-Hodge and Steven Gorelick argue that global food systems are usually monocultures, which "require massive inputs of pesticides, herbicides, and chemical fertilizers." Furthermore, a global food economy requires that millions of dollars be spent on fuel for food transport, thus "making food transport a major contributor to fossil fuel use, pollution and greenhouse gas emissions." In the United States, "transporting food within the nation's borders accounts for over 20 percent of all commodity transport" and "120 million tonnes of CO2 emissions every year" (Norberg-Hodge and Gorelick). In an age of depleted fossil fuel resources and global warming, the logic of "global food" has reached a critical juncture and has caused many food and farming advocacy organizations and environmental groups to advocate for a return to local and regional systems of food production. According to local food advocates like Norberg-Hodge and Gorelick, local or regional food costs less to transport, requires less preservation or modification, and is not as dependent on pesticides and non-organic fertilizers that are common in monocultural production.

While this brief sketch does not do justice to all of the economic and agricultural trade-related trends and patterns currently in play, it outlines the challenges that national and global trade policy poses to small farmers and those concerned with the food system—in other words, to all of us who eat. The current trend toward consolidation and the attendant movement toward global food trade underscores the need for citizens to engage in democratic movements for the protection and sustenance of local food systems, what Vandana Shiva refers to as "food democracy."[2] Not only is the future of small family farms at stake, but also the health of our citizens, the welfare of farm lands and small farms, and the future of the environment.

One significant way to begin addressing such issues is to engage in critical literacy education that will allow us to enact considered change in our global and national political venues, our local communities, classrooms, and in our personal choices at food-outlets. Recently, World Trade Organization protests by farmers and food democracy activists have spotlighted how global agribusiness corporations have disenfranchised many small family farmers, farm workers, rural people, and consumers, leading to the situation described by The Global Policy Forum that appears in this chapter's epigraph. Movements such as local food, slow food, organic farming, community-supported agriculture, community food security, anti-biotechnology, urban gardening, and the revitalization of farmers' markets are slowly shifting people's consciousness and eating habits. Many people are "returning to the local" to meet their basic food needs, thus practicing an alternative agrarian literacy, a form of critical literacy that involves an understanding of the environmental, social, and political consequences of the food system and an endorsement of developing sustainable food systems and sustainable ways of living (Frefoygle xviii). This essay will address alternative

agrarian literacy as achieved through critical literacy instruction as one significant way to address the politics of globalization and its effects on everyday people. Since we all eat everyday and since industrially produced food is resource-
intensive, requiring subsidized water, fertilizer, pesticides, and fossil fuels, it is a
particularly interesting and useful concept through which to address global operations of capital, power, environmental resources, labor, consumption, and literacies.

The Global Food Industrial Complex and Critical Literacy Education: Toward an Alternative Agrarian Literacy

A significant component of the work to address global and local food politics is
influenced by the idea of "literacy" education, an area in the field with which
many of us are acquainted. Literacy, in Deborah Brandt's words, serves as a
resource—"economic, political, intellectual, spiritual—which like wealth or
education, or trade skill or social connections, is pursued for the opportunities
and protections that it potentially grants its seekers" (5). Critical literacy mar-
shals the resources of literacy, in the words of Ira Shor, and "challenges the status quo in an effort to discover alternative paths for self and social development." Critical literacy allows us to analyze and rethink the practices of
everyday life and encourages dissenting perspectives that allow people to connect "the political and the personal, the public and the private, the global and the
local, the economic and the pedagogical for rethinking our lives and for promoting justice in place of inequity" (Shor). Critical literacy, then, "can be thought of
as a social practice in itself and as a tool for the study of other social practices"
(Shor). Following the lead of critical literacy scholars like Brandt and Shor, I see
the practice of critical literacy and the analytic framework it provides as a way
to help our students and communities move toward creating knowledgeable,
literate global citizens who are prepared with the "knowledge and skills for social and environmental justice" (Andrezejewski and Alessio).

Local food activists refer to critical literacy education on food and farming
issues as simply "food learning," and they advocate that food learning be taught
at all levels of schooling (see Winne). Community food educators like Mark
Winne of the Community Food Security Coalition, a 501c3 nonprofit that promotes community food sovereignty, believes that it should be a "matter of national educational policy that every child understands how and where their food
is produced, and that they have the requisite skills to critique those systems of
production." He further argues that students should have the chance to read the
authors that address food production, such as "Jim Hightower as well as Joan
Gussow, Frances Moore Lappe, Marion Nestle, Eric Schlosser, Wendell Berry,

Walt Whitman and, God forbid, Marx and Engels." Although Winne's call is largely focused on K-12 educators, he includes public educators in his manifesto and calls for integrated and wide-reaching models of food and nutrition education:

> I would argue, however, that any attempt to reform our approach to food and nutrition education must be comprehensive and saturate every fiber of **our** public education institutions. We should not succumb to the temptation to limit our endeavors to isolated and discreet projects, as worthy as they may be. Unfortunately, it is simply not enough to yank the soda machines out of the schools, run a school garden for a few weeks, ban irradiated food, establish a school breakfast program here and there, install an organic salad bar in the school cafeteria. Yes, we need those projects and they must be multiplied a thousand fold. But we have to also worm, no, not worm, **bust** our way into the circles of power, nationally as well as locally. We must make our schools the breeding ground for millions of food competent, healthy, and happy children who retain those attributes as adults and become demanding, knowledgeable food consumers, voters, and, in some cases, farmers, nutritionists, chefs, policymakers, and members of the local school boards that control the curricula.

Winne's manifesto for food learning is a call not only to educate young people, but a call to provide critical literacy education on food production for all levels of society. Winne's extended vision of food learning has been realized, to some degree, by farmers, non-profit agencies, fair trade activists, farmers' market directors, USDA employees, community gardeners, public school teachers, college and university professors, and college students. At the Community Food Security "Farm to Cafeteria" Conferences, which took place on June 16-18, 2005, at Kenyon College in Ohio, I had the opportunity to see a branch of the national "food democracy" movement in action. At the conference, hundreds gathered to discuss processes and models for bringing local, family farmed food into their local hospitals, K-12 schools, colleges and universities, and prisons. At several sessions, college faculty and K-12 teachers across the disciplines shared syllabi and assignments that address food, farm, and sustainability issues. At several sessions as well, college student activists spoke with great vigor about how they have set up local food projects on their campuses. In addition, K-12 teachers and farmers addressed how they have used provisions in the federal school lunch program to bring locally farmed food to school cafeterias. The Farm to Cafeteria conference made it clear that there is a nationwide movement to feature local foods and to teach and discuss food and farm issues across the disciplines, to practice an alternative agrarian literacy instead of a neoliberal literacy. The conference also renewed my interest in bringing these issues into my writing and research courses at Syracuse University.

Inspired by this work of student activists, by my own agricultural background, and by an abiding interest in taking up issues of globalization, I began to integrate content and research projects on the global food industrial complex in my Writing 205 Critical Research and Writing course. Over the past three times I have taught the course (Spring '03, Spring '04, and Spring '06), I have designed a second unit that examines the rise of global agribusiness, the shift from a local to global food system, policy and activist debates over international trade agreements, alternative globalization and food democracy movements, farm worker movements, and a host of other issues.

One of the most significant ways to begin to understand the global food industrial complex is to survey with students the public policies and patterns surrounding agricultural production. This is a challenging task as national farm policy and global trade agreements are complex and multi-layered. The main text I have assigned to introduce debates and issues in the food industry is Eric Schlosser's *New York Times* best-seller *Fast Food Nation*, a book that persuasively guides students through the history of the rise of fast food as an American institution and systematically unpacks its political, social, environmental, and global consequences. A number of chapters in the book focus on the American agricultural system: on corporate consolidation in agribusiness, on the loss of small cattle ranches and the rise of large confined animal feeding operations (or CAFOs), the exploitation of Mexican and Central American slaughterhouse workers, and other topics, all of which connect back to the burgers and fries that many Americans consume on a daily basis. Schlosser promotes an alternative agrarian literacy by showing what lies behind our consumer choices. For instance, as he narrates the tragic story of the Colorado rancher Hank who committed suicide in the wake of losing his ranch, we also learn of the suburbanization of Colorado ranch lands and the global economic pressures and policies that Hank and other small ranchers face. As Schlosser puts it:

> It would be wrong to say that Hank's death was caused by the consolidating and homogenizing influence of the fast food chains, by monopoly power in the meatpacking industry, by depressed prices in the cattle market, by the economic forces bankrupting independent ranches, by the tax laws that favor wealthy ranchers, by the unrelenting push of Colorado's real estate developers. But it would not be entirely wrong. (146)

Fast Food Nation brings to light the structure of the food industrial complex and balances it against the environmental and human costs it bears, encouraging readers to begin thinking critically about the food system.

To round out the discussion of food and farm issues, I also assign supplemental readings on issues of globalization to open up questions of global trade, labor, and the role of the international community in addressing issues of agriculture and fair trade. Assigned chapters of Naomi Klein's book *No Logo* introduce students to debates over globalization, multinational corporate branding, and consumerism. Visits to the online archive of The World Trade Organization (WTO) History Project at the University of Washington also provide students with a glimpse into the protests that took place on November 29-December 3,

1999, in Seattle, Washington, at the World Trade Organization Third Ministerial Meeting. Students have the opportunity to view and analyze protest announcements, fliers, pamphlets, interviews, and other organizing and informational literature that was distributed before and during the protests. Excerpts from Klein's more recent book *Fences and Windows* detail her observations about the alternative globalization movements and their fight for fair trade, not just free trade. In *Fences and Windows* Klein models an integrated global analysis that is based on understanding of "global linkages." Understanding "global linkages," says Klein, is "about recognizing that every piece of our high-gloss consumer culture comes from somewhere. It's about following the webs of contracted factories, shell-game subsidiaries, and outsourced labor to find out where all the pieces are manufactured, under what conditions, which lobby groups wrote the rules of the game and which politicians were bought off along the way" (30). While Klein's comments about understanding "global linkages" address the manufacture of consumer goods specifically, her comments can be applied to the food industrial complex as well and offer an interesting connective thread with Schlosser's analytic approach to the food industrial complex.

To round out Schlosser's book with multimedia texts, I show three films that help students visualize how the food industrial complex impacts workers, consumers, and the environment. The first is *Fast Food Women,* which provides an analysis of the lives and working conditions of Southern women working in three fast-food outlets. The second is Morgan Spurlock's *Super Size Me,* which details Spurlock's declining health as he subsists on fast food from McDonald's for thirty days. The final film is *The Meatrix,* a flash film that humorously but compellingly describes the rise of factory farms. Mimicking the plot and characters of the cult-classic *The Matrix, The Meatrix* details the hidden truth about our food supply: that the idyllic small family farms of our national unconscious have been replaced by factory farms run by large agribusiness corporations. The film is interesting not only for its content, but also its quick-moving style and its spoof of popular culture. In conjunction with showing this film, I often discuss with my students the potential of new media as a tool for educating and persuading the public about food and farm issues. Together these readings and films—and there are many more produced in recent years that could be used such as *The Future of Food* and *Food, Inc*—combine to help students gain increasing insight into how citizen-activist movements have responded to questions of the global food industrial complex.

The writing assignments that accompany this unit include weekly two- to three-page typed responses to the assigned readings as well as a formal writing assignment that involves students in collectively researching and writing a "research anthology" on a particular topic of concern that arose from their reading of *Fast Food Nation*, the other assigned readings, and the films. Although the anthology is a collective assignment, with students collaboratively authoring an introduction and conclusion and composing a cover, each student contributes a well-researched analytical essay of approximately eight pages that introduces a specific issue appropriate to their anthology topic and provides informed perspectives on their chosen issue. Students have composed anthologies that investigate a number of agriculturally related topics, including a comparative analysis of factory farming of beef cattle versus organically raised range-fed beef, the rise of Mad-Cow disease in light of contaminated feed and lapsed food safety inspection standards, French farmer Jose Bove's nationalistic resistance to McDonald's and the global celebrity status he has acquired through his protests, Bush's immigration policies and their impact on Mexican farm workers, and the conditions of banana workers in Costa Rica in light of free trade agreements. One of the chief advantages of this assignment is that students constantly move back and forth from their individual essay writing and research to thinking about the collective project as a whole. This mix of collective and individual research efforts challenges students' preconceived notions about writing and research as a single-minded enterprise and helps them figure out how to consider a topic from multiple angles. The group also gives a presentation on their anthology at the end of the unit, offering their ideas for discussion and critique. Often few of my students are from rural backgrounds and few are from farming communities, and few coming into the course are initially aware of the issues raised in the Schlosser's book, Klein's books, and the films. Most students agree, however, that the writing and reading assignments have made them think about and critically engage with food in a way that they have never thought about it before: in systematic, critical, and interconnected ways and in ways that help them combat the neoliberal literacy framework.

In thinking through the questions of power, access, and the environment posed by a writing-related inquiry into food, I am also inspired by J.K. Gibson Graham's notion of the connection between feeling, action, and ethical self-making. Gibson-Graham argues that thinking involves structures of feeling and action, that our responses are conditioned by our "stances," our "affective dispositions," our "curiosity and openness" to new ideas and positions versus our sense of constraint: "To cultivate new attitudes and practices of thinking is to cultivate a new relation to the world and its always hidden possibilities" (xxix). Food can bring to the fore "new attitudes and practices of thinking" because of the interconnection of thinking, feeling, and action surrounding it. Food is often intimate and emotional, connected to the body, family, community, culture, and, whether we realize it or not, place. Food elicits strong feelings of like, dislike, need, desire, want, and intimacy. Food, thus, has an affective and place-based dimension that can be complicated and interrogated by a consideration of "food politics": how eating is a political, social, and material act.

Because of food's affective dimension, a writing class focused on food politics is a charged space. Course readings, films, and writing assignments "pull the veil" away from the industrialized, globalized food system and ask class members to account for how they are implicated in the system's benefits as well as its environmental, social, and political costs. As I note in a forthcoming essay on teaching the flash film *The Meatrix*, an analytic encounter with the industrialized and globalized food system is a disturbing and often dystopian experience for students. Many students are strongly affected by the analyses and images of the factory farms or CAFOs in the course readings and films. Some students are compelled by ethical arguments for animal rights and sustainable farming and are persuaded by the readings and films to consider different choices. In fact, some students have already made those choices individually or with their families earlier in life—choices to not eat meat or processed foods, for instance. Other students mightily resist the materials we read and view in the course, arguing that neoliberal logic of the industrial food system is the best and most efficient way to feed the most people. Many students note that concern about their food choices and the globalized food system is relatively low on their priority list as they confront the realities of economic survival: paying tuition, passing their classes, and getting jobs after graduation. Food is just "there" for them to consume, and they don't want to think about it much even as they encounter arguments about the costs of not caring or thinking about it. This leads the class into larger discussions of how such sentiments are borne out of privilege given the fact that many across the globe and in our community are worried about *if* they will eat rather than *what* or *when* they will eat. Within a few miles of the university where my classroom sits are several local food pantries that provide basic foodstuffs to families who have to balance paying for rent and heating oil against buying food. Thus, part of the learning in the course is articulating and questioning our assumptions about food—how it is that many students have not thought much about food other than assuming it will be there when they want it. What kind of privilege does that signify, and what kinds of responsibilities do students have within that privilege? For instance, what responsibility do we bear for the fact that hunger is a growing issue locally, nationally, and globally? What responsibility do we bear for the fact that food transport, as mentioned earlier, accounts for a large part of carbon emissions?

Moreover, debates often break out in class over what real food choices and options are provided to college students as they live, study, and eat in an institutionalized setting at dining halls, campus convenience stories, campus fast-food locations (of which our campus has an abundance), grocery stores they can reach by foot or bus, and small apartment kitchens. I encourage students to discuss the class politics of food—the time, money, and access they have to healthy food. I urge them to critique some of the positions taken by local food advocates, some of whom aim their arguments at middle-class and upper-middle-class, largely white consumers who are raising families or living independently in their own homes with cars they can drive to farmers' markets or supermarkets like Whole Foods that have expensive organic produce. As a class, we analyze the class and racial privilege that is often present in some local food literature.

Even though my students do not tend to agree about the argumentative stance that they and other class members should take toward the industrialized food system, they tend to agree by the end of the course that public information campaigns are necessary to address the problems and questions the industrialized system poses. Some students go on to become active in local food movements, others modify their individual eating habits, and others proceed with their same habits, often noting the significant discomfort and discord they feel in doing so. Students often stop me on campus and confess that they guiltily think of my course every time they eat a fast-food meal. It is my hope, along with Schlosser's claim for his book *Fast Food Nation* that he hopes readers and, in my case, students, "think about where the food came from, about how and where it was made, and about what is set in motion by every fast food purchase" (270).

At the same time, I know that not all students will engage in the alternative agrarian literacies that my course seeks to engage. The rhetoric of neoliberalism is strong, and it is a rhetoric that will win the day for many of our students. My hope is to "jam"[3] up the system and help students encounter perspectives on the food system that allow them to connect and integrate the global and the local. In doing this work, I strive to connect my pedagogy to movements for place-based globalism, which Michal Osterweil describes as part of the movements around the globe to "reinvent what counts as political as well as what has global reach" (27). Osterweil notes that place-based globalism works "locally, in the everyday, and in the present—connecting in intricate networks—to build new worlds globally" (27). In a future version of the course, I would like to further the connection to place-based globalism by creating opportunities for students to get involved in direct action in the local and regional food initiatives that are ongoing in the local Syracuse community. In recent semesters, other instructors have taught a version of the food politics course at Syracuse that involves work to integrate the classroom learning with a community linking project involving local farmers, representatives from a local Community Supported Agriculture organization (see Winslow), food banking organizations, and other organizations that address food, agriculture, migrant labor, and hunger issues (see Winslow).

While my WRT 205 course has changed from semester to semester and is still under development, I have found this work on the food industrial complex provides students with a productive and practical way of understanding the local and global linkages and power relations that currently shape our lives as global citizens. Considering the consequences of the global food system in our writing classrooms also allows the field of composition studies to engage more directly with efforts toward making sustainability and environmental literacy issues more central to our writing classes and to our university and college core curricula. What we eat has a direct and daily impact on the planet, and critical literacy education on the global food industrial complex can become a means toward creating a more just and equitable food system and a more just and equitable society.

Notes

1. A handful of dissertations addressing agricultural rhetorics and communicative practices have been written in our field, including Adrienne Lamberti's published dissertation "Talking the Talk: Revolution in Agricultural Communication" (Nova, 2007), initially completed at Iowa State University, and Robert Chiaviello's dissertation "Narrative, Metaphor, and Fantasy Themes in Environmental Rhetoric: Critiquing a Livestock-Grazing Conflict in the American West," completed at New Mexico University. Dianna Winslow is currently writing a dissertation at Syracuse University that addresses food literacy and pedagogy in a service-learning project that involved a community-supported agricultural association.

2. Food democracy, Shiva argues, is a food justice movement that supports local and regional food systems and fair trade policies that do not penalize two-thirds world countries such as Shiva's native country of India.

3. My use of the word "jam" is deliberate here and is inspired by the idea of culture jamming—using the terms of the dominant commercial culture against itself in spoofs and critical literacy counter-campaigns. The organization Adbusters and culture jamming activist Andrew Boyd have popularized the idea of culture jamming as a form of activism. Boyd offers workshops on culture jamming to activists and college students nationwide. He visited Syracuse University to give a workshop in Fall 2008

Works Cited

Andrezejewski, Julie, and John Alessio. "Education for Global Citizenship and Social Responsibility." *Progressive Perspectives* 1,2 (Spring 1999): 1-23. Accessed 15 January 2010. <http://www.uvm.edu/~dewey/monographs/glomono.html#EducationforGlobalCitizenshipandSocial >.

Bartlett, Peggy F., and Geoffrey W. Chase, ed. *Sustainability on Campus: Stories and Strategies for Change.* Cambridge, MA: MIT Press, 2004.

Berry, Wendell. *The Unsettling of America: Culture and Agriculture.* San Francisco: Sierra Club Books, 1977.

Boyd, Andrew. "Culture Jamming 101: A Hands-on Workshop on the Tactics and Techniques of Creative Action." Accessed 15 January 2010. <http://www.wanderbody.com/culturejamming101/description.html>.

Brandt, Deborah. *Literacy in American Lives.* Cambridge: Cambridge UP, 2001.

Brooke, Robert, ed. *Rural Voices: Place-Conscious Education and the Teaching of Writing.* New York: Teachers College P, 2003.

Chiaviello, Anthony Robert. "Narrative, Metaphor, and Fantasy Themes in Environmental Rhetoric: Critiquing a Livestock-Grazing Conflict in the American West." Diss. New Mexico State University, 1998.

Cockburn, Alexander, and Jeffrey St. Clair, eds. "Food Central: How Three Firms Came to Rule the World." *CounterPunch.* 8 July 2006. 20 November 1999. <http://www.counterpunch.org/food.html>.

Dobrin, Sidney L., and Christian Weisser, eds. *Ecocomposition: Theoretical and Pedagogical Approaches.* Albany: State U of New York P, 2001.

Donehower, Kim, Charlotte Hogg, and Eileen Schell. *Rural Literacies.* Southern Illinois University Press, Studies in Rhetoric and Writing Series, 2007.

————. Eds. *Reclaiming Rural Literacies.* Under review at Southern Illinois University Press.

Edmondson, Jacqueline. *Prairie Town: Redefining Rural Life in the Age of Globalization.* Lanham, MD: Rowman & Littlefield, 2003.

Fast Food Women. Dir. and prod. Anne Lewis Johnson. Appalshop Film & Video, 1991.

Focus on Food, spec. iss. of *College English* 70,4 (2008).

Food, Inc. Documentary. Dir. Robert Kenner. Magnolia Pictures, 2008.

Frefoygle, Eric T. "Introduction: A Durable Scale." *The New Agrarianism: Land, Culture, and the Community of Life.* Ed. Eric T. Frefoygle. Island Press/Shearwater Books, Washington, DC, 2001.

The Future of Food. Documentary Dir. Deborah Koons Garcia. Lily Films, 2004.

Gibson-Graham, J.K. *A Postcapitalist Politics.* Minneapolis, MN: University of Minnesota Press, 2006.

The Global Policy Forum. "Hunger and the Globalized System of Trade and Food Production." Accessed 15 January 2010. <http://www.globalpolicy.org/socecon/hunger/economy/index.htm>.

"Global Warming as a Justice Issue." New Community Project. 1 July 2006. <http://www.newcommunityproject.org/global_warming.shtml>.

Gorelick, Risa P., and Lisa DeTora, Eds. *Foodsumptions: Fun, Games, and the Politics of What We Eat.* In-progress.

Hanson, Victor Davis. *Fields without Dreams: Defending the Agrarian Ideal.* Free Press, 1997.

Johnson, June. *Global Issues, Local Arguments: Readings for Writers.* New York: Pearson Publishing, 2007.

Kellner, Douglas. "Globalization and the Postmodern Turn." Accessed 15 January 2010. <http://www.gseis.ucla.edu/courses/ed253a/dk/globpm.htm>.

Kingsolver, Barbara, with Steve L. Hopp and Camille Kingsolver. *Animal, Vegetable, Miracle: A Year of Food Life.* Harper Perennial, 2007.

Klein, Naomi. *Fences and Windows: Dispatches from the Frontlines of the Anti-Globalization Debates.* New York: Picador, 2002.

———. *No Logo: Taking Aim at the Brand Bullies.* New York: Picador, 2000.

Lamberti, Adrienne. *Talking the Talk: Revolution in Agricultural Communication.* New York: Nova Science Publishers, 2007.

Lappe, Frances Moore. *Diet for a Small Planet.* Ballantine, Rev. ed. 1991.

The Meatrix. Animated Film. 15 Aug. 2005 <http://www.themeatrix.com/>.

Nestle, Marion. *Food Politics: How the Food Industry Influences Nutrition and Health.* Berkeley, CA: University of California Press, 2002.

Norberg-Hodge, Helena, and Steven Gorelick. "Bringing the Food Economy Home." *The International Society for Ecology and Culture.* Accessed 15 January 2010. <http://www.isec.org.uk/articles/bringing.html>.

Osterweil, Michal. "Place-based Globalism: Theorizing the Global Justice Movement." *Development* 48,2 (2005): 23-28.

Owens, Derek. *Composition and Sustainability: Teaching for a Threatened Generation.* Urbana, IL: NCTE, 2001.

Pollan, Michael. *In Defense of Food: An Eater's Manifesto.* New York: Penguin Press, 2008.

———. *The Omnivore's Dilemma: A Natural History of Four Meals.* New York: Penguin Press, 2006.

Rice, Jeff, and Jenny Rice. "CFP: Food Theory." *Pre/Text* Special issue. Accessed 15 January 2010. <http://call-for-papers.sas.upenn.edu/node/33778>.

Riedner, Rachel. "Women's Survival Economies and the Questions of Value." Blog. 16 Feb 2009. Accessed 15 January 2010. <http://www.womeninandbeyond.org/?p=305>.

Schell, Eileen E. "Cyberactivism, Viral Flash Activism, and Critical Literacy in the Age of the Meatrix." *Complex Worlds: Digital Culture, Rhetoric, and*

Professional Communication. Ed. Adrienne Lamberti and Anne R. Richards. Amityville, NY: Baywood Press, forthcoming.

——. "Every Week Should Be Campus Equity Week: Toward a Labor Theory of Agency in Higher Education." *Works and Days* 41/42 (Spring/Fall 2003).

——. "Gender, Rhetorics, and Globalization: Rethinking the Spaces and Locations of Women's Rhetorics." *Teaching Rhetorica.* Ed. Kate Ronald and Joy Ritchie. Heinemann-Boynton/Cook, 2006. 160-73.

——. "Toward a New Labor Movement in Higher Education: Contingent Labor and Organizing for Change." *Tenured Bosses and Disposable Teachers: Writing Instruction in the Managed University.* Ed. Marc Bosquet, Leo Parascondola, and Tony Scott. Carbondale, IL: Southern Illinois University Press, 2003. 100-110.

——. Toward a New Labor Movement in Higher Education: Contingent Labor and Organizing for Change." *Workplace: The Journal for Academic Labor.* Spec iss. on Composition as Management Science. 4.1. Accessed 15 January 2010. <http://www.louisville.edu/journal/workplace/issue7/issue7frontpage.html>.

Schlosser, Eric. *Fast Food Nation: The Dark Side of the All-American Meal.* New York: Perennial, 2002.

Shiva, Vandana. *Stolen Harvest: The Hijacking of the Global Food Supply.* Boston: South End Press, 1999.

Shor, Ira. "What Is Critical Literacy?" *Journal for Pedagogy, Pluralism, and Praxis* 4 (Fall 1999). 15 January 2010. <http://www.lesley.edu/journals/jppp/4/shor.html>.

Spurlock, Morgan. *Don't Eat This Book!: Fast Food and the Supersizing of America.* New York: Putnam, 2005.

Super Size Me. Dir. Morgan Spurlock. The Con, 2004.

Winne, Mark. "Education for Change." Community Food Security Coalition. 15 January 2010. <http://www.foodsecurity.org/views_education.html>.

Winslow, Dianna. "Sustainability, Public Teaching and Food Literacy: A Community Engaged Study." Diss. Syracuse University. Forthcoming.

The World Trade Organization History Project. Accessed 15 January 2010. <http://depts.washington.edu/wtohist/>.

The WPA as Broker:

Globalization and the Composition Program

Bruce Horner

broker. I. 1. A retailer of commodities; a second-hand dealer. 2. A retailer;
contemptuously, Pedlar, petty dealer, monger. . . . I. One who acts as a mid-
dleman in bargains. 4. A go-between or intermediary in love affairs; a hired
match-maker, marriage-agent; also a procurer, pimp, bawd; a pander general-
ly. Obs. 5. A middleman, intermediary, or agent generally; an interpreter, mes-
senger, commissioner. (OED)

In the field of composition studies, writing program administrators (hereafter
WPAs) figure prominently. They are the ones who, at large and medium-sized
U.S. research universities, public and private, are responsible for the design and
management of the programs of first-year undergraduate composition (FYC),
and all those who teach and all those students who take courses in the programs—in most schools, virtually the entire undergraduate student population.
While the majority of actual composition teaching in the United States takes
place at other types of institutions (two-year "community" colleges and small
colleges and universities), the size of composition programs at research universities and the dominant role those types of institutions play in the popular imagi-
nary of U.S. higher education have led those managing those programs to take
center stage in discussions of composition writ large: what any one WPA de-
cides, and what happens to any one WPA, not only can and does have effects on
significant numbers of composition teachers, courses, and students in one fell
swoop at a particular institution but also has repercussions felt beyond the

WPA's specific institution, as stories of these events circulate over listservs, at conferences, and in the scholarly literature. It is thus that scholarship on, by, and for WPAs dominates the field of composition studies in its representations of and for the work of those teaching and taking composition.

The work WPAs do managing composition programs is, not surprisingly, shaped by and responds to changes to the economic and cultural landscape. In this chapter, I address the ways in which that work confronts those forces affiliated with free market fundamentalism and so-called "fast" capitalism, in particular the insistence of these on the privatization and commodification of education as part of the move to a "knowledge" or "information" economy, and the demands of these for efficiency in the global communication of goods, services, and knowledge, efficiency often attributed to reliance on a standardized English as the "lingua franca" for communication.

As I will show, much of the work of WPAs has always consisted of "brokering" writing and its learning and teaching. And as others have shown, composition programs have long been noted for their exploitation of labor, focus on language standardization, and drive for efficiency (see, for example, Connors). That said, however, increases in the speed and scope of the flow of capital and labor associated with current globalizing of communication technologies, the market economy, and its concomitant privatization and commodification of all aspects of education, including knowledge work in English, mandates that WPAs take into account the global context in which their brokering is conducted in order to resist those effects of globalizing that threaten the value of the work of writing and its learning and teaching. Using dominant WPA discourse on the challenge of achieving program coherence and combating exploitation of composition labor, I show how dominant approaches to addressing these challenges in strictly local institutional terms prevents substantive resistance to the forces that largely account for these challenges in the first place. And I recommend ways to define the meaning of composition programs in WPA brokering that work against, rather than solely within, the common (de-)valuation of composition work as commodities for exchange in the current marketplace of globalizing capital.

While I focus on the work of WPAs, I want to be clear from the outset that I am concerned with how that work is being structured, not with the ethics or validity of decisions individual WPAs might appear to be making on their own, as individuals. In other words, I am interested here in what WPAs find themselves having to cope with in their positions as WPAs, and why, and by implication what tactics might best be deployed from such positioning. That WPAs always have resisted and continue to resist the material social constraints of their position is a given. But my concern here is first with determining the nature of those constraints in order to identify the ways in which these constraints themselves shape the kinds of tactics WPAs find themselves deploying, as well as alternatives to these tactics. I am not interested in adding to the many narratives of the lone WPA, heroic and/or tragic, with which much WPA literature is rife (see George), but with the material historical situation of WPA work in the current, globalizing era.

* * *

WPAs work as "brokers" in the sense of being "intermediaries" or "middlemen" insofar as they mediate between the work conducted in the programs they direct and the demands made on that work. As Geoffrey Chase warns in an essay appearing in a popular collection intended as a sourcebook for new as well as experienced WPAs,

> WPAs have the unenviable task of serving many constituents [faculty and instructors within the writing program, colleagues in the department, colleagues from other departments, department chairs, other university administrators, students, and parents], all of whom have different perceptions, and often contradictory expectations, about the aims and goals of composition. Meeting [their] expectations and demands . . . and serving as a mediator between these many stakeholders are both critical and stressful. (243)

In a model he proposes for analyzing how best to address this task, Chase warns that WPAs must understand "local [institutional] conditions," achieve "internal coherence" within the program being directed, and ensure that the program also has "external relevance," advising that WPAs "must become spokespersons for writing who are able both to listen carefully to external expectations and to articulate clearly how those expectations might better line up with internal program goals" (246). In this sense, WPAs' brokering also includes the work of interpretation, as they explain the relationship, or "line up," between what might seem to be competing, even contradictory, expectations. In Joyce Kinkead and Jeanne Simpson's contribution to the same collection, they advise WPAs to prepare for this work of interpretation by learning how to "'talk the talk'" of "admin-speak" by mastering the acronyms it uses to name the currency of school administrative budgeting (such as FTEs [full-time equivalents] and SCHs [student credit hours]) as well as administrators' preferred genres of proposals and bulleted memoranda and the intricacies of institutional governance (68 and passim; see also Schwalm "Writing" 16-22). Similarly, in Doug Hesse's contribution to the same collection, Hesse provides WPAs with a guide to organizations and publications that are likely to be contributing to these administrators' thinking so that WPAs' own ideas for their programs can appear more likely to be "fitting" to the worlds in which these administrators move (311 and passim).

Such discourse locates WPA brokering at three sites: 1) within the program directed by the WPA, as WPAs mediate courses and course sections within their programs; 2) within the local academic institutional site, as WPAs broker the relationship between their program and the various other administrative units comprising their home institutions (e.g., in struggles for funding and program control); and 3) within the network of other postsecondary institutions with which the WPA's home institution has relationships, including, for state schools, other state colleges and universities with which the WPA's school has articulation agreements. However, brokering also occurs, and increasingly so, within a fourth, much larger spectrum of private and public schools and testing services. As David Schwalm warns new WPAs in his essay for the same collection,

> [Y]ou must recognize that your institution is not totally independent. Students constantly move back and forth among institutions. . . . Your campus will be involved with other universities, colleges, and community colleges in statewide (if not national) "articulation agreements" that govern the transfer of courses from one campus to another. . . . Because first-year composition is the course most frequently transferred from one institution to another you will need to become very familiar with the transfer processes and the procedures whereby course equivalences are established. You must be willing to work collegially with faculty from other institutions (and other kinds of institutions) to conduct the business of articulation. . . . Similarly, you will be involved in determining how your institution handles credit earned through advanced placement, international baccalaureate, CLEP, or other test-based sources of credit. ("Writing" 15)

Though Schwalm identifies this network as extending only nationally, the privatization and commodification of all aspects of education affiliated with the current globalizing of the market economy mandates that this brokering network be understood as extending globally—at the very least, for example, involving the traffic and exchange of academic credit and students globally as postsecondary schools compete for international status, students, and funding (see Ziguras, Raduntz).

In a study of the work of "literacy brokers" in the production of English language-medium scholarly texts by central and eastern European scholars—such as the scholars' peers, copy editors and translators, and nonprofessionals offering informal support to the scholars—Theresa Lillis and Mary Curry note that such literacy brokering is constrained by particular power relations not only at the individual and institutional but also geohistorical levels (29-30), including those power relations "privileging English-center literacy and rhetorical practices and the differential power relations between center-periphery relations regarding knowledge production" (30). For example, in the process of brokering the production and publication of these central and eastern European scholars' texts in English-medium international journals, brokers were in a position to make significant changes to the knowledge claims made by the scholars, even to the point of redefining claims as constituting confirmation of existing knowledge rather than new contributions to knowledge (Lillis and Curry 30).

While WPAs do not work as literacy brokers in quite the same way, their brokering of the work of the writing and learning and teaching of writing conducted in their programs is likewise constrained by such power relations. Perhaps most obviously, the globalizing of the market economy has increased the demand for a standardizing of English—Lillis and Curry's "privileging of English-center literacy and rhetorical practices"—but also the commodification of the "skill" in producing this standardized written English as the new "lingua franca" of global commerce, and for the commodification of the skill of instructing students in this skill (see Lu, "Essay"). Insofar as universities are now charged with producing knowledge workers with this skill, and with ensuring the standardization of English as a means to efficient communication of information as well as goods and services, then WPAs broker these as well.

WPA brokering thus involves them as not just mediators and interpreters but also retailers of commodities. They have to broker commodifications of both writing and the teaching of writing at the local institutional level and oversee the exchange of these in the marketplace of academic courses and credits in the negotiation of articulation agreements with other schools regarding course and credit transfer, arguing for specific terms for the exchange of these as "equivalent" commodities. Labor, recall, is commodified when the value of the product of that labor is identified as an objective property of the product itself and the concrete labor involved in producing the value is occluded (see Marx, *Capital*, I: 153-54). In commodity fetishism, "the commodity reflects the social characteristics of men's own labour as objective characteristics of the products of labour themselves, as the socio-natural properties of these things. . . . the products of the human brain appear as autonomous figures endowed with a life of their own, which enter into relations both with each other and with the human race" (*Capital* I, 164-65). WPAs engage in commodity fetishism insofar as they occlude the concrete labor involved in producing particular values in writing—the concrete labor of readers and writers and the social relations necessary to the production of such values—and instead treat writing abstractly as having in itself particular values irrespective of the work of readers, writers, or the social relations in which the writing is produced. But likewise, the work of teaching and learning writing is fetishized insofar as the value of such work is treated as independent of the social characteristics of the concrete labor of those involved. With the "marketization" of education, as Helen Raduntz observes, "the knowledge of educators is commodified and packaged," "because capitalist forms of exchange "cannot deal with quality education nor with social, ethical, or equity concerns. . . . [but] only with quantifiable 'things' as commodities" (242). This fetishizing of the teaching and learning of writing is manifested in the transformation of the concrete labor practices of a particular writing course involving specific students and instructors into units of abstract labor, or academic credit, with exchange value within the economy of academic credits and graduation requirements within and outside the WPA's institution, and, simultaneously, into the production of abstract skills of writing (say, for example, the skill of "effective" argumentation, treated as universally applicable) for exchange in the globalized job market.

The dilemma to which such fetishizing leads is revealed in a recent discussion on the WPA-listserv ("New Brand Composition"). Prompted by someone enthused by a 2008 WPA conference presentation on (commercial) "branding" by Keith Rhodes, the discussion focused on the difficulties of selling the value of composition programs to administrators, colleagues, students, and their parents in light of the inability of these programs to be "accountable" by showing they produced what was expected of them—"good" or "better" writers, understood in the abstract as writers who are always "good" at producing writing always recognized as having inherent ("good") value. Faced with this dilemma, listserv participants debated the possibility and desirability of various strategies by which the composition "commodity" might be branded, or re-branded, so that it would sell more easily and for a higher price (in the form of more funding for programs) in both the local institutional and public sphere despite the actual, contingent use-value of the commodity being sold.

Eliding the "social characteristics" of the concrete labor involved in the work of both writing and the teaching of writing through commodification of these as abstract skills exchangeable on the marketplace occludes the arbitrary and contingent character of the valuations of those commodities and, more problematically, the demands of fast capitalism in the production of such valuations: the demand for writing that is clear (to all) and (thus) efficient in its communication of knowledge globally. Such valuations of writing overlook what Anna Haupt Tsing, in her critique of dominant, fast capitalist models of global exchange, calls the necessity of "friction" in any exchange. For any kind of movement, she explains, friction is in fact necessary, yet it is neglected in fast capitalist ideology's accounts of the "fluidity" of capital. In the case of writing, we can identify this friction in the necessary concrete labor readers and writers must undergo of "translating" any material instantiations of writing, in English or any other language, into various meanings (see Pennycook). Far from representing a neutral and friction-free conduit of fixed meanings, writing (and reading) are social practices in which the friction of difference and resistance are crucial contributors to the production of meaning. Likewise, teaching (and learning), far from representing the neutral and friction-free transmission of fixed skills, constitutes a site of necessary friction as meanings and skills are reworked through the concrete labor of teachers and students.

In brokering exchanges of commodified skills of writing English and its teaching, WPAs risk earning the more unsavory meanings that have attached to "brokers" as being not just "middlemen" and "retailers" but procurers, pimps, and panders: those who prey on weakness by pretending to offer, or treat, what they know are not commodities as if they were. After all, WPAs have known for some time now that, as Susan Miller put it back in 1991, "good" writing

is the result of established cultural privileging mechanisms, not of pure "taste,"
. . . . that a mixture of ideas, timing, entitlements, and luck have designated
some rather than others as "important" writers/thinkers. . . . [that] [t]he field's
most productive methods of evaluation also judge writing by situational rather
than by universal standards. (*Textual* 187)

WPAs bring their knowledge of what Miller refers to as "the arbitrariness of
evaluations [of writing] and their relativity to particular power structures" (*Textual* 187) to their brokering of the value of writing and its learning and teaching.
However, brokering the value of writing and its learning and teaching as commodities belies the contingent character of the value of what is offered (and the
necessity of the concrete labor of "translation" in any act of reading and writing
and the "translation" of specific practices of reading and writing teaching and
learning involve). Such brokering allows the operation of such power relations
in conferring value on writing and its teaching to go unopposed, with deleterious
effects to both the achievement of internal program coherence and the decent
working conditions for composition instructors.

The pervasive reliance on exploited labor for composition instruction is illustrative in this regard. A number of critics, of course, have articulated the ways
that dominant gender, class, and race ideologies have contributed to the continuation of composition's exploitative labor practices (see, for example, S. Miller,
"Feminization"; Schell; Strickland; Tuell; Horner, *Terms* 1-18, 146-47). But the
privatization of postsecondary education and the development of communication
technologies for "delivery" of such education in keeping with the globalizing
market economy adds to the pressure on institutions, and by implication WPAs,
to accommodate such ideologies (see Raduntz, Ziguras). Schooling is no longer
seen as a "public" but a "private" good, with the consequence that less and less
public funding is made available for schooling. Schools faced with less and less
public funding are forced to look for ways to cut costs. Institutions' efforts to cut
costs work in concert with ideologies that have long denigrated the teaching of
composition as "women's work" undeserving of pay to demand more and more
of composition teachers in exchange for less and less. (The privatization of the
costs of teachers' health care and retirement, of course, furthers this deterioration of working conditions.) The privatization of postsecondary education has
also led to an increase in the number of "for profit" schools and the development
of "distance learning" schools.[1] As Schwalm warns WPAs further, "You will
also be among the first who will have to address the transfer of a whole range of
courses delivered via technology by a range of mysterious providers" ("Writing"
15). Most traditional colleges and universities must now compete with these
"mysterious providers" for not only students but their tuition dollars as well as
other funding, increasing pressure on them to pay less to composition instructors
(who for ideological reasons have less cultural and social capital with which to
resist such treatment) and to search for ways to "outsource" this work elsewhere
to achieve even greater cost-savings (see Jaschik, Rai). In short, globalizing of

the market economy encourages institutions to view composition instructors as so much "flexible" labor, as indicated by the various terms used to name those now responsible for the majority of postsecondary composition instruction—"adjunct," "temporary," "part-time," "contingent."

I am arguing that both the treatment of composition instructors as "flexible" and the treatment of the work of composition courses as the production of commodities constitute responses to the same pressures of a globalized market economy for efficiency in production of English writing skills understood as a commodity for information communication. To the extent that composition courses at any university are treated as readily exchangeable for composition courses at any other, then those teaching these courses can be drawn from anywhere, and are thus in competition with their peers anywhere (again, see Jaschik, Rai), so long as they are imagined to have the equivalent skills.

We see this dynamic operating in one section of Richard Miller and Michael Cripps' essay "Minimum Qualifications: Who Should Teach First-year Writing," appearing in a collection on the "postmodern WPA." In that section of their essay, Miller and Cripps offer a defense of the decision to staff Rutgers University's first-year composition courses with TAs from departments outside as well as inside English in terms of the equivalence of their teaching abilities. As they put it, "a first-time English TA, drawn to Rutgers by its outstanding graduate program in literatures in English, is not, a priori, better prepared than an advanced graduate student in art history or political science or physics and astronomy to begin the hard work of teaching first-year students how to read with care, how to draft a thoughtful response, or how to use revision to produce a supple argument" (136). Miller and Cripps present this defense not as the "single, overarching narrative" that fully accounts for their program but rather as only one of "four overlapping versions" of their program's "approach to staffing freshman composition" (124). And as I will suggest below and as Miller and Cripps themselves also suggest elsewhere in their essay, there are a number of other ways one might justify hiring TAs from outside English to teach composition. Nonetheless, it is worth attending to the way in which, in this particular justification—one common in WPA discourse—there is an elision of the concrete labor of reading as well as writing and the social characteristics of that labor. That labor is necessary to the construction of what might be deemed a "thoughtful response," "a supple argument," or a careful reading. That elision instead treats the ability to produce these as a commodified "skill." The elision of the concrete labor involved in the production of such entities enables treatment of those involved as embodiments of an equivalent set of commodified teaching skills, readily exchangeable in the globalized marketplace, and denigrated as such depending on their "market" value—a race to the cheapest ensues among all those deemed to possess the equivalent skills, with the added contemporary speedup of that race made possible by current communication technologies which allow for outsourcing of this teaching to other locations globally.

Following this logic, if, say, I as WPA assume that first-year composition courses at all schools train students in the ability to produce what will be assumed to be texts that *in themselves* represent thoughtful responses, supple arguments, and the like, then it would appear safe to assume as well that individuals who can verify that they have taught such courses at any other schools can join the ever-increasing pool of flexible labor on which I might draw in staffing composition courses at my school: for by this logic, composition is composition, just as "a supple argument" is "supple," "effective teaching" "effective," "effective writing" "effective," and so on, no matter the reader or writer or reading or writing practice. Moreover, there is no particular reason to hire back instructors with experience teaching at my school in preference to others if I can hire others who are less expensive and perhaps less recalcitrant more cheaply, or to outsource this instruction altogether—a fact that college and university administrators are fully aware of (see Schwalm, "New Brand"). In other words, globalization of the market economy encourages both the degeneration of courses in the first-year composition curriculum into "general writing skills instruction," easily exchangeable in the marketplace of academic credits and general education requirements, and, concomitantly, the denigration of those involved in its teaching as just as easily exchangeable in the buyer's market for composition instructors. The valuation of each is contingent on the valuation of the other; neoliberal free market fundamentalism's demand for efficiency (often couched in terms of accountability) works to ensure the de-valuation of both. Of course, while this is justified in terms of "flexibility," as Zygmunt Bauman explains, the "flexibility" on the demand side requires a different kind of flexibility from the supply side of the labor market:

> flexibility on the demand side, rebounds on all those cast on the supply side as hard, cruel, impregnable and unassailable fate: jobs come and go, they vanish as soon as they appeared, they are cut in pieces and withdrawn without notice while the rules of the hiring/firing game change without warning and there is little the job-holders and job-seekers may do to stop the see-saw. (*Globalization* 104-5)

The interdependence of curriculum and labor practices in composition programs is mediated within dominant WPA discourse through various forms of professional development to achieve what is identified as program "coherence." Program coherence is often defined in terms of consistency in instruction, assessment procedures, and goals. Instructors are expected to teach all sections of each course in the same way, pursue the same goals, and assess student writing similarly, and different courses within the program are expected to work in concert toward similar goals. Three of the components Chase identifies as necessary to achieving internal program coherence are "common goals specific and detailed enough to be meaningful and useful," "common assignments," and "standard methods for evaluation and assessment across multiple sections"

(245). Miller and Cripps' account of Rutgers' writing program is again illustrative. The concern of the program, they state,

> is not to convert any of its teachers to its method; it does demand, though, a practical adherence to its pedagogy during the term of employment. Consistency in the number and type of writing assignments across all sections of the program's writing courses, consistency in pedagogical approach, and consistency in the application of the shared evaluative criteria are all that is required. These three consistencies make it possible to provide over ten thousand students each year with a common learning experience in their writing classes. (137)

Those failing to offer such practical adherence are judged to be inflexible but, fortunately, easily replaced. A similar consistency to achieve program coherence was pursued at the institution where I served as writing program director. At that time and under my "direction," composition teachers of first-year composition (consisting by default strictly of TAs and contingent instructors) were warned that they must "Follow the curriculum and syllabus approved for the course" and "Use texts approved for the course" ("Responsibilities"). Such consistency was achieved through various forms of instructor mentoring and assessment. For example, at the institution where I served as WPA, course coordinators and I oversaw a barrage of institutionalized procedures to ensure that only the approved curricula and texts were used, and that they were used in consistent ways. This included extensive orientation meetings, mentoring, portfolio assessment, teaching observations, and teaching evaluation instruments. Similarly, Miller and Cripps report that the Rutgers program employs a "highly elaborated program" of orientation, mentoring, midterm and end-of-term folder review sessions to ensure "oversight and quality control" (139).

Frequently, however, such internal program coherence is seen as both vital and yet in competition with the need to claim "external relevance" to the department and university communities within which the composition programs are housed and the public at large. Goals that might be "meaningful and useful" to students, teachers, and WPAs might not be perceived as such by others, nor might the "standard methods for evaluation"—hence the need Chase identifies for WPAs to become "spokespersons for writing" (246). But in light of the pressures to commodify writing and writing instruction as uniform skills for exchange in a globalized market, it is not surprising that WPAs feel pressured to redefine the common goals for their programs in terms of teaching general writing skills. Unfortunately, however, as I have been suggesting, to do so achieves a false coherence through commodification of the work of teaching composition that contributes to denigration of the work of composition, undermining WPAs' own efforts and contributing to the denigration of composition instructors. WPAs yielding to such pressure end up defending claims about their courses that they know belie the complexity of writing and the contingent character of any writing's value, and that in fact undermine their efforts to improve the working conditions of instructors in their programs. Brokering that implicitly accepts a commodified notion of teaching and writing skills puts composition instructors in global competition with one another for jobs "producing" a commodity: writing skills. The poor working conditions resulting from the ensuing race to the bottom then reinforce the difficulty of achieving the program coherence that is sought. For insofar as exploited labor tends to be unreliable—those exploited tending, not surprisingly, either to resist efforts to control their labor or to be unable, as a consequence of their exploited condition, to meet demands made of them—creating or maintaining "coherence" in a writing program staffed with exploited labor eminently "flexible" in light of their ostensible ability to produce the commodity of skilled writing is largely an ongoing exercise in futility— hence the "feeling of disappointment" among WPAs that has become a phenomenon worthy of scholarly investigation (see Micciche). WPAs find themselves in the position of having to broker what they know to be degraded and degrading: the production of ostensible "skills" in what is termed "human capital" by those working under degrading working conditions. The treatment of instructors as embodiments of the commodities of abstract teaching skills belies the need for professional development—why, after all, should instructors in possession of these skills need to re-acquire them? Consequently, WPAs are hard-pressed to justify the expense involved in providing the orientation and mentoring that they know the concrete labor of teaching writing in fact requires.

Of course, there is now a raft of scholarship documenting and posing ways to combat the practice of relying heavily on adjunct instructors and GTAs to staff composition courses at cut-rate pay and few or no benefits, including calls to abolish the first-year composition requirement, unionize composition teachers, and enforce standards for instructor pay and benefits set forth by such professional organization as MLA and CCCC (see, for example, Bousquet et al., Crowley, Schell and Stock). But while in much of this literature the effects of the globalizing of the market economy on postsecondary education generally are acknowledged (see, for example, Bousquet et al., Downing et al., Ohmann xxxvii ff.), accounts of WPAs' responses to what I have been identifying as effects of the globalizing of market economies are typically couched in terms of "local" institutional solutions, understood not in dialectical relation to those forces but rather in ranked relation—a set of "local" phenomena and conditions to which WPAs must perforce adapt. In other words, despite the pervasiveness of similar conditions in a multitude of institutional settings, which suggests the operation of forces beyond the local institutional site, WPAs describe their responses as developing "local" solutions that address what are defined as "local" rather than "globalizing" conditions, and they warn against imagining solutions that would respond to these conditions in ways that define them as, in fact, anything other than "local."

For example, in a model Chase offers for "examining the complex relationships that determine the day-to-day practices in our composition programs . . .

for writing throughout our colleges and universities," Chase emphasizes the
need to "think about the *local conditions* [sic] at our institutions" (244). He defines these as "those features of our colleges and universities that make our institutions distinct from each other. Budgets, teaching loads, requirements, building
design, pay scales, computer availability, and the students themselves" (244-45).
While he acknowledges that "[a]t times, it may seem that because there are general statements we can make about higher education, all our campuses are essentially the same," he asserts that, in fact, "This is, obviously, not the case and we
would be wise as we pursue changes in our program to focus on these differences [between campuses] and how local conditions shape the programs and
opportunities at our schools" (245). Regarding his own program's solutions to
the problem it faced when it was clear "additional resources were not going to
be pumped into the [writing] program to alleviate pressures caused by increasing
enrollment," he warns, "It is unrealistic and unwise to assume that what works
effectively on one campus is well suited to another campus without local adaptation" (251). Miller and Cripps go further. While the conditions they contended
with closely mirror those Chase describes at his institution and those at countless
others—increased enrollments, no improved budgetary climate and thus no increase in faculty lines and virtually complete reliance on TAs and part-timers to
teach burgeoning numbers of sections of first-year composition—on the question of who teaches first-year writing courses, they conclude, "We think that this
question can only be answered locally" (138), arguing that the answer to that
question

> is determined not only by the local WPA's philosophical, pedagogical, and po-
> litical commitments, but also by a host of [local] variables entirely beyond the
> local WPA's control; the pool of possible applicants in the region; the home in-
> stitution's history with writing instruction; the financial well-being of the home
> institution; and who happens to be department chair, area dean, and provost at
> any given moment. (123)

There is, of course, a genuine, practical logic to such a focus on the "local"—understood as one's own institutional conditions. There are indeed, after
all, significant differences as well as similarities in the local conditions obtaining
at different institutions, including those at Chase's school and Miller and
Cripps's school. Moreover, WPAs need to know the "local" institutional landscape of people, procedures, and policies in order to do their work. Knowing a
dean's quirks, or a local institutional funding possibility, or loopholes in hiring
procedures, as well as the specific instructors and the students whom they serve
can be crucial in enabling a WPA to maintain and improve the strength of the
program he or she is "administering." At the same time, such a "practical" response is also susceptible to defining the local in limited ways and thus limiting
the scope of actions to solutions that work only within rather than also against

those economic forces producing or exacerbating the problems in the first place with which the WPA, here significantly imagined as working solo, contends.

In short, the practical logic that dictates attending strictly to the specific institutional conditions obtaining at one's particular location—conditions WPAs would of course be foolish to ignore—can also encourage a kind of fatalism that allows the widespread prevalence of those conditions to continue: here, to accede to "globalism's" insistence that There Is No Alternative to the global hegemony of neo-liberal market fundamentalism ("TINA," a.k.a. "la pensée unique" [see Beck 9, Ramonet]). As Raymond Williams, writing on the term "realistic," observes, "'Let's be realistic' probably more often means 'let us accept the limits of this situation' (*limits* meaning *hard facts*, often of power or money in their existing and established forms)" (*Keywords* 217-18). Chase and Miller and Cripps, for example, all seem to accept as givens that enrollments are up, budgets for public schooling are down, only TAs and adjuncts can be persuaded to teach composition, and no collective resistance to these current practices is possible. Why enrollments are up, funding is down, and WPAs are being expected to hire instructors only from "the pool of possible applicants in the region" remains unchallenged. In attempting to understand and explain what is to be done, at least at their institutions, here and now, WPAs' attention is diverted from both why it is that these conditions currently seem to prevail generally as well as immediately at their individual institutions, and how they might be improved. And while WPAs' immediate concern is understandably likely to be with what is to be done, well, immediately (and locally) within their institutional setting, that focus can mute not only questions, but also answers, addressing the larger forces producing these questions.

Alternatively, WPAs, composition instructors, and their students can examine the relationship between the institutional conditions in which they find themselves locally and the pressures globally to acquire the skill of producing "standard written English" as quickly and cheaply as possible, for example, with the results of burgeoning enrollments, exploited teaching labor, heavy student debt, and so on, and they can develop responses, if not solutions, to those problems that resist these pressures in meaningful ways that do more than simply adapt to them. We can see a move toward finding goals that are meaningful in terms other than skills exchange and that potentially address the relationship between local institutional conditions and the global in the fourth component Chase identifies as crucial to achieving internal program coherence: "a commitment to examining and discussing these shared features [of common goals, assignments, and methods for evaluation and assessment] openly," as in the decision at his institution to focus the first-year writing course on the themes of environmental sustainability (Chase 246, 249). Such a decision would make it possible for students and teachers to identify and pursue writing practices, needs, and interests routinely devalued by, and potentially resisting, effects of global capitalism.

We can see a comparable move in the changes Miller and Cripps describe themselves making to their program's curriculum in one of the accounts they offer of their program's staffing practices. In that version, Miller and Cripps argue that a more appropriate question for WPAs to ask than "Who should teach first-year writing?" is "Who is freshman composition for?" (131). From this perspective, Miller and Cripps's decision to expand the "pool" of TAs on which they drew for composition instruction to include those from disciplines outside as well as inside English is defended not in terms of the ability of any and all TAs to do "the hard work of teaching first-year students how to read with care, how to draft a thoughtful response, or how to use revision to produce a supple argument" (136) but rather as a means to treat writing in ways that might respond more directly to effects of the globalizing of the market economy on students as well as their teachers and to meet needs unaddressed within its terms.[2] When they first started including TAs from disciplines other than English as writing instructors, Miller and Cripps report, these TAs helped them see that the program's approach at the time to teaching writing was "really a discipline-specific methodology that did not readily transfer to writing or history, philosophy, or political science" (131). In other words, we might say that they discovered that the "general writing skills" they thought they'd been teaching were not "general" at all but, in terms of my argument, a commodification obscuring the concrete labor necessary to the realization of any use-value with writing. By subsequently drawing on the expertise of TAs hired from a variety of disciplines, they were able to develop a different pedagogy that "asked students to use their writing to engage with a set of problems that belong to no one discipline," reasoning that "since the first-year course could never prepare students to write in every discipline, the best pedagogical response might well lie with challenging students to build connections across disciplinary boundaries to generate responses to pressing contemporary problems," e.g., "the fate of democracy in the jobless future," "the biogenetic engineering of food and the prospect of environmental devastation" (131).

Miller and Cripps identify this as an "unintended consequence" of their initial decision to hire TAs outside English. Nonetheless, WPAs might argue for the need to hire only those instructors, or a pool of instructors, who have a sensitivity to and thus can contribute to the study of differences and changes in writing, and in writing in English. Those instructors would be hired not because they possessed the "minimum qualifications" for teaching commodified writing skills but because the concerns they would bring to their teaching might have the potential to advance the understanding of writing and what writers might accomplish in addressing effects of fast capitalism unrecognized—unrecognizable, even—within its ideology. In other words, if, as David Harvey observes, "it is important for capital that new skills emerge . . . which allow for flexibility and adaptability and, above all, for *substitutability*—that are non-monopolizable"

(109), then WPAs can interfere with capital by insisting that their programs require teachers with skills that are in fact not substitutable and are *monopolizable*.

These examples suggest that WPAs' articulations of the value of composition courses in their brokering need not simply "line up with" the commodification of knowledge work and its workers and the privatization of education, imagined now as necessary only to individuals' private portfolios of marketable skills. Instead, in their brokering, WPAs might articulate the value of the courses in their programs in terms that resist tendencies toward the commodification of writing and the learning and teaching of writing while being responsive both to WPAs' own understanding of that work and to effects of globalization—e.g., environmental destruction—unacknowledged within the ideology of global capitalism. It does not immediately follow from the literature challenging the legitimacy of the teaching of "general writing skills" that required first-year composition courses should be abolished. It does, however, mean that some other value for them must be articulated (see Bazerman; Horner, *Terms* 54-57, 127-33; Horner, "Redefining").

In addition to the valuations suggested in the programs described by Chase and by Miller and Cripps, let me pose an alternative which responds to challenges to the standardizing of English and linguistic imperialism which are themselves brought on by globalizing of the market economy and which might better enable WPAs to achieve program coherence without colluding with the exploitative labor practices in their hiring of instructors. Globalizing of the market economy has led not only to demands for a standardized English "lingua franca" but also to challenges to the monolithic view of standard written English by the burgeoning number of Englishes and the increasing awareness of the complex power relations involved in the negotiation of differences among Englishes and between English and other languages in writing. WPAs might use such challenges in conjunction with the knowledge they have of the contingencies of the value of any writing with any language to argue for a universal first-year composition requirement, not on the basis that these courses will give students (and certify them as possessing) some general and readily exchangeable writing skills on the global job market (e.g., the ability to produce "Standard Written English"), but by arguing that the complexity of writing and the role of power relations in judgments about it, the shifting nature and burgeoning multiplicity of written forms of English(es), the growing need for translation between Englishes as well as between Englishes and other languages, and the pervasiveness of literacy in a globalized world merit some of the attention of all undergraduate students for sixteen or thirty-two weeks—something like arguments for why students should learn world history, or the arts.

In other words, in addition to addressing issues related to globalization thematically in their writing, as students in the courses described by Chase and by Miller and Cripps are asked to do, composition courses might be the site for explicitly negotiating conflicts between specific language users' and global market fundamentalists' definitions of writing and its value, both thematically and practically, in the writing produced, activating students' and teachers' sense of the importance of writing practices and interests devalued by global capitalism. (For accounts of related pedagogy, see Canagarajah, and Horner and Lu.) And, of course, WPAs might design their programs and train instructors in ways that are in accord with such a conceptualization of the value of their programs. By the same token, WPAs directing such programs, faced with the task of evaluating whether or not courses from elsewhere might "transfer" as equivalent to composition courses at their home institutions, could legitimately reject, say, the equivalence of courses that do not seem to address writing in ways that honor that complexity. For such courses, however valuable in many respects, would conceive of the value of writing, and thus a writing course, differently, and not at all equivalent to the value of the writing courses offered in the WPA's program.

How might articulating the value of writing program courses in terms other than writing skills affect the valuation accorded those teaching them? First, insofar as the writing program is not valued simply as one site among, and in competition with, many others for the production of abstracted "general writing skills," then those teaching in the program would not so easily be exchanged for, and in competition with, others teaching at those other sites. Even within the terms of capitalist "free market" logic/ideology, greater job security and pay would thus be merited for these teachers. Secondly, insofar as composition programs were not assigned the dubious task of "skills instruction" but of teaching about a subject—writing—whose nature is complex, whose valuation is politically and socially contingent, and consequently whose study is even more complex, the teaching of writing would be less susceptible to ideologies that denigrate such work—which is to say that WPAs who make such different claims about the value of their program would face strong opposition from others, including some within their ranks, making more traditional ascriptions of the value of their programs, just as they would face opposition from those within and outside their institutions claiming "equivalency" between very different types of composition courses. The "collegiality" that Schwalm calls for between WPAs at different institutions might thus be strained.

Thirdly, in a program that imagined its subject in more complex ways than in a program offering to do no more than teach "general writing skills," usually denigrated as "the basics," there would be a more likely recognition of the need for initial and ongoing professional development and training for those teaching the program's courses.[3] For example, qualifications for teachers to be sensitive to and able to contribute to the study of differences in writing and the negotiation of global as well as local language relations in confronting these differences, and to engage their students in such study and negotiation, would justify a demand for greater support for initiating instructors to the program and keeping them, unlike what most "freeway flyers" report experiencing in moving from school to school. There would be greater reliance on veterans to the program because of their knowledge of and experience in teaching its particular focus, and greater need for giving instructors continued opportunities for professional development in the form of course reductions, travel to conferences, and the like to further instructors' own study of differences in writing. Thus a program defining itself in such ways would be able to justify demanding not only such qualifications from its instructors but the improved working conditions of job security and opportunities for professional development that would further instructors' ability to do the work demanded of them in their teaching.

In making hiring decisions, such a program would not exclude instructors from around the world nor seek them out as cheap competition for local labor. Instead, it would value their input differently. For example, while a more traditional composition program might question the qualifications of an instructor for whom English is a second language to teach standardized English writing skills, a program that recognizes and takes as its charge addressing the complexity of English(es) globally would view such an instructor as at least potentially bringing valuable insights on what it might mean to write "in English" to the program, let alone that instructor's potential insights into the challenges of translating between languages and the power relations involved in all of these issues, just as Miller and Cripps found that TAs from disciplines outside English brought valuable insights into the parochial character of the writing instruction that their program had been offering. WPAs might argue for the need to hire only those instructors, or a pool of instructors, who have a sensitivity to and thus can contribute to the study of differences and changes in writing, and in writing in English, and to give those instructors working conditions of pay, teaching load, benefits, and opportunities for professional development making it possible for them to study and teach of such matters—i.e., on the basis of curriculum.

* * *

I have argued that the much of the normal "brokering" work WPAs are called upon to do is at odds with WPAs' own understanding of the nature of writing and its teaching and assessment, and that normal practice works in collusion with the globalizing of the market economy that tends to the denigration of composition courses and those who teach them by participating in the commodification and privatization of the work of composition—writing, English, and its learning and teaching. At the same time, I am suggesting that WPAs might heed other effects of the globalizing of the market economy, such as recognition of writing differences and power relations operating in the mediation of those differences, in their design of composition courses and in their brokering—in hiring, training, supervising, and pleading on behalf of—those involved in the teaching of these courses. The challenges of being a WPA are often treated as a balancing act: WPAs attempt to address different audiences with different demands, and to speak the language appropriate to each, all under unpromising conditions, and hoping all the while that no one will notice the difference and subterfuge. While it would be foolhardy, in light of the extreme circumstances prevailing at some institutions, to deny the need for such balancing, and even subterfuge, I'm suggesting that WPAs can achieve a more coherent balance and redeem their reputation as brokers and simultaneously the work they broker by mediating the work of writing and the learning and teaching of writing on terms that address more directly the contradictions of globalization and the necessary friction of the labor of reading and writing as meaning production rather than communication commodity. WPAs can in their brokering resist the forces of privatization and commodification of writing and its learning and teaching while drawing on the challenges posed by differences with and within writing in English that global capitalism has itself unleashed.

Notes

1. For an example of breathless advocacy of such for-profit, "distance ed." providers, see Taylor, ch. 8. For more sober analyses of distance education, see Cornford and Pollock, and Crook.

2. For a discussion of the effects of current economic changes on college composition students and composition curricula to address these, see Lu and Horner.

3. This is not to give credence to the popular belief that teaching (or learning) "the basics" of writing is simple. There is now a significant body of scholarship demonstrating the complexity of producing as well as interpreting those aspects of writing commonly categorized and denigrated as "basic skills" (see, for example, Bartholomae; Horner, "Rethinking"; Hull, "Acts" and "Research"; Lees, "Proofreading" and "Exceptable"; Lu, "Professing"; Shaughnessy; Tricomi; Joseph Williams). In short, treating writing in terms of "basic skills" is of a piece with the commodification of writing and reading as social practices, which, as I have been arguing, contributes to the denigration of the work of composition in which teachers and students engage.

Works Cited

Apple, Michael W., Jane Kenway, and Michael Singh, eds. *Globalizing Education: Policies, Pedagogies, & Politics*. New York: Lang, 2005.

Bartholomae, David. "The Study of Error." *College Composition and Communication* 31 (1980): 253-69.

Bauman, Zygmunt. *Globalization: The Human Consequences*. New York: Columbia UP, 1998.

Bazerman, Charles. "Response: Curricular Responsibilities and Professional Definition." *Reconceiving Writing, Rethinking Writing Instruction*. Ed. Joseph Petraglia. Mahwah, NJ: Erlbaum, 1995. 249-59.

Beck, Ulrich. *What Is Globalization?* Trans. Patrick Camiller. Cambridge: Polity, 2000.

Bousquet, Marc, Tony Scott, and Leo Parascondola, eds. *Tenured Bosses and Disposable Teachers: Writing Instruction in the Managed University*. Carbondale: Southern Illinois UP, 2004.

Canagarajah, A. Suresh. "The Place of World Englishes in Composition: Pluralization Continued." *College Composition and Communication* 57 (2006): 586-619.

Chase, Geoffrey. "Redefining Composition, Managing Change, and the Role of the WPA." *Writing Program Administration* 21 (Fall 1997): 46-54. Rpt. Ward and Carpenter 243-51.

Connors, Robert. "Rhetoric in the Modern University: The Creation of an Underclass." *The Politics of Writing Instruction: Postsecondary*. Ed. John Trimbur, Richard Bullock, and Charles Schuster. Portsmouth, NH: Boynton/Cook Heinemann, 1991. 55-84.

Cornford, James, and Neil Pollock. "The University Campus as a 'Resourceful Constraint': Process and Practice in the Construction of the Virtual University." Lea and Nicoll 170-81.

Crook, Charles. "Learning as Cultural Practice." Lea and Nicoll 152-69.

Crowley, Sharon. *Composition in the University: Historical and Polemical Essays*. U of Pittsburgh P, 1998.

Downing, David B., Claude Mark Hurlbert, and Paula Mathieu, eds. *Beyond English Inc.: Curricular Reform in a Global Economy*. Portsmouth, NH: Boynton/Cook, 2002.

George, Diana, ed. *Kitchen Cooks, Plate Twirlers, & Troubadours: Writing Program Administrators Tell Their Stories*. Portsmouth, NH: Boynton/Cook, 1999.

Harvey, David. *The Limits to Capital*. London: Verso, 2006.

Hesse, Doug D. "Understanding Larger Discourses in Higher Education: Practical Advice for WPAs." Ward and Carpenter 299-314.

Horner, Bruce. "Redefining Work and Value for Writing Program Administration." *JAC* 27 (2007): 163-84.

——. "Rethinking the 'Sociality' of Error: Teaching Editing as Negotiation." *Rhetoric Review* 11 (1992): 172-99.

——. *Terms of Work for Composition: A Materialist Critique.* Albany: State U of New York P, 2000.

Horner, Bruce, and Min-Zhan Lu. "Resisting Monolingualism in 'English': Reading and Writing the Politics of Language." *Rethinking English in Schools: A New and Constructive Stage.* Ed. Viv Ellis, Carol Fox, and Brian Street. London: Continuum, 2007. 141-57.

Hull, Glynda. "Acts of Wonderment: Fixing Mistakes and Correcting Errors." *Facts, Artifacts and Counterfacts: Theory and Method for a Reading and Writing Course.* David Bartholomae and Anthony R. Petrosky. Upper Montclair, NJ: Boynton/Cook, 1986. 199-226.

——. "Research on Error and Correction." *Perspectives on Research and Scholarship in Composition.* Ed. Ben W. McClelland and Timothy R. Donovan. New York: Modern Language Association, 1985. 162-84.

Jaschik, Scott. "Outsourced Grading." *Inside Higher Ed.* 22 September 2005. <http://insidehighered.com/news/2005/09/22/outsource.html>.

Kinkead, Joyce, and Jeanne Simpson. "The Administrative Audience: A Rhetorical Problem." Ward and Carpenter 68-77.

Lea, Mary R., and Kathy Nicoll, eds. *Distributed Learning: Social and Cultural Approaches to Practice.* London: Routledge, 2002.

Lees, Elaine O. "Proofreading as Reading, Errors as Embarrassments." *A Sourcebook for Basic Writing Teachers.* Ed. Theresa Enos. New York: Random, 1987. 216-30.

——. "'The Exceptable Way of the Society': Stanley Fish's Theory of Reading and the Task of the Teacher of Editing." *Reclaiming Pedagogy: The Rhetoric of the Classroom.* Ed. Patricia Donahue and Ellen Quandahl. Carbondale: Southern Illinois UP, 1989. 144-63.

Lillis, Theresa, and Mary Jane Curry. "Professional Academic Writing by Multilingual Scholars: Interactions with Literacy Brokers in the Production of English-Medium Texts." *Written Communication* 23 (2006): 3-35.

Lu, Min-Zhan. "An Essay on the Work of Composition." *College Composition and Communication* 56 (2004): 16-50.

——. "Professing Multiculturalism: The Politics of Style in the Contact Zone." *College Composition and Communication* 54 (1994): 442-58.

Lu, Min-Zhan, and Bruce Horner. "Composing in a Global-Local Context: Careers, Mobility, Skill." *College English* 72,2 (2009): 109-29.

Marx, Karl. *Capital, I: A Critique of Political Economy.* Trans. Ben Fowkes. New York: Vintage, 1976.

Micciche, Laura. "More Than a Feeling: Disappointment and WPA Work." *College English* 64 (2002): 432-58.

Miller, Richard E., and Michael J. Cripps. "Minimum Qualifications: Who Should Teach First-year Writing?" *Discord & Direction: The Postmodern*

Writing Program Administrator. Ed. Sharon James McGee and Carolyn Handa. Logan: Utah State UP, 2005. 123-39.

Miller, Susan. "The Feminization of Composition." *The Politics of Writing Instruction: Postsecondary.* Ed. John Trimbur and Richard Bullock. Portsmouth, NH: Boynton/Cook, 1991. 39-54.

———. *Textual Carnivals: The Politics of Composition.* Carbondale: Southern Illinois UP, 1991.

"New Brand Composition." WPA Listserv Thread, #227-231. 25-30 July 2008.

Ohmann, Richard. Introduction to the 1995 Edition. *English in America: A Radical View of the Profession.* Hanover, NH: Wesleyan UP, 1996. xiii-lii.

Pennycook, Alastair. "English as a Language Always in Translation." *European Journal of English Studies* 12,1 (2008): 33-47.

Raduntz, Helen. "The Marketization of Education." Apple et al. 231-45.

Rai, Saritha. "A Tutor Half a World Away, But as Close as Keyboard." *The New York Times* 7 (September 2005). <http://www.nytimes.com/2005/09/07/education/07tutor.html>.

Ramonet, Ignacio. "La pensée unique." *Le monde diplomatique* January 1995.

"Responsibilities of Teaching Assistants and Academic Staff." University of Wisconsin-Milwaukee English Department Composition Advisory Committee, 2004.

Rhodes, Keith. "Marketing Composition for the 21st Century." *WPA: Writing Program Administration* 23,3 (2000): 51-69.

Schell, Eileen E. *Gypsy Academics and Mother-Teachers: Gender, Contingent Labor, and Writing Instruction.* Portsmouth, NH: Boynton/Cook, 1998.

Schell, Eileen E., and Patricia Lambert Stock, eds. *Moving a Mountain: Transforming the Role of Contingent Faculty in Composition Studies and Higher Education.* Urbana, IL: National Council of Teachers of English, 2001.

Schwalm, David. "Re: New Brand Composition." WPA Listserv posting, 26 July 2008.

———. "The Writing Program (Administrator) in Context: Where Am I, and Can I Still Behave Like a Faculty Member?" Ward and Carpenter 9-22.

Shaughnessy, Mina P. *Errors and Expectations: A Guide for the Teacher of Basic Writing.* New York: Oxford UP, 1977.

Strickland, Donna. "Taking Dictation: The Emergence of Writing Programs and the Cultural Contradictions of the Composition Teacher." *College English* 63 (2001): 457-79.

Taylor, Mark C. *The Moment of Complexity: Emerging Network Culture.* U of Chicago P, 2001.

Tricomi, Elizabeth Taylor. "Krashen's Second-Language Acquisition Theory and the Teaching of Edited American English." *Journal of Basic Writing* 5,2 (Fall 1986): 59-69.

Tsing, Anna Lowenhaupt. *Friction: An Ethnography of Global Connection.* Princeton UP, 2005.

Tuell, Cynthia. "Composition Teaching as 'Women's Work': Daughters, Hand-maids, Whores, and Mothers." *Writing Ourselves into the Story: Unheard Voices from Composition Studies.* Ed. Sheryl Fontaine and Susan Hunter. Carbondale: Southern Illinois UP, 1992. 123-39.

Ward, Irene, and William J. Carpenter, eds. *The Allyn & Bacon Sourcebook for Writing Program Administrators.* New York: Longman, 2002.

Williams, Joseph M. "The Phenomenology of Error." *College Composition and Communication* 32 (1981): 152-68.

Williams, Raymond. *Keywords: A Vocabulary of Culture and Society.* New York: Oxford UP, 1976.

Ziguras, Christopher. "International Trade in Education Services: Governing the Liberalization and Regulation of Private Enterprise." Apple et al. 93-112.

Anxieties of Globalization: Networked Subjects in Rhetoric and Composition Studies

Rebecca Dingo and Donna Strickland

So there is a general anxiety about globalization because there is a sense that there are changes going on that are touching all of us, and we don't know how, at the end of the day, our families, ourselves, our companies, our communities are going to end up being hit or not hit. (Moises Naím, editor, *Foreign Policy*, in Barfield, Glassman, and Naím)

It's true that many people think of a liberalized approach to trade when they consider globalization, and in recent years economic effects have come to dominate discussion of this phenomenon. But there is also a powerful psychological dimension to globalization. (Clack)

The benefits from globalization are enormous, but so are the obstacles. And we've talked a little bit about the polarization that has occurred in our trade policy here at home, where one side believes that open markets, with the United States leading the world toward economic liberalization, will generate prosperity, growth and political stability. And the other side, concerned about jobs and other social concerns, are seeing that the open markets actually are detrimental to their concerns and believe that an attack on globalization and, to some extent, an attack on the institutions that personify globalization, like the World Trade Organization, advances their cause. (Brookings Institution, "A Prescription to Relieve Worker Anxiety")

If globalization can be said to have a dominant structure of feeling, that structure must surely build upon a generalized feeling of anxiety. As the above epigraphs suggest, feelings of insecurity and helplessness circulate along with globalized neoliberal economic policies. Globalization is associated with changes at once material and intangible: these changes seem to affect all of us and yet seem out of our control. This lack of control contributes to a general sense of anxiety: anxiety about jobs, about the future, and ultimately about powerlessness.

As the above quotation from the Brookings Institution suggests, the dominant arguments that frame globalization appear to follow a polarized cultural narrative suggesting that globalization is either a "good" or "bad" trend. That is, the dominant narratives tend to either assert the goodness of globalization and the inappropriateness of anxiety, or they assert the detrimental effects of globalization and the inevitability of anxiety. However, we suggest that this two-sided narrative of globalization functions more like a Möbius strip that twists the argument but ultimately is non-orienting and inextricable. Rather than offering two sides, the globalization argument is continuous and self-replicating. We hear that globalization, as our above examples demonstrate, produces anxiety among workers, then, with a twist of the ribbon, workers are told not to feel uncertain because globalization will take care things. Still, it's unclear how globalization will take care of things, and so anxiety continues, feeding the loop. The dominant narrative of globalization that the Möbius strip exemplifies thus merely recirculates a never-changing rhetoric of anxiety within a closed system. In short, this globalization narrative never gets outside of itself; it only circulates mutually repetitive and overlapping arguments. If, as Raymond Williams argues, structures of feeling shape and sustain an economic system, then the dominant globalized economics of neoliberalism are shaped by feelings of anxiety, insecurity, and sustained by defensive mechanisms and morale boosting, like the Brookings Instution's "prescription." In other words, these emotional postures of anxiety and defense against anxiety frame any discussion within the ecology of globalization. Whenever discourse is locked in this way, little progress can be made or material effects can be realized. Because the dominant discourse of globalization is locked within an emotionally laden, moralistic frame, any arguments about globalization will simply be recirculated within the twisting Möbius strip; we will not get any new arguments.

We maintain, then, that if attention to the discourse of globalization is to have material effects in rhetoric and composition studies, it will be important to offer an alternative frame—another way of feeling—to the ones circulating in the Möbius strip of anxiety. Our goal, then, is not to identify the bad (or good) effects of globalization, but to demonstrate the affectively driven rhetorical moves that link and sustain three subject positions shaped by globalization and central to the continued emergence and sustenance of rhetoric and composition studies: student, contingent worker, and administrator. In the United States these three subjects come together in introductory-level classes where contingent faculty are more likely to be teaching students in lower-division classes, and where WPAs often serve as overseers of and intermediaries between the two.

In order to observe anxious rhetorics circulating among and constituting the three subject positions of student, teacher, and administrator, we turn to two activist organizations that recently have been in higher education news: Students for Academic Freedom (SAF) and New York University Graduate Student Organizing Committee (GSOC). SAF, a national student organization working to secure student's rights legislation nationwide, is a right-leaning group that attracts students to its cause by framing their arguments in a locked, anxious rhetoric that urges the need for defense against liberal professors. GSOC, a left-leaning graduate employee organization, would seem to be far removed from the politic discourse of SAF, and yet in the public documents released during their ongoing struggle with the NYU administration, a similar rhetoric of anxiety and paternalistic defense is clear. We look at discursive artifacts produced by SAF and those produced as part of a management/labor dispute at NYU to demonstrate that the anxieties of globalization circulate in the context of higher education in a locked Möbius strip where expressions of anxiety are often assuaged by paternalistic reactions. Because the politicization of students has been a significant discourse within rhetoric and composition studies, and because the administration of programs and the question of contingent workers is also significant, we argue that observing these discourses feeding off each other provides the exigence for producing an alternative model for working with globalization in our field.

The alternative model we offer is the network. While the network can be seen as the free market run amok, it can also be understood as a system of linkages that allows us to pay attention to the diverse material affects of neoliberal economies. We argue that getting outside the Möbius strip of anxiety and expanding our rhetoric to reflect networks of linked subject positions is an important strategy for teachers and administrators of writing. These networks— what Jenny Edbauer calls "coordinating processes"—comprise not closed rhetorical situations but "rhetorical ecologies [. . .] moving across the same social field and within shared structures of feeling" (20).

In order to make visible the shared structures of feeling within the field of rhetoric and composition studies, we map the links between anxieties expressed by Students for Academic Freedom with those that come across in documents related to the New York University graduate student strike. We see these two instances of rhetorical activism as demonstrative emblems of the tensions and links globalization produces within U.S. higher education. We also briefly suggest alternative pedagogical and administrative practices that respond to the economic insecurity that students feel, contingent faculty endure, and administrators juggle.

Globalization and Linked Subject Positions in the Corporate University

Globalization comprises the social field for all discursive practices (whether in or out of the classroom), and mapping the circulation of affect structuring that field provides an essential tool for understanding globalization. Of course, many scholars have mapped the political, economic and cultural circulation of the logic of neoliberal transnational capital, both abroad and in the United States. Specifically, the United States has undergone significant economic and cultural changes as corporations move operations out of the United States, creating a new middle class in second and third world nations, just as the U.S. labor market demands that workers be able to adapt their skills to new technologies or downplay their skills for service sector jobs, and as the nation-state has withdrawn from the financing of education and welfare (see, for example, Sassen and Ong). These very examples demonstrate that the constricted globalization narrative circulating around the Möbius strip—globalization is good/bad—does not adequately address globalization's material realities. For example, job loss in the United States threatens citizens here, but in India the technology and telecommunication boom has created new wealth for an expanded middle class. And yet India itself maintains a caste system that keeps many in poverty. We don't mean to imply, then, that globalization has not contributed to inequalities, but that its effects are not clearly cut.

In higher education, too, globalization's effects are uneven. Globalization, for example, has necessitated a new, more inclusive awareness of global dependencies that inform our research and teaching practices. At the same time, globalization has transformed universities into what are variously called "corporate" or "managed" universities—institutions that follow the logic of markets more than the logic of nonprofit organizations. According to Sheila Slaughter and Larry L. Leslie, the flow of public monies toward higher education has decreased as globalization has made "increasing claims on government funds" (7). This decrease in public funding has led to increases in at least two kinds of entrepreneurial activities: universities more aggressively market themselves in order to get what government money is available in the form of student aid, and universities more aggressively seek private funding to compensate for the decrease in federal and state funding (see Slaughter and Leslie, especially pp. 8, 11-12). Both activities tend to put more focus on research (and the management of resources) than on instruction. As Slaughter and Leslie explain,

> Research money is a critical resource for universities not only because most research money is raised competitively, but also because universities are prestige maximizers. Since most faculty teach, and many faculty perform public service, but fewer win competitive research funds from government or industry, research is the activity that differentiates among and within universities. (17)

In other words, the flow of public monies away from universities has led to an increased dependence on research as a source for both economic and cultural capital.

The effects of globalization on the university are thus far-reaching, leading to increased emphasis on research and graduate education and decreased attention to undergraduate instruction. In fact, between 1976 and 1992, expenditures dedicated to instruction decreased 3.2 percent at public four-year institutions, even as expenditures dedicated to research increased 2.7 percent and to administration 2.2 percent (see Slaughter and Leslie 96-97). As Slaughter and Leslie point out, "Given that the recent decades were periods of major enrollment growth in the United States, these are profound declines [in expenditures for instruction]" (86).

As we in rhetoric and composition studies are deeply aware, this decline in expenditures for instruction has led to the hiring of increasing numbers of contingent faculty, including graduate student and adjunct instructors, who often teach the bulk of lower-level classes for less pay and fewer benefits than full-time, tenure-line faculty. What we may be less attuned to is the way that this decline creates another inextricable circle of materially significant affect:

> The shift away from instruction may have negative direct consequences not only for students, but it also contributes to increased university alienation from the general public, thereby reinforcing secular tendencies to reduce state general support even more, which in turn further destabilizes the universities and ultimately renders them more dependent upon and answerable to contracting and granting organizations. (100)

In short, federal and state responses to neoliberal economic policies of globalization have put pressure on universities to seek private funding, which in turn has led to decreased emphases on the popularly recognized mission of universities (undergraduate education), which in turn may lead to yet further withdrawal of state support. This shift in priorities has directly affected the teaching of composition, as it has led to increased reliance on contingent faculty and increased employment of administrators to coordinate their work. Marc Bousquet points this out in "Composition as Management Science"—an article that itself sparked an anxious reception:

> [I]f we are to locate rhet-comp's ascendance in the years 1975-1995, then we must also acknowledge that this is a period of time in which undergraduate admissions substantially expanded while the full-time faculty was reduced by 10 percent, and the number of graduate-student employees was increased by 40 percent. [...] The discipline's enormous usefulness to academic capitalism—in delivering cheap teaching, training a supervisory stratum, and producing a group of intellectuals theorizing this scene of managed labor—has to be given [...] credit. (16-17)

While some within rhetoric and composition studies have objected to Bousquet's "blaming" of the field for supplying cheap labor and program administrators, it nonetheless must be admitted that the field *does* produce administrators of programs who *do* manage the labor of contingent faculty. Rather than getting caught up in a defense of the field in the wake of globalization (or a defense of Bousquet's position, for that matter), turning to the linkages among these subject positions produced in the corporate university provides an alternative to these polarized yet mutually reinforcing arguments.

As the field of rhetoric and composition studies has expanded, however, it has become increasingly difficult for scholars in the field to see their work as connected. Writing program administrators have an organization separate from CCCC, and some complain that theoretical work is out of touch with the practical demands of directing programs. Locke Carter, for example, has urged that scholars in the field take a harder look at the free market in order to develop programs that are more financially competitive and responsive to market changes. His approach, however, emphasizes the positive effects of neoliberal economics, thus keeping the conversation within the closed Möbius strip. We consider this move a mistake and call instead for a rhetorical strategy of linking. As important as economics is, a purely economic response simply cannot account for the differences in the effect of globalization even as we observe the similarities in affect. Indeed, as Caren Kaplan and Inderpal Grewal have recognized in their call for transnational feminist cultural studies methodology, economic models that adhere to neomarxist (and antimarxist) arguments simply replay "old divides" that do not account for the ways that "one's subject position [. . .] is constituted through links among thoroughly unequal social forces" (356).

To understand how these links work in rhetoric and composition studies, we suggest looking not simply at isolated scenes (the scene of the writing classroom as workplace or the scene of the writing classroom as site of hegemonic struggle), but at the ecologies—Edbauer's "co-ordinating processes," "shared structures of feelings" in which students, teachers, and administrators connect, interact. Attending to these links will allow for the creation of rhetorics that respond to, sustain, and sometimes undermine these ecologies. Because affect circulates within and sustains ways of thinking about globalization, it demands our attention. And calling attention to affect is necessarily calling attention to linkages. As Edbauer puts it, "To say that we are connected is another way of saying that we are never outside the networked interconnectedness of forces, energies, rhetorics, moods, and experiences. In other words, our practical consciousness is never outside the prior and ongoing structures of feeling that shape the social field" (10). But as Kaplan and Grewal make clear, attending to these connections also demands paying attention to the inequalities that circulate within the shared social field:

> Linkages suggest networks of economic and social relations that occur within postmodernity vis-à-vis global capital and its effects. Linkages does not require

a reciprocity or sameness or commonality. It can and must acknowledge differentials of power and participation in cultural production, but it also can and must also trace the connections among seemingly disparate elements. (359)

Thus, we examine the circulation of discourses that affectively and economically connect three sometimes opposed but nevertheless clearly linked subject positions of special significance to composition studies: the right-tending discourse of the student-consumer, the left-leaning discourse of the contingent academic worker, and the moderate (and, sometimes, moderating) discourse of the beleaguered administrator.

Linked Anxieties: Administrator-Teacher-Student

In her book about university students' activism, Liza Featherstone describes the contemporary university's ecology: "A prominent feature of the corporate university is students' alienation and powerlessness; universities often treat them as anonymous consumers, rather than as members of a community who deserve a say in its policies. When administrators do that, they can expect student customers to act like politicized consumer activists" (31-32). Although Featherstone describes students working against sweatshop labor, her observation similarly characterizes the undergraduate student activist and lobbying group SAF and graduate employee union activists, including those who are currently on strike at NYU. We want to be careful here: in identifying graduate employees as "student activists," we don't intend to reinforce the binary propagated by the NYU administration—that graduate employees are principally students, not workers. Indeed, graduate employees *are* both students and workers: their subject position is constituted through the linking of unequal social forces. Similarly, the subject positions of the undergraduate student members of SAF are constituted through the linking of consumer and student activist. In this section, we observe the circulation of moralistic, rights-based discourse among both groups of activists, together with bureaucratic, paternalistic responses. What stands out in the public documents associated with each group is the affective contagion: the way in which opposing discourses circulate in almost predictable ways. While this discourse certainly serves to reinforce the felt sense of each of the parties, it does little to sway the emotional stance of the other. In other words, the *public* discourse, at least, works to reaffirm already established positions. And, on the part of the university administrators, this paternalistic discourse serves to obscure economic linkages.

In his upbeat guide to graduate employee unionizing, William Vaughn lists "five reasons why you should not begin a campaign" to form a union, with "trendiness" topping the list. "Face it," Vaughn writes, "I wouldn't be writing this piece and you wouldn't be reading it if grad employee unions, and academic labor issues in general, didn't happen to be 'hot' at the moment" (266). This "hot" intensity, this "trendy" aura connected to the discourse of graduate employee unionization signals a dynamic circulation of affective discourse in the neoliberal ecology. In fact, perhaps few issues connected directly to English studies, and especially to the teaching of first-year writing (where so many graduate teaching assistants earn their living), currently carry such emotional weight.

The union movement itself currently is "hot," though not always in positive ways. An organization calling itself "Union Facts" has recently launched an ad campaign and website, offering support to workers who wish to fight forced unionization. In an economy that exports industrial jobs transnationally and a federal administration that appoints anti-union judges to the National Labor Relations Board, it would seem hard to believe that unions are currently in a position to force the hand of workers. Yet, this hate campaign, a "hot" discourse itself, is surely an anxious reaction to the increasingly prevalent discourse of unionization, particularly as this discourse circulates in new scenes, extending to service and knowledge workers. Graduate employee unions (as well as adjunct faculty unions) are a response to the corporate university. Graduate student numbers have swelled as graduate education (allied with research) has gained greater emphasis; simultaneously, more contingent faculty are employed (for less money) as undergraduate education has received less funding.

The circulation of anxious, conflicted, "hot" discourses of unionization and anti-unionization has recently gained attention in the case of the New York University graduate employee strike. The NYU administration ended negotiations with the Graduate Student Organizing Committee (GSOC), a United Auto Workers local, in August 2005, and the union began a strike in November of that year (see Nolan and GSOC). The union members, like many workers under globalization, appeal to their right to organize to gain workplace benefits. In the FAQs to explain their reason for striking, they write, "Our first contract raised stipends by 40% on average, provided employer-paid health care, paid leave, workload protection, paid TA-training, child care benefits, a grievance resolution procedure and many other important workplace rights. . . . After working with a contract for four years, GSOC members do not want to work without one" (GSOC). In support of the GSOC, The American Association of University Professors (AAUP) works to make a transnational appeal as they draw from the United Nations' 1948 Universal Declaration of Human Rights:

> Among the fundamental rights enshrined in that document was the right to unionize. "Everyone has the right to form and to join trade unions for the protection of his interests" (Article 23). That graduate employee unions are appropriate to the Academy is evidenced by more than three decades of graduate employee unionism in the United States and by the AAUP's Statement on Graduate Students, which explicitly provides that "graduate student assistants,

like other campus employees, should have the right to organize to bargain collectively." (American Association of University Professors)

Although this appeal draws from a historical document, rights discourse, Wendy Brown argues, tends to operate "in an ahistorical, acultural, acontextual idiom," appealing to an "enduring universality rather than provisionality or partiality" (Brown 97). In other words, rights discourse—in its appeal to universal values—tends to be self-enclosed rather than linking. Moreover, rights discourse tends to maintain the dynamics of the existing power structure, putting the group asking for rights in the position of the subaltern.

At the same time, an appeal to rights has a long history as a response to paternalistic discourse that seeks to keep subalterns in subordinate positions. In this way then, GSOC's and the AAUP's rhetoric is an apt response to the university administrators' paternalistic discourse. This paternalistic rhetoric is deployed throughout the documents related to the strike that the NYU administration has posted to their website. In these documents, graduate employees strategically become "our students," and the union becomes a threat to the paternal relationship between "faculty" (or is that management?) and students. This slippage—Is the faculty the same as management? Are "students" not also equally employees?—reveals the difficulty of negotiating complex identities in the global ecology that shapes the corporate university. Indeed, the June 2005 document "To the NYU Community" struggles to create links. After establishing that the university would no longer enter into collective bargaining ("with the UAW," not with "our students"), the administrators take pains to demonstrate their willingness to establish common ground with graduate student employees. Like patient parents, the vice president and provost acknowledge that they've learned a great deal through this rebellion of "our students," writing that, "the experience gave graduate assistants a strong collective voice, providing the University with a mechanism to better understand their desires, needs, and concerns." And part of what they've learned is that graduate students at times "feel" like employees:

> From the University's standpoint, the general principle is unwavering: all graduate students, whether or not they are GAs, are students of the University. However, as our GAs carry out their duties, many of them, understandably, also feel like employees. There needs to be clarity about their role, their rights, and their responsibilities. We must ensure that their work as GAs is related to their course of study, that they are treated with the respect and dignity accorded colleagues, and that they are accountable to NYU, just as NYU is accountable to each of them. ("Relationship")

What's needed, then, is a clarification of just what a graduate student is in relation to NYU; thus, the university developed a draft of rights and responsibilities "to give clarity to and achieve agreement on the nature of their relationship to the University." Ultimately, however, none of these rights and responsibilities deals directly with their status as economic subjects of the university; rather they simply reaffirm Brown's observation that rights discourse reaffirms subaltern relationships.

Indeed, what NYU seems to wish to remind graduate employees is that their primary economic relationship to the university is that of product: they represent a kind of cultural capital that is threatened by their wish to affiliate themselves with labor: many members of our community have expressed deep reservations about the impact of the collective bargaining framework on our academic programs. These reservations include the difficulty of reconciling a non-academic intermediary between faculty mentor and student, and the introduction of the one-size-fits-all approach – traditional in the labor context—into a University that values distinctive scholarship and prides itself on the diversity of its graduate programs ("Relationship"). As we point out above, in the words of Slaughter and Leslie, universities are "prestige maximizers": thus, to lose cultural capital to the less prestigious realm of "labor" represents a major loss.

What is perhaps even more striking about this correspondence is that it is publicly available on the Internet. This transfer of information provides opportunities for linking—linking anyone in the "NYU community" to the events, whether that person is in the city or on another continent. This performance of openness, combined with the rhetoric of paternalism, is also certainly a defense mechanism, an anxious response to the threat of loss—both material economic loss and cultural capital loss. Administrators seek to regain cultural capital through this performance of openness, this ostensible linking outward by making their documents publicly available. Our point here is not so much to reprimand the NYU administration, but to demonstrate the failure to link outside the corporate university's anxious, defensive rhetoric even as the discourse clearly gestures toward openness.

Paternalistic rhetoric, however, is not the sole domain of administrators. As SAF members make clear on their public website—wherein students are invited both to "lodge complaints" against professors and join the struggle to pass the "Student Bill of Rights" at the state and federal levels— students imagine their professors as power-hungry, abusive, and overtly paternalistic. They describe teachers who merely "rail against capitalism" and do not consider students' own authority or experiences. While activist-oriented scholars in composition studies may feel compelled to defend the activism of graduate employees, they may tend not to see their own links with conservative students, like those in SAF. As scholars like Jennifer Trainer point out, activist-oriented teachers might in fact have difficulty interacting with such students, potentially feeling defensive in response to them.

Yet, reactively dismissing conservative students as misguided or innocent evokes the very arguments about graduate employees put forth by administrators. Rejecting students who are either overtly or implicitly aligned with SAF-like stances while identifying with graduate employee activists simply replicates the anxious rhetoric of globalization rather than observing the ways that these subject positions are linked and mutually constructing of the complex subject positions inhabited by administrators-teachers-scholars of rhetoric and composition studies. If rhet-comp professionals identify with the politics of graduate employees and are dismissive of SAF as an organization that unfoundedly puts students at odds with teachers, then our professional discourse replicates the NYU administration's paternalistic rhetoric that pits "our students" against the interfering UAW. Administrators, teachers, scholars, students: all are mutually linked and constituted through the neoliberal corporate university. It is crucial to see that just as administrators and graduate employees are feeling the effects of the corporate university, so are undergraduate students. Indeed, as Slaughter and Leslie point out, as the economy has changed and universities divert money away from undergraduate instruction, the experience of students in classrooms is necessarily changing. The rights-based discourse of SAF, then, must be understood not simply as a symptom of neoliberalism but as an apt response to the paternalistic stance teachers might make.

As it happens, composition scholars and teachers do not often attend to student organizations such as SAF or to students who share SAF's beliefs. Activist-oriented composition teachers may seek to empower students to criticize the university constructively—through public writing, for example—not acknowledging that in fact many students enter our classrooms already empowered. SAF demonstrates that some students are indeed *acting* as empowered subjects by being publicly and actively critical of the university. In their "Mission Statement" and "Student Bill of Rights," SAF members employ a rights discourse similar to that utilized by GSOC and the AAUP. However, unlike GSOC and AAUP, SAF's arguments make links between consumer rights and academic rights. SAF's mission statement, for example, links student's academic rights and campaign finance reform:

> The principle of campaign finance reform is recognized in the society at large but is currently absent from campus affairs where the vast preponderance of general student funds is devoted to promoting ideas at one end of the political spectrum. Students for Academic Freedom will advocate reforms that make the "public square" of the university a more inclusive and representative marketplace of ideas. ("Mission and Strategy")

SAF's focus on campaign finance reform as a means to secure the "marketplace of ideas" demonstrates how the rhetoric of consumerism has extended beyond the boundaries of economic policy; SAF's use of this rhetoric illustrates how they themselves are not only persuaded by it, but it has become part of their lived sense, part of their ecology. SAF's rhetorical choices suggest that student identity has been directly affected by the shifts in globalization: students see themselves as consumers who have a right to a "diverse education" simply because they pay for it (whether out of pocket or via state taxes); indeed, at the top of their website is a quote by David Horowitz stating: "You can't get a good education even if you are paying $30,000 a year."

SAF's mission statement goes on to make the following argument: "The state legislatures and publicly appointed boards of trustees have a fiduciary responsibility to taxpayer-funded institutions and their tax-paying supporters. [...] It is illegal under state patronage laws to use state-funded institutions for partisan purposes" ("Mission and Strategy"). Interestingly, at the very moment that SAF makes this argument, the state is actually reducing funding of universities. As a result, tuition at state institutions has exponentially increased, thus driving the consumeristic discourse of SAF.

Throughout SAF's Mission Statement they employ rights discourses and name themselves as victims of professors' whims, yet as the above examples illustrate, these students also demonstrate that because they are ultimately the consumers of education they deserve a particular type of education. As adept rhetoricians, these same students appeal to university boards and administrators by making their arguments resonate with the university's changing identity as a corporate entity. By drawing a parallel to their identities as victimized consumers and the current debates on campaign finance reform, SAF articulates further their rights in ways that all members of their audience (students, professors, and administrators) might recognize.

But just as the GSOC use of rights discourse keeps them in a paternalistic relationship, so does SAF's appeal to rights. This persistent power relationship is most clear in the testimony for the website's "abuse center," where SAF rhetorically constructs professors as intellectual-ists, a form of discrimination that—like racism or sexism, for example—places students in a compromised power position. Consider the following complaint:

> The professor rails against capitalism and deceptively encourages classmates to blame the problems of the world on US imperialism by way of white man. Insists on degrading the Constitution and the US Government by way of saying it was designed to keep white men in power, offering no empirical or compelling proof. Told the class the electoral college was rigged for Bush in the 2000 election. ("Complaint 1")

The student, recirculating the Möbius strip of anxiety, is actively working to differentiate herself/himself from the "liberal" identities of her/his professors. Unselfconsciously, the student above complains about her/his professor not giving specific examples, but the student does not actually supply tangible examples of how it is that the teacher has abused the student. The "abuse" is contingent upon the professor not listening to the student and holding a differing view than the student does. The student's complaint also demonstrates that perhaps the professor as well might be stuck in the non-orienting and repetitive Möbius strip argument and unable to reframe globalizations' affect. Given the power dynamics of the student-teacher relationship, extricating themselves from a paternalistic stance is certainly difficult.

Instead of either discounting, bemoaning, or paternalistically trying to sway students who might share SAF's concerns, we suggest that their arguments for academic freedom and the "abuse" testimonies they publish on their website might challenge the pedagogical practices of the composition classroom and the default assumptions circulating in rhetoric and composition studies. In fact, as our reading of the SAF documents alongside those from NYU demonstrates, multiple identities are linked and constituted through a common anxiety circulating in the corporate university. This anxious discourse leads to a closed, defensive system alternating between rights and paternalism. Rather than remaining caught in reactivity, rhetoric and composition teachers-scholars-administrators need to find ways to pay attention to linkages and invite others into these conversations. While we can't escape the paternalistic institutions we inhabit, we can more productively negotiate these structures by mapping networks and taking action based on these maps.

In particular, program administrators and union activists both may be able to make more strategic arguments for improved conditions when they can more fully see specific ways that their institutions have responded to the neoliberal economy. In other words, rather than being forced only to appeal to the right to better working conditions, they might employ new strategies that address the complex circulation of global capital, recognizing that the university itself is merely a node in a larger global network. For example, if the state legislature has recently responded to global exigencies by slashing the university budget, WPAs and union members might join with university administrators in creating arguments that demonstrate the need for additional state funds.

Likewise, writing teachers might take advantage of the linking technologies of new media to invite students to take on projects that trace connections throughout this global network. For example, Rebecca has asked students in her writing classes to choose an image with resonance for them and to connect that image with multiple contexts and stories. They then use Photoshop or other digital media software to create layered images that illustrate the links that they found. Donna uses blogs as interactive sites to encourage students to engage in and see how they exist in networked relationships. Ultimately, globalization requires that we all, as administrators-teachers-scholars, engage in more networked conversations, recognizing our uneven linkages, rather than remain in the constricted and closed Möbius strip arguments that reify old anxieties.

Works Cited

American Association of University Professors. "AAUP Grad Student Committee Speaks Up for NYU Grads." 17 February 2006. AAUP website. Accessed 15 August 2006. <http://www.aaup.org/newsroom/press/2006/gradcmtstatement.htm>.

Barfield, Claude, James Glassman, and Moisés Naím. "A Conversation about Globalization." *eJournal USA* (February 2006). Accessed 15 August 2006. <http://usinfo.state.gov/journals/itgic/0206/ijge/globalization.htm>.

Bousquet, Marc. "Composition as Management Science." *Tenured Bosses and Disposable Teachers: Writing Instruction in the Managed University*. Ed. Marc Bousquet, Tony Scott, and Leo Parascondola. Carbondale: Southern Illinois UP, 2004. 11-35.

Brookings Institution and the Institute for International Economics. "A Prescription to Relieve Worker Anxiety: Wage and Health Insurance for Displaced Workers. A Luncheon Discussion." Brookings Institution website. Accessed 15 August 2006. <http://www.brook.edu/comm/transcripts/20010306.htm>.

Brown, Wendy. *States of Injury: Power and Freedom in Late Modernity*. Princeton, NJ: Princeton UP, 1995.

Carter, Locke. "Rhetoric, Markets, Value Creation: An Introduction and Argument for a Productive Rhetoric." *Market Matters*. Ed. Locke Carter.

Clack, George. Introduction. *eJournal USA* (February 2006). Accessed 15 August 2006. <http://usinfo.state.gov/journals/itgic/0206/ijge/introduction.htm>.

Edbauer, Jenny. "Unframing Models of Public Distribution: From Rhetorical Situation to Rhetorical Ecologies." *Rhetoric Society Quarterly* 35 (2005): 5-24.

Featherstone, Liza. *Students against Sweatshops*. New York, NY: Verso, 2002.

GSOC Strike FAQ. Accessed 15 August 2005. <http://www.2110uaw.org/gsoc/gsoc_strike_faq.htm>.

Kaplan, Caren, and Inderpal Grewal. "Transnational Feminist Cultural Studies: Beyond the Marxism/Poststructuralism/Feminism Divides." *Between Woman and Nation: Nationalisms, Transnational Feminisms, and the State*. Ed. Caren Kaplan, Norma Alarcón, and Minoo Moallem. Durham, NC: Duke UP, 1999. 349-63.

Nolan, Terrance J. Letter from NYU to UAW. 5 August 2005. New York University Office of the Provost. Accessed 15 August 2006 <http://www.nyu.edu/provost/ga/lettertouaw080505.pdf>.

Ong, Aihwa. *Flexible Citizenship: The Cultural Logics of Transnationality*. North Carolina, Durham: Duke UP, 1999.

Sassen, Saskia. *Globalization and Its Discontents: Selected Essays 1984-1998*. New York: New Press, 1998.

Slaughter, Sheila, and Larry L. Leslie. *Academic Capitalism: Politics, Policies, and the Entrepreneurial University.* Baltimore: Johns Hopkins UP, 1997.

Students for Academic Freedom. "Abuse Center." Accessed April 2, 2005. <http://www.studentsforacademicfreedom.org/comp/complaints_form.asp.>

———. "Academic's Bill of Rights." 15 Jan. 2005. <http://www.studentsforacademicfreedom.org/essays/sbor.html>.

———. "Complaint One." 2 April 2005. <http://www.studentsforacademicfreedom.org/comp/viewComplaint.asp?complainId=241>.

———. "SAF Home Page." 21 November 2004. <http://www.studentsforacademicfreedom.org/>.

———. "Mission Statement." 15 January 2005. <http://www.studentsforacademicfreedom.org/essays/pamphlet.html>.

———. "Student's Bill of Rights." 20 December 2004. <http://www.studentsforacademicfreedom.org/essays/sbor.html>.

Trainor, Jennifer Seibel. "Critical Pedagogy's 'Other': Constructions of Whiteness in Education for Social Change." *CCC* 53,4 (2002): 631-50.

Vaughn, William. "Need a Break from Your Dissertation? Organize a Union!" *Chalk Lines: The Politics of Work in the Managed University.* Ed. Randy Martin. Durham, NC: Duke UP, 1998. 264-304.

Mapping Everyday Articulations:
Gender, Blackness, and the Significance of Space in Washington, D.C.

L. Hill Taylor, Jr.

> When we are laid open to global forces, we confront ourselves differently. As the nation loosens its hold on us, we encounter new possibilities of community. In this moment it is possible to ask what is possible—besides economic victimhood and social incivility. Can we find other ways to be? Can we be other than what globalization makes for us? These questions are challenging ones that ask for daily practices of learning to live differently. I hear them as a call for an "ethics of the local." (Gibson-Graham)

> I hate to sound wimpy (is that a girl thing?), but aren't there shuttles from the airport to the Palmer House, for those of us who aren't quite brave enough to try the subway? (WPA Listserv post prior to annual College Composition and Communication Conference)

> This society eliminates geographical distance only to reap distance internally in the form of spectacular separation. (Debord)

Stepping off of the Van Ness/UDC Metro escalator, I am venturing further into state space. My subterranean journey to the English Department at the University of the District of Columbia originates in the city of Arlington in the Commonwealth of Virginia, from a portion of land that was once part of "Federal City" or rather the District of Columbia (until allegiance to pro-slavery factions prompted a reclamation of territory by the state of Virginia in 1847). UDC, a

Historically Black College/University (HBCU), exists as one of the few urban, open-admissions, land grant universities in the United States and sits in affluent Northwest D.C. surrounded by international embassies and offices of fortune 100 companies. Most of UDC's students have traveled on the Metro as well, though most not from Virginia; they have come from other places like Ward 7 and Ward 8 in Southeast D.C, the places where news crews venture when a story of inner city crime and decay is needed.

The students that I meet with are mostly black, either from inner city D.C. or recently emigrated from places like Cameroon, Sierra Leone, Nigeria, and Ethiopia. Many speak multiple languages deftly, though more out of necessity as vestiges of colonialism and empire, than out of progressive curriculum and choice. Most are women, many of them single mothers working and taking classes. These students are, in many ways, the abstractions that some (though certainly not all) curriculum theorists and educators at suburban colleges and universities do not know but write about and construct anyway; for these students, the design and implementation of curriculum has very much "tended toward the abstract" (Pinar 165) without much recognition or accommodation for their specific aspirations, needs, and challenges. Without knowing or being of this place, and knowing the lived spaces that inform it, much curricular consideration for these students has come through racial simulation and "knowing" vis-à-vis electronic mediation rather than localized corporeal interaction or experience (McCarthy & Dimitriades 191). The processes of globalization that result in the prolific and rapid circulation of racialized and gendered scripts and images result in such simulation and inaccurate "knowing."

An answer in part, at least in these students' situations, is to foster a progressive mandate in education. Such a mandate seeks to provide students access to full dimensions of their most immediate spaces as well as possible future spaces. To that end, it is interesting and important for these students to have access to this space, to have a place, at this HBCU situated next to the embassies of Israel and China, and on the fringe of Cleveland Park with its multi-million dollar homes (these places and spaces exist as abstractions to the students just as the students exist as abstractions to these places and spaces). It is very troubling and problematic as their presence and access in this space are strictured and relegated in ways that mine, and that of others like me, are not. Often times, and increasingly more so within the current manifestation of globalization, state space and its ideological accoutrements "puts us in our place" and creates a way of knowing that "puts us in our space" too. To figure out how curriculum and school might map onto a broader global hegemony, it seems useful to look at Neil Smith's *The Endgame of Globalization*. Smith writes of " 'endgame global America' as a culmination of a US-centered (but not exclusively American) political and economic globalization" (12). I write this essay as a meditation on how racialized space in public education operationalizes an overt and hidden curriculum theory, and how Composition might benefit from theories of the spatial to address globalized circulation of oppressive social scripts and assumptions about "other" places and identities.

Looking in All Directions at the Same Time OR Theory to Reconceptualize Curricular Space

I recently left Washington, D.C. to teach at one of those suburban research universities that I have "indicted" as dealing in abstraction when it comes to race and gender experience in urban space. Not a day passes when I do not use and think about the lessons learned with regard to how the functioning of identity, space, place, and curriculum broadly defined are inextricably linked. Central to my education is the awareness that cultural, technological, and material machinations prompted by the processes of globalization amplify the impact of assumptions about everyday life and educative concerns for students whose existence is truly at risk of being hidden, misrepresented, or occluded from curricular decisions and understandings. To avoid such perils, I have found myself continuously turning to theories of the spatial in efforts to accommodate the "mutually constitutive dynamics of local-global flows of knowledge, power, and capital, of systematic as well as unsystematic and uneven 'effects', and of local histories that always embed 'the new' in existing and generative material-economic and cultural condition" (Luke & Luke 276). Luke and Luke highlight the fact that the process of globalization does not exist partitioned from historical relations and processes; rather globalization maps onto older hegemonic relations and amplifies disparities vis-à-vis a more rapid circulation of social and economic capital.

In this globalized context, it is more difficult to identify and unravel the relations and reasons that position individuals, groups, and institutions as "other," and it is even more confounding to clearly identify how our participation may support this "othering." So as curriculum "marches on" at the research one university where I now teach, there is no recognition of relation or connectedness to the students who inhabit these other spaces, like the ones in D.C. that I have described. Their curriculum, its content, and the aptitudes it fosters are typically "other" to WPAs at R1 universities. If the curricular space of the "other" school is familiar, it is because the HBCU (in this instance) has taken from the status quo "best in field" Composition scholarship that seemingly can only be produced and properly executed by those at the "excellent" schools. Curriculum is indeed hegemonic, lest we forget. The violence of this neoliberal arrogance and self-delusion can be seen easily if one were to only visit and talk to these other students in places like D.C., or to simply teach as if one knew these lives existed in the ways that they do. But such a social justice curriculum concerned with global relations is not the work of "serious" scholars at esteemed universities. So now that some readers' "twinge-o-meters" have gone off, my bold claim is that it is not unfathomable that the neoliberalism of the "progressive" WPA works in concert with scalable neoconservative aspirations of global hegemony. To address this challenge, Compositionists must use theories of the spatial to think through contradictions inherent in this new globalism.

In *The Production of Space*, Henri Lefebvre outlines his geographic approach to examining our lived experiences and possibilities. He defines representations of space as "conceptualized space, the space of scientists, planners, urbanists, technocratic subdividers and social engineers, as of a certain type of artist with a scientific bent—all of whom identify what is lived and what is perceived with what is conceived" (Lefebvre 38). For Lefebvre, and me, this conceived space is the dominant space in any society. It is also the dominant space of curriculum. Educators find themselves in here daily (whether they recognize it or not). This space can be immediately radical by simply engaging in classroom practice that decontextualizes dominant meanings/readings while under stricture (e.g., while teaching to the test) or by proffering an outright subversion for social justice. In *Thirdspace*, his remediation of Henri Lefebvre's spatial trialectics, Edward Soja highlights the importance of conceived space, stating that it is:

> a storehouse of epistemological power. This conceived space tends, with certain exceptions, "towards a system of verbal (and therefore intellectually worked out) signs," again referring to language, discourse, texts, logos: the written and spoken word. In these "dominating" spaces of regulatory and "ruly" discourse, these mental spaces, are thus the representations of power and ideology, of control and surveillance. (Soja 67)

Given a current environment where urban spaces and subjects are increasingly positioned as sites of struggle and conjecture (and almost always without their voices participating), we have a mandate to be seriously concerned with the functioning of ideology articulated by conceived space in relation to identity.[1] Compositionists need to understand how curriculum functions as conceived space and within current curriculum as well as how certain "ideology hails or interpellates concrete individuals as concrete subjects, by the functioning of the category of the subject" (Althusser 174). For urban students in D.C. the risk is that representational, ideological, and curricular scripts will stand in for them when unsituated (and thereby uninformed) curriculum is designed and implemented.

In a globalized era characterized by increased electronic communication, perceived (and real) connectedness, and access to information the "category of the subject" can become actualized by "racial simulation," thereby animating a curriculum informed by assumptions about such students rather than an essential knowing of such students. My thesis is that by understanding how situated materiality (i.e., place) and contestations of identity matter when conceiving global and curricular space, writing teachers as critical educators may interrupt and rearticulate practices and systems of oppression.

The globalized spaces that we inhabit, spaces characterized by curricular trends toward measurement, assessment, and standardization, normalize a certain way of conceiving and perceiving, ultimately yielding an instance of "spectacular separation" (Debord 120). This separation is most readily apparent in critiques of globalization as an apparatus to further alienate labor and as a mechanism to exploit the labor of individuals and groups in "less developed" locales. Most readers are probably familiar with popular critiques and definitions, especially ones that stress the ubiquitous and frictionless collaboration and communication that can be made possible through the processes of globalization (Friedman 2005; Giddens 2000; Stiglitz 2002). This trajectory, hopefully a familiar one, is not the source of my exposition. Rather, the by-products of myopically engaging this debate are my concern. In focusing on globalization writ large there is danger of leaving unattended some important concerns of the local, and thereby failing to see how processes of globalization exacerbate already problematic and oft-hidden curricular issues such as achievement of better spaces when gender and race are involved. This potential diversion typifies the most insidious quality of the current form of globalization: that is, an articulation of ubiquitous, uniform, and systemically oppressive social scripts. This is the focus of my inquiry.

Hardt and Negri claim that "the failures of representation at the local and national levels increase geometrically in the processes of globalization" and that "mechanism of connection and instruction in the new realms of globalization are much more tenuous than even those of the old patriarchal representation" (Hardt & Negri 271). Assuming this is the case, as well as assuming that within the contemporary landscape of curriculum theory there is (still) possibility for "creative social practices" (Hardt 41) that deploy efforts with an emphasis on a "revolution of everyday life,"[2] I am concerned with the need to help students as globalized subjects/citizens access their most immediate environments at a time of unprecedented change (i.e., economically, scientifically, and technologically).

I envision a curriculum where spaces of representation may emerge as counterspaces, meaning "spaces of resistance to the dominant order arising precisely from their subordinate, peripheral or marginalized positioning" (Soja 68). It seems fruitful to think in terms of interstices, namely as the social scripts within discourses as these interstices that can be hijacked, detourned,[3] rerouted, essentially made available for new possibilities of justice and equality. Thinking of the globalization debate by way of discourse may prove useful to Composition theorists who want to address areas of gender and race on the local level but who also want to make sure that they accommodate for the influence of the global. To that end, on a structural level, discourse as I am using it here means: a set of ideas and practices that when taken together organize both the way a society defines certain truths about itself and the way it puts together social power. This means race, gender, and sexuality have ideological dimensions that work to organize social institutions (Collins 17).

In Collins's critique of contemporary ideology and what she labels as *The New Racism,* social scripts (the aforementioned interstices) serve as vehicles "that show people appropriate gender ideology as well as how to behave toward one another" (18). My argument for a change in curriculum and the theory that informs curriculum is built upon the plea that we not dismiss language or the "givens" of communication that enable and encourage readings and "recognitions" (Gee 142) of rhetorical situations in the everyday, be it in inner-city D.C. or across the Potomac River in the exurban enclaves of Fairfax County.

My inquiry is a continuation and response to influential meditations on curriculum theory. In *What Is Curriculum Theory?* Pinar asserts curriculum theory is "the interdisciplinary study of educational experience" (2) and that "curriculum studies are very much embedded within nations and regions" (158). Pinar's move to address international concerns in curriculum and education by way of local practice is, in a way, a direct response and resistance to the processes and intimations of globalization that aim to invoke a standardization of curriculum worldwide. Writing programs can fall prey to such standardized curricular devotions as well. Recently, Pinar (*Intellectual*; "Crisis") has also advocated for a "return to disciplinarity," whereby a reclamation of educative space is made, not by educators operating primarily horizontally as transdisciplinary individuals, but as educators working horizontally *and* vertically toward collective best practices in curriculum studies. This return to disciplinarity depends on open acknowledgment and privileging of respective disciplinary strengths within the context of locale (but with an understanding of the international or global). Given present circumstances and the increasing standardizing strictures of policy, progressives are obligated to undertake such approaches to curriculum; understanding that educators and curriculum theorists certainly do not exist outside of hegemony, we must engage hegemonic forces that ask "what knowledge is of most worth?" ("Crisis" 25).[4] By doing this, we can articulate our curriculum and pedagogies, as opposed to them being articulated for us.[5] For those cultural workers looking to participate progressively in response to the processes of globalization, this practice of recognizing and creating discourse using a rearticulation of social scripts is a "way in." The student writing that I will share later in this essay comes from writing projects in an English class where students are arguing through and against the dominant representations of their lives.

Many of the following student writings and comments exemplify failures to provide an appropriate liberatory discourse for the concerns, problems, and even dreams of many women and people of color. To remedy this, and to identify what challenges and problems exist for the multitude, we must start with the local, be it the city or other environs, as a "possibilities machine" (Soja 81), where "to change life we must change space" (Lefebvre, *Production* 190). Composition theorists must come up with a pedagogy that operationalizes a curriculum concerned with an "ethics of the local"[6] that addresses inequities (both local and universal) within the immediate situatedness of students' lives. Curriculum that makes lives better should be *centered*. In my students' lives this means centering issues of gender, race, safety, and health. Relevantly, the hidden spaces of the city, standing in as metonyms for the intentionally hidden problems of globalization, are alien and occluded from many educators' current lifeworlds.

By addressing the mediating processes of global forces, from cultural texts on gender performance to the meanings of material conditions in one's neighborhood to the use of technology to build empowering communities, a curriculum can become flexible yet universal. Theories of the spatial are readily available to inform such curriculum. Borrowing from the work of Giles Deleuze, one might privilege a "haptic" versus "optic" curriculum. As I have argued previously (Taylor 103), a "haptic" curriculum is predicated on contingency and participation versus standardized curriculum that tends to be "optic" and assumes that phenomena repeat, or are measurable, assessable representations of an ideal form, resulting in a simplification and homogenization of cultural identity as well as a cultural-deficiency perspective where gaps and "deficient" literacies exist (Sleeter 246).

Gradients of haptic space are contingent upon the local and "produced region by region, neighborhood by neighborhood, through connections, deterritorializations, intensities and observances" inducing "new becomings, and is reciprocally produced by such becomings" (Roy 31). The local and immediate are the spaces for immediate liberation. Creative curricular and creative social practices may run counter to or in concert with pre-existing curricular mandates, but ultimately the impact of the practices should become paramount. To realize the promise of curriculum for students in places like inner-city D.C. these new practices should aim to become hegemonic in their own right. By remembering that places and spaces differ, we can construct curricula that are contingent on difference and recognition. By letting abstractions stand, we fall prey to assumptions, one-dimension mapping, and uncritical measurement that further occlude those so critical to our journey toward better words and worlds.

Narrative Space, Cultural Representation, Authenticity and Simulation

In the local literacy projects that dominate my curriculum the epitome of Debord's *spectacular* representation, and its attendant demands, is readily apparent. For instance, several years ago when writing in my course blog space about the removal (from inner-city Los Angeles) of Paramount's billboards advertising 50 Cent's 2005 film, *Get Rich Or Die Tryin'*, one student remarked:

> I do understand the billboards being removed because him holding a gun in one
> hand and a microphone in another depicts that you can be a gangster out on the
> streets toting a gun and you can make it to the music industry in one piece. I am
> pretty sure that the movie is rated R so it is up to the parents to tell their chil-
> dren the odds that that kind of stuff happens. Despite the rating children are still
> going to see it in the movies or on bootleg. They need to know that that is one
> man's story of fact not fiction and that is not the only way to be famous. Even
> though the billboards were taken down those children already know 50 Cent's
> story by heart, have his cds and know all of his lyrics.

Note that school is not mentioned. We're not even in the ballpark. If you saw
this billboard or promotional poster, you would notice "Fiddy" with a micro-
phone in one hand and a gun in the other. Rhetorical questions and positionings,
scripts rather, abound. What can a black man do or be? Relationally, what does
this mean for women? Spaces of entertainment or violence seem to be privileged
and certainly are materially more real (and even appealing) than school and the
possibilities it represents. Where are the pathways/discourses to the utopias we
profess at conferences and in academic journals? Who is committed to living
them and making them real? Doing so would mean giving up privilege of
course. And too often contemporary globalized curricular space is all about privilege, whether it manifests as an overt and obvious concern with assessment and
evaluation or as a hidden curriculum of "taken for granted" racism and sexism
buttressing the hidden foundations of our ivory tower.

At the most extreme fundamental level, this seems a failure of curriculum
theorists to conduct an adequate analysis of their immediate surroundings and
practices. This is an extreme characterization, but may be helpful hyperbole toward better curriculum and resistance of ill-serving pedagogies. For instance,
and at the very least, a starting point could be the discourses of "fast capitalism"[7]
and globalization, and how such scripts have created an environment "characterized by the exacerbation of the sexual politics of global capitalist domination
and exploitation" and how one might find pathways to a "renewed politics of
hope and solidarity" (Mohanty 29). Failing this vigilance of language and appropriate pedagogy equates to forgetting that, indeed,

> ideology 'acts' or 'functions' in such a way that it 'recruits' subjects among the
> individuals (it recruits them all), or 'transforms' the individuals into subjects (it
> transforms them all) by that very precise operation I have called interpellation
> or hailing, and which can be imagined along the lines of the most commonplace
> everyday police (or other) hailing: 'Hey you there!' (Althusser 175)

Of course, and entirely appropriate here, Althusser is using the verbiage of a
policeman hailing a "suspect." This characterizes our current era of ubiquitous
policing and paranoia due to endless wars on terror; however, this social policing along lines of race and gender has been around for some time. My students
in D.C. were used to this and "see" this much more clearly and much differently

than most, as they are suspects in so many discursive formations from life in their neighborhood to *individuals* exiting a metro stop in Northwest D.C. to *subjects* of conjecture and positioning in the white patriarchal spaces of Research-One universities.[8] Curriculum has yet to offer such students any sort of repose. One student writes:

> To tourists, the media represents D.C. as this wonderful place to be with lots to do. Don't get me wrong, there are some beautiful places in D.C. to see such as the museums, monuments, gardens, and other historic places. This is not D.C. as a whole. This is a problem because leaving out important details is a lie; "lying by omission". To the white residents, D.C. also seems to be this great place to live, but if there are problems the reason it is going down hill is because of the minorities. All the crime you usually see broadcasted on the news in our area are committed by minorities. Like White people don't commit crime.

While the ideology that supports racism, and the conceptualization of racism, is apparent at times, the ideology that makes suspects and subjects of women is nearly invisible due to the inattentiveness to language and the inability to see simultaneous relations between sexuality, gender, race, and materiality. One way in is to identify the interstices and remap these phalogocentric scripts, creating the possibility to acknowledge that, "woman, a type of embodiment, is antecedent to a conceptualization and delineation of the category 'woman', then the possibility emerges for a discussion of how 'woman' materializes through the spontaneous bodily performances of racialized identities at points of geographic specificity on the ground" (Saad & Carter 49). A better (and more accessible) way to see this within the scope of this article is to read what one female student wrote about a reading on pornography and domestic/sexual violence. With globalization facilitating many things, including increased proliferation of pornography and human trafficking, a discussion and critical representation of this makes sense for a "content area" in new curriculum. This is what we should be educating for if we were truly critical and anti-hegemonic in globalized times. My student illuminates:

> Porn serves as a social script because porn usually portrays women as being passive and submissive, and men believe that women are supposed to be this way and think that women are supposed to do what they say when they say. Porn also portrays women as being property which is very dangerous because that is usually why there is a lot of domestic violence because men think women are their property.

Certainly, one could substitute race for gender and sexuality here, yielding a materialization of the familiar reprise of America's historical racial exploitation and oppression. What is significant, though, is that globalization ensures an expedited proliferation of practices and literacies on scales never before dreamt of. This includes systemic forms of oppression, namely racism and sexism, proving

Hardt and Negri's point that in globalized spaces fair and socially just representation is truly at stake. And what a recently emigrated male student wrote illuminates this calculus:

> I think men's violence against women is a sign of unequal power relations between men and women. It has also led to discrimination of women by men. Images in the media of violence against women, in particular those that portray rape or sexual slavery as well as the use of women and girls as sex objects, including pornography, are factors contributing to the continued widespread of such violence, harmfully influencing the community at large, in particular children and young people.

The visual rhetoric of pornography fixes subordinated identities and possibilities while ensuring the ubiquity and spatiality of patriarchy. Globalizing processes, if not interrupted, accelerate these systems of exploitation and oppression. Images of terrorist acts committed by dark-skinned "others" and anti-American sentiment at gatherings in the faraway towns of the Middle East are not the only "texts" that fix relations in globalized space. One need not look far to find examples, such as human trafficking and trade, as well as predatory web-based pornography. These are real issues with much at stake for people of color and women especially; we must offer a curriculum and pedagogy aimed at interrupting these systems and practices.

Granted, this is a theoretical frame and, as always, the challenge to link theory to praxis looms. But, even a critical educator operating under the stricture of mandated curriculum can work against the reception of oppressive gender scripts that get circulated quicker through globalized mediums. Doing so, that is embracing the notion of discourse in this way, "allows a re-reading of 'woman' as the trace of conglomerated mimetic acts within contingencies that stabilize places as particular by codifying boundaries between raced and emplaced identities." The result is a curricular stand that emphatically notes that "places are stabilized through repetitions of these mimetic acts, by the work of bodies acting in space. 'Races', then, can be assumed to be sexed and gendered bodies who literally take place(s) on the surface of the earth at any point in time" (Saad & Carter 49). Spatial theory gives us a way to enact new spaces and identities, ones that compete to make better places. The structure of curriculum is repetitive, as with the deluge of media images, and it is curriculum's repetitive mimetic nature that can be fertile anti-hegemonic ground. In similar more direct spirit, a student does us one better when he observes:

> The media, as usual, only portrays the political and "white" side of DC when they have something positive to say. If it is something negative, it will inevitably focus on a minority group, especially blacks. As the media ignores the reality of poverty, crime and delinquency in DC it will only be delaying solving the problem and allow it to fester. This was clearly seen in New Orleans when America "woke up," even if for a few days to the reality of black poverty and

desperation in this country. Sadly, after Katrina the media will go back to their old ways and this should change.

In just about every community, but especially those located in urban environs, we are increasingly witnessing the emergence of extreme segregation epitomized by a New Orleans or Washington, D.C. where there exists "a dual city spatially, as well as socially and economically" (Lipman 28). To remedy this, the student mappings that take place in my classroom serve as a critical meaning making, or urbanism as social practice (Lefebvre, *Urban* 6), and are juxtaposed with the dominant articulation of place, specifically that of Washington, D.C., that strictures and erases already marginalized identities. This is a way to enact new spaces and identities, ones that compete to make better places. Continuing the commentary on the stabilization and mimesis that fuels this sequestering and segregation, and eventual hiding or erasure, another student comments:

> The media posts what they want. They also choose what they will and won't air. My organization, The Black Panthers, held a rally and a food drive...they would not air it on the news. They didn't want to show The Black Panthers doing positive work. If we were involved in a shoot-out they would be first on the scene to expose to the world our negative doings.

I have tried to get at the production of experiences and the meaning we make of them; this has been the centerpiece of my pedagogy. Derek Owens highlights the importance of knowing where our students are writing from when he discusses what "success" is in the English classroom. Owens mentions that success depends "on how effectively the teacher and students work together to create a writing environment that they find intellectually and culturally related to their local conditions" (180). Just as "education" doesn't just happen in Building 39, Room 110, there are limitless and different contexts of writing and writing environments with all existing contingent on place and particularity. Owens follows Eric Zencey's advocacy for a shift toward "rooted education," which takes to task what non-black universities often perpetuate in the name of "multicultural inclusiveness," that being a "politics of placeless identity rather than a politics of rootedness in place" (Zencey 17). In a process of globalization, where space and time appear to be compressed at dizzying rates, the "inferior" or "deficient" places (just like "inferior" or "deficient" literacies) tend to be occluded or "corrected" through spectacular abstraction and separation (Debord 1994). Identity is treated as an abstraction by curriculum designers in far too many instances. Rather than have a curriculum that is not centered on place, I argue for a continued pursuit and extension of Pinar's call for a focus on place, one achieved through a treatment of the spatiality of globalization. This, of course, is not to say curriculum should be focused exclusively on place; rather, the curriculum should be rooted in the conjuncture of the immediately local and imminent global while endeavoring toward more hopeful futures on all fronts. This is probably the most difficult task for curriculum theorists and designers to pursue and adhere to since it requires ever-present contingency and flexibility, characteristics foreign to most institutions subject to most accountability and assessment/evaluation mandates.

In a class, I often ask students to write about their communities and/or a community of which they are a part; I then give them a choice of giving a brief presentation about their exegeses. I have incorporated this into other classes taught at other institutions with different demographics and in different environs, but consistent throughout the assignments I have asked students to think relationally and spatially with regard to how they are "entered into the fray." Essentially, I have asked them to consider their stretched out social relations and how certain globalized assumptions, scripts that is, reinforce these relations for better or worse—where these scripts take us and where they prevent us from going. Regardless of the differences based along lines of race, gender, and materiality, the student accounts are amazingly similar in some global systemic respects. The disconnect between dominant contemporary curriculum and lived experience is apparent in the following passage, especially how dominant contemporary suppositions about literacy interpellate, inaccurately and unjustly, already subordinated individuals. A female student writes:

> My biggest fear is being a single mother again…of my children needing to depend only on me. These along with different feelings of emotion, anxiety, fear, and helplessness to name a few, are sometimes too much. Although it was the best thing that I could have done, I wouldn't want to go through that again, and I will explain as I go along with the story.

The woman is detailing her experiences in an abusive, unhealthy, and all too common relationship (predicated on the historical patriarchal discourse of marriage), and ultimately her difficulty in leaving and making it as a woman of lower socio-economic status in a phallocentric society. She continues:

> I was young when I first married, which did not bother me at all; it was everything that went along with it. I couldn't do a lot of things with other neighborhood mothers who had kids close to my children's ages. I was left with a list of things that he wanted done before he got home as well as dinner being ready. No if, ands, or buts. You just do not answer back. Going to my mother's was a privilege I had to earn. I put up with that for years, until I finally said enough! Along with my two children, who were two and five we had to leave everything we owned…our clothing, shoes, toys, etc. I was allowed to leave with just what we were wearing. Me, I was just happy to be out of there. I was very scared, how would I support my kids? I was never allowed to get a job, so I didn't know what to do.

This piece moved me as a rhetorician; it made me question the discourse I was providing to people like this student and how, in a larger sense, any sort of privileging of English Studies' historical pedagogy of (phallogocentric) rationalism was not serving as empowering education. These traces of living, manifest via her essay, should put critical educators on watch for ways that their pedagogies may not serve students and may actually work to reinforce subordinating structures for certain groups of students (i.e., women, relational institutions that privilege contemporary definitions of masculinity). For me, the rhetoric of this artifact and of her talking about her fear with the class while holding up the jacket that she wore the night she left her abusive husband seems powerful and profound. It is important. And maybe representations like these are the new and appropriate critical pedagogies, form and content changing for the better. Brave communication of such relations may be a way to tap in to the conduits of globalized communication and representation. If it seems like an odd curricular choice, it is only because *sustained* centering of such topics has not been done before. In globalized curricular space her representation is anti-hegemonic and more in line with the call for a concern for the non-discursive made by Cornel West in a critique of Jean Baudrillard's extreme form of postmodern skepticism. Here, West is well worth quoting at length as he states:

> Baudrillard seems to be articulating a sense of what it is to be a French, middle-class intellectual, or perhaps what it is to be middle class generally. Let me put it in terms of a formulation from Henry James that Fredric Jameson has appropriated: there is a reality that one cannot know. The ragged edges of the Real, of Necessity, not being able to eat, not having enough shelter, not having enough health care, all this is something that one cannot know. The black condition acknowledges that. It is so much more acutely felt because this is a society where a lot of people live a Teflon existence, where a lot of people have no sense of the ragged edges of necessity, of what it means to be impinged upon by structures of oppression. To be an upper-middle class American is actually to live a life of unimaginable comfort, convenience, and luxury. Half of the black population is denied this, which is why they have a strong sense of reality. (277)

Obviously, West is acknowledging the importance and reality of material conditions and relations, but of unrecognized value for curriculum studies is his critiquing the "role of representation in forming subjects who bring these conditions interpretive frames" (Berlin 72). What gets left out of the discourse, namely the subaltern and her representation, is critical to note; but the medium and logic of the discourse is oftentimes the bigger impediment to accurate signification as hegemony is constructed through the logic of the medium, and in the contemporary educational project this is the logos of rationalism. In the environment like the one I am profiling, an appropriate pedagogy for the students seems quite different than that which is commonly advocated; mandated mainstream curriculum only sets subordination stronger for the students in my class. To enact such traditional curriculum would be akin to selling the students bogus goods.

New Grammars for Continuing Struggles

Our historical and dominant curricular grammar, or way of understanding curriculum, ensures only the possibility of subordination for the students I have described; a more revolutionary pedagogy would embrace the notion of a changing grammar, one that highlights historical becoming through opening the field of history (Derrida 27). While the various processes of globalization often amplify already oppressive relations and patterns, there do appear to be openings that can be used to reroute curriculum and ways of knowing. In order to foster a curriculum that promotes transformative understandings about power relations in which sexuality, femininity, and masculinity are embedded, in urban locales and otherwise, educators should work toward a fundamental recognition of the way language and social scripts function where the common positionality is that of "the Spectator, the passive viewer and consumer of a social system predicated on submission and conformity" (Best and Kellner 12). I would like to see Composition take a stand with a curricular project that interrupts the globalized decimation of egalitarian and accurate representation, while at the same time fostering creative possibility and alterity. I believe that educators need to be able to articulate a spatial practice that links locality to global relations.[9] In order to resist homogenization and standardization (in curriculum and in culture), we need to collectively "champion active, creative, and imaginative practice" and "counterpoise the activity of the radical subject which constructs its own everyday life against the demands of the spectacle" (Best and Kellner 12). As intimated in the brief detailing of my classroom, such a curriculum movement could start with an effort to dismantle globalized scripts of patriarchy and racism. Curriculum's examination of everyday life can do this only when forced to reconstruct our positionality with regard to our support, or rerouting, of the scripts that enable globalized systems of oppression and occlusion.

Current standardized curriculum, by its very nature, discourages revolution and rearticulation not in line with the historical patriarchal project; there is no momentum or encouragement to change the hegemonic grammar. Obviously I am arguing that dominant pedagogy seems to result in disconnecting the writing/communication from the identity, action, and experience of the speaker. This language of action should be revolutionary and empowering for those previously disaffected, and I am in agreement with Derrida here in believing that there is a dominant history and system of scripts. And, that mostly this system has been seen as a disconnected rationality, separate from actual experience (when in fact it is not). The claim for social justice and appropriate pedagogy that I am making is a theoretical, open-ended, curricular one. It represents a fundamental shift aimed at creating recognition that, given our current cultural landscape and conditions of engagement, the better way of representing identity is "by the effacement of the representer and the personal presence of the represented" (Derrida 305). This radical foregrounding that makes curriculum contingent upon the local and corporeal, but informed by the global's tendency toward mass simulation and circulation of social scripts, runs counter to a lot of what is happening in classrooms, which makes the task much more formidable. It is asking a lot. But a lot is at stake, and the mandate is impossible to ignore for any teacher invested in the project of democratic and liberatory education.

Notes

1. These students have historically been referred to as "at risk"; and, of course, they still are referred to as such. For me, this moniker is problematic but also portends a horizon much more dire in these globalized times. These students, their attendant literacies, and possible unique and creative futures are "at risk" of being occluded and "left behind." At the same time that globalization is connecting and homogenizing, it is also hiding, obscuring, and erasing identities, histories, and futures.

2. Guy Debord wrote: "The spectacle is not a collection of images but a social relation among people mediated by images.... The spectacle in general, as the concrete inversion of life, is the autonomous movement of the non-living.... The liar has lied to himself." It is this way of knowing and mediating things like curriculum and everyday life that I advocate interrupting.

3. Detournement can occur when images produced by the spectacle get altered and subverted so that rather than supporting the *status quo*, their meaning becomes changed in order to put across a more radical or oppositionist message.

4. To help facilitate this articulation of best practices in curriculum studies, Pinar has created the Canon Project, which can be found at http://csics.educ.ubc.ca/projects.html.

5. By no means is this a new call. Raymond Williams and the Birmingham School aimed to operationalize cultural studies by creating a recognition or critical oppositional consciousness of hegemony. On the topic of resistance, Williams wrote "it thus affects thinking about Revolution in that it stresses not only the transfer of political or economic power, but the overthrow of a specific hegemony: that is to say an integral form of class rule which exists not only in political or economic power, but the overthrow of a specific hegemony.... This can be done, it is argued, by creating an alternative hegemony— a new predominant practice and consciousness" (Williams 145).

6. In hashing this "ethics of the local" J.K. Gibson-Graham comments: "Globalization discourse situates the local (and thus all of us) in a place of subordination, as "the other within" of the global order. At worst it makes victims of localities and robs them of economic agency and self-determination. (I)magine what it would mean, and how unsettling it would be to all that is now in place, if the locality were to become the active subject of its economic experience" (50).

7. For a detailed account of "fast capitalism" and how discourse analysis works see *The New Work Order: Behind the Language of the New Capitalism* by James Paul Gee, Glynda Hull, and Colin Lankshear.

8. This hailing occurs along lines of race, most obviously, but I am fretful that all too often the occurrence of this dangerous and oppressive hailing along lines of gender is overlooked.

9. I subscribe to Doreen Massey's notion that "'The spatial' ...can be seen as constructed out of the multiplicity of social relations across all spatial scales, from the global reach of finance and telecommunications, through the geography of the tentacles of national political power, to the social relations within the town, the settlement, the household and the workplace" (4).

Works Cited

Althusser, Louis. "Ideology and Ideological State Apparatuses (notes toward an investigation)." *Lenin and Philosophy and Other Essays.* New York: Monthly Review Press, 1971.

Berlin, James A. *Rhetorics, Poetics, and Cultures: Refiguring College English Studies.* Urbana, IL: NCTE, 1996.

Best, Steven, and Douglas Kellner. "Debord and the Postmodern Turn: New Stages of the Spectacle." Illuminations: The Critical Theory Website, 2002. <http://www.uta.edu/huma/illuminations/kell17.htm>.

Collins, Patricia Hill. *African Americans, Gender, and the New Racism.* New York: Routledge, 2005.

Debord, Guy. *The Society of the Spectacle.* New York: Zone Books, 1994.

Derrida, Jacques. *Of Grammatology.* Trans. Gayatri Chakravorty Spivak. Baltimore, MD: The Johns Hopkins University Press, 1976.

Friedman, Thomas. *The World Is Flat: A Brief History of the Twenty-first Century.* New York: Farrar, Straus, & Giroux, 2005.

Gee, James. *Social Linguistics and Literacies.* London: Falmer Press, 1990.

Gibson-Graham, J. K. "An ethics of the local." *Rethinking Marxism* 15 (1), 2003: 49-74.

Giddens, Anthony. *Runaway World: How Globalization Is Reshaping Our Lives.* New York: Routledge, 2000.

Hardt, Michael. "The Withering of Civil Society." *Social Text* 45 (Winter 1995): 27-44.

Hardt, Michael, and Antonio Negri. *Multitude: War and Democracy in the Age of Empire.* New York: Penguin, 2004.

Lefebvre, Henri. *The Production of Space.* Oxford: Blackwell, 1991.

———. *The Urban Revolution.* Minneapolis: U of Minnesota P, 2003.

Lipman, Pauline. *High Stakes Education: Inequality, Globalization, and Urban School Reform.* New York: Routledge, 2003.

Luke, Allen, and Carmen Luke. "A Situated Perspective on Cultural Globalization." In Nicholas C. Burbules and Carlos Alberto Torres (Eds.) *Globalization and Education: Critical Perspectives.* New York: Routledge, 2000. 275-298.

Massey, Doreen. *Space, Place, and Gender.* Minneapolis: U of Minnesota P, 1994.

McCarthy, Cameron, and Greg Dimitriades. "Globalizing Pedagogies: Power, Resentment, and the Re-narration of Difference." In Nicholas C. Burbules and Carlos Alberto Torres (Eds.) *Globalization and Education: Critical Perspectives.* New York: Routledge. 2000. 187-204.

Mohanty, Chandra Talpade. "Women Workers and Capitalists Scripts: Ideologies of Domination, Common Interests, and the Politics of Solidarity." *Fem-

inist Genealogies, Colonial Legacies, Democratic Futures. Eds. M. Jacqui Alexander and Chandra Talpade Mohanty. New York: Routledge, 1997.

Owens, Derek. *Composition and Sustainability: Teaching for a Threatened Generation.* Urbana, IL: National Council of Teachers of English Press (Refiguring English Studies series), 2001.

Pinar, William F. "Curriculum as Social Psychoanalysis: On the Significance of Place." In Joe L. Kincheloe and William F. Pinar (Eds.). *Curriculum as Social Psychoanalysis: The Significance of Place.* Albany: SUNY P, 1991. 167-86.

——. *What Is Curriculum Theory?* Mahwah, NJ: Lawrence Erlbaum, 2004.

——. *Intellectual Advancement through Disciplinarity: Verticality and Horizontality in Curriculum Studies.* Rotterdam: Sense Publishers, 2007.

——. "Crisis, Reconceptualization, Internationalization: U.S. Curriculum Theory since 1950." From the Centre for the Study of Internationalization of Curriculum Studies homepage. <http://csics.educ.ubc.ca/PDFs/China2007(ECNU)1.pdf. 2007>.

Roy, Kaustuv. "Power and Resistance: Insurgent Spaces, Deleuze, Curriculum." *JCT: Journal of Curriculum Theorizing* 21,1 (2005): 27-38.

Saad, Tobie, and Perry Carter. "The Entwined Spaces of 'Race', Sex and Gender," *Gender, Place and Culture* 12,1 (2005): 49-51.

Sleeter, Christine. "How White Teachers Construct Race." In Cameron McCarthy, Warren Crichlow, Greg Dimitriadis, and Nadine Dolby (Eds.) *Race, Identity, and Representation in Education.* 2nd edition. New York: Routledge, 2005. 243-256.

Smith, Neil. *The Endgame of Globalization.* New York: Routledge, 2005.

Soja, Edward. *Thirdspace: Journeys to Los Angeles and Other Real-and-Imagined Places.* Malden, MA: Blackwell, 1996.

Stiglitz, Joseph E. *Globalization and Its Discontents.* New York: W. W. Norton, 2003.

Taylor, Hill. "Black Spaces: Examining the Writing Major at an Urban HBCU." *Composition Studies* 35,1 (2007): 99-112.

West, Cornel. "Interview with Cornel West." *Universal Abandon? The Politics of Postmodernism.* Ed. Andrew Ross. Minneapolis: University of Minnesota P, 1988. 269-286.

Williams, Raymond. *The Long Revolution.* New York: Columbia University P, 1961.

Zencey, Eric. "The Rootless Professors." *Rooted in the Land: Essays on Community and Place.* Eds. William Vitek and Wes Jackson. New Haven, CT: Yale UP, 15-19.

"The People's Challenge": Rhetorics of Globalization from Above and Below

Daphne Desser

It is not the short term we look for as Hawaiians, it is the long. Anything else is a mistake pushed by minds that do not understand the essence of water or the finite nature of our human resources. It will always, always be a mistake to base a movement on money. Always. This is an epistemological point—that relationship is more important than the more modern sense of efficacy, money. (Meyer, "Our Own Liberation" 126)

This chapter examines the rhetoric of protest from the vantage point of the unique context in Hawai'i, focusing on the clash of the ideologies of globalization with indigenous cultural values and epistemologies. Native Hawaiian culture, language and identity have been under ongoing threat and degradation since the arrival of the missionaries in the nineteenth century. I investigate the particular threat globalization poses to indigenous values and ways of knowing by examining the dynamics of a grassroots protest that took place in Hawai'i in response to an international conference located in Honolulu and sponsored by the Asian Development Bank (ADB) in 2001. What the decision-makers overlooked in this case, as is often overlooked by the predominantly tourist-oriented gaze upon Hawai'i, is that Hawai'i, of all the states in the union, has the most complex relationship to colonization and globalization and their impact on indigenous peoples and is thus a most appropriate locale for both the meeting and the questioning of the meeting's contents and goals. This article will use this moment in globalization's evolving history to put globalization in the historical context of colonization and conquest, to examine its impact on local and indigenous communities, and finally to analyze the form and content of social protest in these communities against the negative effects of globalization on their lives, futures, and communities.

In examining the rhetorical strategies as well as the specific arguments made by indigenous protest groups against this symbol of globalization, this chapter aims to shed light on how rhetorics of globalization interact with rhetorics of the indigenous to create an emerging battleground of cultural values and epistemologies. Ultimately, I argue that in order to teach the writing of English in Hawai'i effectively and responsibly, the writing teacher must take this battleground into consideration in the classroom, making both local and mainland students more aware of its dynamics, and encouraging students to situate themselves, their rhetorical positions, their arguments and their writing within this complex context. For readers outside of that context, this chapter can serve as one exemplum among many of how educators can productively and proactively engage in globalization's history and, to be sure, its future—by focusing critical, analytic, and rhetorical work on the local and the global contexts in which they occur and to which they contribute.

I begin by defining the terms *globalization from above* and *globalization from below* for the purposes of situating my position amongst current conversations. I then provide a brief introduction to relevant Native Hawaiian history and current circumstances in order to provide context for my analysis. Next I discuss the discursive strategies of the ADB conference and local and/or indigenous grassroots protests as exempla of competing rhetorics of globalization from above and globalization from below. I then analyze the petition "The People's Challenge" in light of these rhetorical strategies and argue that its arguments are grounded in globalization-from-below values that resonate well with Native Hawaiian epistemologies. Subsequently, I examine how the petition argues against the "dominant," "mainstream" values of globalization from above by setting up three core sites of rhetorical contestation: 1) land for profit vs. land as a source for spiritual knowing; 2) individualism vs. interdependence; and 3) emphasizing corporate profits vs. prioritizing human rights and interests. As a conclusion, I discuss resistance to what Neil Smith has called "the endgame of globalization" (from above) as well as implications for future disciplinary directions.

Globalization: From Above and Below

Globalization and *anti-globalization* are themselves contested terms. I prefer not to use the term *anti-globalization*, having been convinced by Noam Chomsky that international communication, information sharing, and solidarity building is not the problem. He explains:

The term "globalization" has been appropriated by the powerful to refer to a specific form of international economic integration, one based on investor rights, with the interests of people incidental. That is why the business press, in its more honest moments, refers to the "free trade agreements" as "free investment agreements" (*Wall St. Journal*). Accordingly, advocates of other forms of globalization are described as "anti-globalization"; and some, unfortunately, even accept this term, though it is a term of propaganda that should be dismissed with ridicule. No sane person is opposed to globalization, that is, international integration. Surely not the left and the workers movements, which were founded on the principle of international solidarity—that is, globalization in a form that attends to the rights of people, not private power systems. ("Interviewed")

Similarly, scholars such as Brecher, Costello, and Smith in *Globalization from Below* argue that cultural, political, and economic transnational connections made possible by globalization are irreversible and not necessarily destructive in intent or effect; they assert that this interconnection could potentially serve the interests of people and the earth, not just the ruling powers. They distinguish between *globalization from above*, which serves the interests of global capitalism without regard for local or indigenous concerns, from *globalization from below*, which describes the internationally connected grassroots community that has arisen to critique the inhumane aspects of globalization from above.

Activists who support globalization from below argue that global financial institutions and trade agreements negatively impact local decision-making. In addition, they oppose the ways in which corporations make use of privileges not granted to human beings, such as moving freely across borders and having easy access to human and natural resources. Not surprisingly then, globalization-from-below activists seek an end to the legal status of "corporate personhood" and to free market fundamentalism, while also opposing economic privatization measures sponsored by organizations such as the World Bank, the International Monetary Fund, and the World Trade Organization ("Anti-globalization Movement").

Sociology scholar Amory Starr compares and analyzes the methods and goals of activists concerned with the negative effects of globalization in *Naming the Enemy: Anti-Corporate Movements Confront Globalization*, proposing three major forms of protests to global capital: restraining it, democratizing it, or building local alternatives to it. In the first category, which she calls "contestation and reform," she examines movements that seek to restrain global capital through state regulation. Here she discusses movements against structural adjustment, peace and human rights groups, movements for land reform, the explicitly anti-corporate movement, and cyber-punk. Her second category is "globalization from below," or movements that seek to democratize globalization by making governments and corporations accountable to the people rather than to the interests of the transnational ownership class. In this section, she focuses on environmental and labor movements, socialist movements, anti-free trade movements, and the Zapatistas. Her final category is "delinking," in which she analyzes movements that want to separate from global capital and build locally based alternatives to it, such as the anarchist movement, movements for sustainable development, the small businesses movement, sovereignty movements, and religious nationalist movements.

These sorts of definitions and categorical divisions of globalization are useful for scholars who are engaged in researching and teaching rhetorics of social movements. In particular, the concept "globalization from below" can be productively applied to local and/or indigenous instantiations of rhetorical actions that have a hand in shaping the local in the context of the global, and vice-versa. If we look, for just one example, to a case study of globalization from below, we can extract from it lessons in intervention that we can in turn use in our own research, teaching, and service in our disciplinary work. In the section that follows, I examine one such case study: the grassroots protests that emerged in Honolulu as a response to the ADB Conference.

The ADB Conference in the Context of Native Hawaiian History and Current Social Injustice

The grassroots protests that emerged in Honolulu in response to the ADB Conference combined elements of various of Starr's categories as peace and human rights groups, land reform groups, environmental and labor movements, anti-free trade movements, sustainable development groups, and Native Hawaiian sovereignty groups were all involved. Their critiques and suggestions focused on making entities such as the ADB more aware of local and indigenous experience and more accountable to their interests, with Native Hawaiian sovereignty groups in particular using the opportunity to recast Hawai'i's history from their perspective: as a story of colonization, cultural theft, and destruction.

To begin to understand the full extent to which the ADB conference organizers and the grassroots group were informed by contrasting rhetorics and disparate values and worldviews, it is helpful to examine their use of core terms and key definitions. On their public website, the ADB defines the indigenous as "groups with social or cultural identities distinct from those of the dominant or mainstream society" ("Indigenous Peoples"). Within this opening definition one can already ascertain a positioning in which the non-indigenous is valued as dominant or mainstream, rather than being posited as foreign or destructive. This bias, that the indigenous must conform and reshape itself in the face of what is called "dominant," "mainstream," or "modern," is at the heart of the problem. This prevalent perspective devalues the indigenous and misunderstands its place. The "dominant," "mainstream," and "modern" in, for example, Hawai'i has no inherent value for this particular location; rather these foreign cultures, languages, and ways of lives must be seen for what they are: impositions—violent and unwanted ones at that—forced upon the Native Hawaiian culture, way of life, and language that arose from this location and were sustained for centuries because they are in harmony with Hawai'i's land, sky, and ocean in a way that the "mainstream," "modern," and "dominant" can never be. To begin to understand the motivations behind grassroots protests against the ADB, one must first grasp this distinction and realize and come to terms with the great loss of Native Hawaiian language, culture, identity, lives, livelihoods, and ways of life "mainstream" culture represents.

One of the primary ways in which "dominant," "mainstream" culture, which now includes the basic tenets of globalization from above, defines itself is through altered concepts of place which can be more accurately described as "abstracted place" or "deferred place" or even "placelessness." A modern, "globalized" point of view assumes that place is no longer relevant, that we are all citizens of a world in which our primary life goal is the pursuit of happiness through assimilation into western-dominated values that include individualism, materialism, and capitalism. The spread of certain, undeniably valuable ideals such as democracy, liberty, and human rights are linked to the more questionable values of instant immediate access to information, striving for material goods and status, the prioritization of the individual over the community, and the use of new technologies, the English language, and the American dollar to advance these goals. The flipside—loneliness, uprootedness, isolation, greed, and cultural superficiality—is what indigenous groups, among others, find unappealing about the spread of global capitalism.

It is thus not a desire to preserve quaint and almost forgotten traditions, languages, cultures or ways of life, nor a knee-jerk political correct compunction to align oneself with the oppressed or the loser in cultural battles, that motivates indigenous resistance to globalizing forces. Rather, the driving force is a clash in values. The globalization-from-above movement cannot and does not recognize the ways in which people are shaped—intellectually, morally, emotionally, politically, and spiritually—by their relationships to the land, language, cultures, and traditions with which they identify. The real losses associated with global citizenship—national identities, languages, and spiritual traditions, a sense of belonging to a particular parcel of land—must be studied, recognized and responded to if we are to avoid the negative consequences of globalization's presence—the rise of terrorism, fundamentalism, and fanaticism—in response to the "dominant," "modern" culture. The resistances expressed by indigenous grassroots movements can give us some insight into the nature and depth of those losses and perhaps indicate ways of mitigating globalization's most destructive effects.

Sentiment against globalization from above resonates in Hawai'i (and with Native Hawaiians in particular) because the environment is constantly threatened by ongoing luxury development for non-Native Hawaiians purchasers of real estate and by continuous construction, sometimes on sacred sites, designed to keep tourists coming back to Hawai'i. Watered down versions of Native Hawaiian culture have become yet another commodity to market, sell, and purchase, while the material conditions of Native Hawaiians do not improve and while Native Hawaiians are increasingly displaced from their own land.

Local practices regarding law and language were taken over by the United States in the mid-1800s, allowing for the easy spread of capitalism to the islands, from which an oligarchy of white businessmen and government officials primarily benefitted (Schamel and Schamel). Disparities in income, access to education, healthcare, and employment opportunities persist to this day, while arguments regarding state ownership and sale of land previously held by Native Hawaiians are heard in contemporary courts. The evolution of Hawai'i into its contemporary incarnation as a site for transnational commerce based largely on global tourism is directly connected to this history of exploitation. Contemporary Hawai'i is thoroughly enmeshed in what Jameson describes as the cultural logic of late capitalism; it has moved beyond the buying and selling of actual products (sugar, pineapple) to the marketing of image, idea, and experience. Today, tourists outnumber Native Hawaiians by about thirty-to-one (Trask) and nearly every economic enterprise in Hawai'i is controlled by overseas capital (Kent 186). Being more aware of some of the historical, cultural, and economic forces that have played a significant part in the shaping contemporary Hawai'i and that continue to be largely responsible for its future allows one to better understand the source of the grassroots protests against the ADB as well as their proposed solutions.

Honolulu in 2001: The Site of Struggle

In January 2001, the Honolulu Police Department (HPD) began to prepare with special riot training for the arrival of the upcoming ADB conference, which was to take place May 9-11. This was the first indication that the local authorities did not understand, any better than members of the ADB, the motivations behind the grassroots protests. From their actions, it is clear they imagined and feared an unruly and violent mob, and a great deal of time, money, and work was put into preventing something that never occurred, nor was ever intended to occur. A local television station, KITV, reported that "the training included hands-on simulations in which police, sheriffs and firefighters dressed in riot gear including gas masks and bulletproof vests to confront a crowd. ...The mock protestors chanted, taunted and threw fruit at the officers" ("Kanahele to Be Insider at ADB Meeting").

By the time the conference took place, HPD officials reported that they had trained for ten months along with virtually every other law enforcement agency in the state. 40 to 50 percent of the police force was assigned to activities related to the conference. The riot gear and training, both of which would prove to be unnecessary, came at a cost of $500,000 for new equipment to taxpayers. Another media outlet, *Hawai'i Indymedia*, reported that "...about $14,000 per protester [was] spent by local police and tourism groups to ensure tranquility..." ("Hawaiian Protestors"). These types of expenditures in time, money, and resources demonstrate the ways in which both ADB participants and organizers, as well as state and city government agencies, misunderstood the goals and purposes of the protest movement. As we will see, the protesters' goals were peaceful, community-minded, and focused on information sharing and improved communication. Violence, upheaval, and destruction were never in the picture; however, in preparing for the upcoming protests in this way, the local authorities perpetuated and indulged in the stereotypical image of protestors as unruly, expensive, laughable, and irrelevant. What if that time, money, and energy had gone into meeting with the grassroots environmental and Native Hawaiian groups to understand better their goals and motives? Instead the HPD chose to rely upon the hegemonic and thus often unexamined rhetorical construction of protestors as violent trouble-makers with whom it is not worth attempting to communicate. This was a rhetorical construction based in a particular ideology, one to which competing rhetorics can provide alternatives and correctives if and when they are allowed to be voiced and heard (Di Alto).

In April, the ACLU had to step in to protest the Honolulu City and the Hawai'i State governments' attempts to create a censored-speech zone around the convention center, to block off the entire sidewalk in front of the convention center to protestors, and to close off the promenade along a nearby canal, the Ala Wai. In the end, after filing suit, the ACLU was successful in negotiating permission for protestors to march in a parade in front of the Hawai'i Convention Center. A week before the conference in Hawai'i, conference organizers' and local authorities' concerns regarding potential protests were intensified due to widely reported violent clashes between police forces and protestors that took place in Quebec City in response to the Summit of the Americas. Local activist Cha Smith of the group ADB Watch, a Hawai'i-based coalition of indigenous, peace, social justice, and environmental groups, sought to reassure everyone of the nonviolent nature of the protest planned for Hawai'i, stating "our every intent is to get the word out about what globalization is and the impact that it's having on people." At that point, however, the rhetorical construction of the protestor as violent, scary, and unpredictable had firmly taken hold, and the actual protestors were unable to argue effectively against it.

Organizers had wanted to avoid grassroots resistance similar to what was experienced in Seattle in 1999 in response to the World Trade Organization conference by moving the conference to Hawai'i—"the most isolated archipelago in the world"—hoping thereby to undermine the national and international network of activists supporting globalization from below. ADB officials privately conceded that they picked Honolulu because it is in the middle of the Pacific Ocean surrounded by large military bases, which they hoped would discourage protesters from flying in (Mutume). Home to the U.S. Pacific Fleet, Hawai'i has over fifty surveillance stations. Unbeknownst to many tourists and even to some residents, the islands serve as "storage areas for nuclear and biological weapons, incineration sites for weapons disposal, sites for bombing exercises, and training areas for tropical mountain and jungle combat" (Bello and Guttal). Moreover, land "has been taken from native and other local residents in the name of 'national security,' and parts of the islands have experienced devastating environmental destruction and contamination as a result of military exercises and storage. The US supplies 24-hour security to protect these investments" (Bello and Guttal).

The ADB conference organizers were correct in their assumption that shifting the locale of their meeting would decrease the influence and numbers of protesters arriving from outside of Hawai'i. However, what the organizers did not foresee is that local, environmental, and/or Native Hawaiian grassroots organizations would step up to the plate, seeing an opportunity to highlight the concerns and experience of indigenous peoples. The ADB Watch organized a march, with a *Kanaka Maoli* (a person of Native Hawaiian descent) blowing the *pu* (conch shell). In addition, the ADB Watch organized a conference on indigenous rights and struggles, a teach-in on globalization coordinated with the International Forum on Globalization (IFG), a seminar on globalization and militarization, and a two-day series of talks, "Voices of the South," featuring speakers from across Asia and the Pacific. Observers remarked that the participation of native peoples and the theme of native people's rights distinguished the mobilization against the 34th ADB conference from previous protests. Indeed, about half of the participants in the May 9th march were Native Hawaiians, and a prominent theme in the weeklong anti-ADB events was protest against the U.S. destruction of their national sovereignty. A group of protesters headed in part by activist Dennis "Bumpy" Kanahele and former state Democratic Party chairman Walter Heen, 'Aha Ho'okele Huli'au, positioned themselves inside the conference, directly presenting Native Hawaiian cultural and social issues to conference delegates.

The ADB was and continues to be criticized for promoting neoliberal macro-economic policies and for financing huge infrastructure projects, such as roads and dams, which displace people and harm the environment. Indigenous groups contend that the unequal power relationships between developed and developing nations are unjust; in particular they oppose protectionist global trade agricultural policies in developed countries. They argue that the heavy subsidization of developed countries' agriculture and the aggressive use of export subsidies by developed nations to make their agricultural products more attractive on the international market were major causes of declines in the agricultural sectors of many developing nations. Anti-debt organizations have indicated that more than 10 percent of the $800 billion in external debt owed by Asia Pacific nations is owed to the ADB ("Hawaiian Protesters").

In response to the marches, protests, pamphlets, and chants, the ADB invited Native Hawaiians into its meeting to make a formal presentation before those in attendance. The advocacy group 'Aha Ho'okele-Huli'au made a two-hour presentation to ADB delegates on the third day of the meeting. The group's presentation "focused on the role of the United States in ending recognition of the international status of the sovereign nation of Hawai'i and its effects on the Hawaiian people. It explored opportunities to manage Native Hawaiian trust assets, introduced the concept of socially responsible investment, and fostered discussions of Hawaii's future leadership in the Asia-Pacific region" (Heen, et al.). Some Native Hawaiian leaders, among them noted poet, professor, and scholar, Haunani-Kay Trask, contended that the group had been co-opted by the ADB, raising the issue of whether and to what extent Native Hawaiian groups ought to collaborate with representatives of institutions and cultures that have done them harm.

"The People's Challenge"

Walden Bello, a Filipino author, political analyst, and professor of sociology and public administration at the University of the Philippines Diliman, as well as executive director of Focus on the Global South, presented the ADB with a petition that demanded the cancellation of four controversial projects: the Samut Prakarn Wastewater Management Project in Thailand, which was seen as corrupt and which threatened irreparable damage to a sensitive coastal ecosystem; the Cordillera Highland Agricultural Resource Management Project in the Philippines (CHARM), whose support of cash-cropping served to undermine traditional community-based farming; the Chashma Right Bank Irrigation Project in Pakistan, which resulted in the involuntary resettlement of villagers; and the Sri Lanka Water Resource Management project, which threatened serious ecological disruption to local communities ("Hawaiian Protestors").

My focus is not on the particulars of these projects, although they are clearly significant and bear closer examination in their own right, but rather on the rhetorical constructions and arguments that involve these projects; that is, how these sites function rhetorically in the "People's Challenge" to represent globalization from below's alternative value system and ways of knowing. My purpose in the rest of this chapter is to analyze recurring rhetorical strategies in the petition used to argue against the "dominant," "mainstream" values as articulated by institutions which embrace the goals of globalization from above, such as the ADB. These rhetorical strategies serve to question and undermine the hegemony of "prevailing" values by articulating alternative values and belief systems, ones that often correspond with key indigenous values and epistemologies. Through the analysis of this petition and of similar protest documents, we can learn from the rhetorical appeals, epistemologies, and value systems offered by indigenous peoples and/or globalization-from-below activists, so that what we find is (1) of course, an argument in response to globalization from above, but also (2) a competing framework or set of values or epistemologies for considering economic and social arrangements in globalization. In the following section, I highlight and interpret rhetorical gestures in the "People's Challenge to the Asian Development Bank" that demonstrate, embody, and encourage others to see the impact of globalization from above in new ways. And that, ultimately, is the value of this analysis, both for better understanding rhetoric in the era of globalization and for teaching rhetorical production in the era of globalization.

The following categories of rhetorical strategies recur in the petition; I contend that they correspond well to Native Hawaiian values and epistemologies as these are articulated by scholars of Native Hawaiian culture and language. These categories include the following groupings of understandings, experiences, attitudes, priorities, and practices, each of which I have not labeled but see as inherently related in foci and as reflective and formative of particular epistemologies and values: 1) an emphasis on people's experience and emotions rather than money; the desire to prioritize people over corporate interests; corporate responsibility (i.e., the argument that international corporations should bear responsibility to local citizens and not be unduly aided by national governments); consumer and worker rights; limits on the influence of capital; valuing people's experience over corporate profits; 2) the idea that people can be emotionally, spiritually, and culturally connected to location and community and thus can experience displacement; valuing and validating local experiences and articulations; respecting local, national, sovereignty interests and/or rights; 3) the belief in economic and social justice (i.e., that there should be compensation for losses experienced due to negative effective of globalization); compassion for the poor; government regulation of global corporate interests; 4) valuing transparency in proceedings and decision-making; accountability; integrity; public discussion and debate; 5) equality over competition (i.e., community collaboration); international solidarity; community input, participation and oversight; community oversight of government regulation; democratization; and 6) the protection of land and natural resources; international environmental guidelines and restrictions; sustainable economies; supporting developing countries' agricultural efforts.

It is important to consider these rhetorical constructs in the "People's Challenge" in light of scholarly treatments of indigenous values and epistemologies—not because they can be mapped alongside one another; that oversimplifies. I argue instead that there are interesting correspondences and resonances to be found, and that if one is listening carefully, one can hear the influence of indigenous values and epistemologies in the petition. That there is a clash of worldviews is evident; Native Hawaiian scholar Manulani Meyer states, uncompromisingly: "The truth is, Hawaiians were never like the people who colonized us. If we wish to understand what is unique and special about who we are as cultural people, we will see that our building blocks of understanding, our epistemology, and thus our empirical relationship to experience is different. We simply hear, feel, taste, and smell the world differently" (3). In "Our Own Liberation" Meyer creates the following categories for her discussion of Native Hawaiian epistemologies: 1) spirituality and knowing; (2) the cultural nature of the senses and expanding notions of empiricism; (3) relationship and knowledge; (4) utility and knowledge; (5) words and knowledge; and (6) the body/mind question. Meyer sees these as sites of empowerment and resistance. I don't think that each of these are present in the "People's Challenge," nor do I think it would be useful to attempt to map the petition along each of these categories. Instead I want to highlight a few key resonances where significant values and worldviews overlap. I point out core common discursive gestures, which embody and make known alternative ways of understanding our relationships and responsibilities to land, money, and each other.

In the following sections, I explore three core resonances between Native Hawaiian epistemologies and values and the worldviews expressed via the argument presented in the "People's Challenge." I then show how each of these commonalities in perspective provide a rhetorical counterpoint to "dominant" or "mainstream" values typical of globalization from above movements and, as one example, articulated in the words and actions of the ABD, the HPD, and the Hawai'i state, city, and county governments. These three sites of contention are 1) land as profit-making real estate vs. source of spiritual knowing and cultural belonging; 2) individualism vs. interdependence; and 3) prioritizing corporate profits and interests over human needs and concerns vs. valuing people's experiences and lives over the interests of global capitalism.

Before embarking on this analysis, however, I should acknowledge that drawing from a source like Meyer for this kind of work necessitates one further caveat: her categories are valuable and undoubtedly representative, but they are surely not complete. According to Native Hawaiian scholar Puakea Nogelmeier "Hawai'i stands out among all Pacific island groups for the massive extent of literature written in the native language, a pastiche of historical native production exceeding one million pages of printed text (1-2)." And yet, Nogelmeier laments: "A *discourse of sufficiency* exists in relation to knowledge about Hawai'i, meaning that modern scholarship has long accepted a fraction of the available sources as being sufficient to represent the whole [. . .]. The sum of these works makes up only a fraction of one percent of the available primary material, and yet for decades these few extracted and translated texts from a handful of authors have been accepted as representative of Hawaiian cultural and historical knowledge" (2). Meyer herself makes clear that the depictions of Native Hawaiian epistemologies she offers are not her own opinions but rather are views shared "by twenty Hawaiian educational leaders" (4) whom she interviewed for her article, at once acknowledging the paucity of sources and attempting to compensate for the lack in archival resources by making use of human connections.

"Location, location, location" vs 'Aina

For Meyer and the Native Hawaiian scholars she interviews, location is significant, primarily because human beings draw sustenance from their connections to particular parcels of land, through their care of it and respect for it. This is also connected to Native Hawaiian spiritual beliefs. Meyer explains that Native Hawaiian epistemology draws from "cultural beliefs about our place and purpose in the hierarchy of family, deified or mundane; our land, animistic or static; and our gods, plural or singular" (6) and that "the most difficult to explain is the notion of *'aina*, land— *'aina* as origin, *'aina* as mother, *'aina* as inspiration" (128). She cites Hannah Kihalani Springer, noting that "our cultural as well as physical geography is the foundation of our creativity, of our problem solving, of our knowledge building" (129), and she further explains how the Native Hawaiian conception of knowing is connected to place:

> How one knows, indeed, what one prioritizes with regard to this knowing, ends up being the stuff of identity, the truth that links us to our distinct cosmologies, and the essence of who we are as Oceanic people. It is a discussion of place and genealogy. It is a way to navigate the shores of what is worth knowing and it is particularly important as we enter the new millennium where information will no longer be synonymous with knowledge, but rather how that information helps us maintain our sense of community in the daily chaos of access and information overload. (125)

The act of valuing land for what it can give people spiritually and for what it can give them in terms of knowledge, identity, and a sense of belonging is articulated in the "People's Challenge," serving as a direct contradiction to the "prevailing," "dominant" view that sees land as real estate to be invested in or developed for the sake of turning a profit. For example, the challenge states: "Development must not be a process that creates refugees. The ADB creates refugees through physical displacement of peoples as well as alienating them from their communities, livelihoods and culture"; and "The ADB should acknowledge that ADB-financed projects have displaced peoples and created a new class of 'development refugees.'" Some possible alternatives to displacement and alienation from communities, livelihoods, and culture include required job creation for those whose means of support are negatively affected, as well as sustainable architecture and planning. The core values underlying these proposals is that people matter, that their connections to their communities and land matter, and that place is often connected to economic as well as cultural survival. This resonates well the Native Hawaiian emphasis on respecting *'aina* and people's spiritual, emotional, economic, and cultural connections to it. Indeed the extent to which unchecked, irresponsible development negatively impacts the lives and experiences of people, as well as their history, their sense of selves and their futures, is articulated throughout the "People's Challenge, " sometimes in striking detail:

> The Asian Development Bank...is an institution that is now widely recognized as having imposed tremendous sufferings on the peoples of the Asia-Pacific. In the name of development, its projects and programs have destroyed the livelihoods of people, brought about the disintegration of local and indigenous communities, violated ancestral domains, undermined sovereign self-determination, promoted a sharp rise in inequality, deepened poverty, and destabilized the environment.

The full cost of displacement, with its far-reaching consequences, is effectively outlined in the above passage: the breaking down of local and indigenous communities, the damaging of sacred sites, the loss of faith in self-determination, sharp increases in inequality, increased poverty, and significant damage to the environment. The petition draws on the core value of respecting the land to argue for transparency and public discussions, support for and recognition of sovereignty movements, and the value of prioritizing national concerns over external forces. In this way, the document demonstrates the interrelatedness of core values such as respecting the land, interdependence, and prioritizing the human experience over global capital, stating, for example, that

> the ADB should open to public scrutiny decision making and agreements between the ADB and host governments about projects and programmes. The ADB should review past and current decision making processes in light of their impacts on national sovereignty and where found wanting, these decision making processes must be changed to respond to national, rather than external interests.

The Native Hawaiian perspective of connection and relationship to land and the particularity and concreteness of place resonates with the values used as rhetorical constructs in the above passages taken from the petition. Of her treatment of Native Hawaiian concepts related to epistemology, Meyer explains "embodied knowing": "It is 'knowing' that is not divorced from awareness, from body, from spirit, from place [. . .]' (145).

Individualism vs. Interdependence

According to Meyer, many Native Hawaiian scholars view epistemology as connected to relationship; it is through relationship that one learns about oneself and others, as well as how one acquires ethical practices. The Native Hawaiian worldview emphasizes interdependence over independence. Meyer articulates it this way: "Relationships or interdependence offered Hawaiians opportunities to practice reciprocity, exhibit balance, develop harmony with land, and generosity with others" (134). In a similar way, one can find arguments in the "People's Challenge" that question the Western, capitalist, neo-liberal assumption that independence is to be valued above all else and that competition rather than collaboration and cooperation provides for the best results. In contrast, the document emphasizes shared responsibility, economic justice, and community collaboration, stating for example that "full direct compensation must be provided to all people negatively affected by ADB funded hydropower and other infrastructure projects in the Asia Pacific region. This must be done in a timely and transparent manner, in consultation with local peoples, and with ongoing monitoring and input from truly independent observers." In this passage, the petition articulates the need for and significance of transparency, the power and potential of community oversight, as well as the desire to respect and preserve local experience, expression, and knowledge. What all of these admittedly lofty goals have in common is that they question and destabilize the "dominant" and "mainstream" prioritizing of individualism characteristic of globalization from above and replace it with a vision of what collective action, cooperation, and collaboration could look like. This act of rhetorical reimagining of neo-liberalism's core values resonates with the Native Hawaiian emphasis on interdependence rather than independence as a way of knowing.

Interdependence as it is articulated in the petition is not just confined to the local, either; true to globalization's dedication to international solidarity and economic justice, the petition works to define the scope of one's ethical responsibilities beyond national borders, while still maintaining a commitment to one's immediate community:

> We call for an immediate and independent review of the ADB's Private Sector Development (PSD) strategy with special focus on the impacts of this strategy on local populations, the public sector, national and sub-national government capacities and the overall business climate. The results of this review should feed directly into a fundamental rethinking and reworking of this strategy to serve local, sub-national and national economic priorities and needs, rather than those of external investors and foreign governments.

The petition does not always remain on the terrain of the lofty and the ideal, however. Rather, it balances visionary goals and statements inspired by the ideal of interdependence with concrete arguments for particular financial transactions and the need for specific reparations. Pragmatic community participation and transparency are linked to interdependence, as in the following passage:

> The ADB must put into place appropriate mechanisms to monitor the environmental, social and economic impacts and costs of all projects and programs it supports in any manner or form. These mechanisms must include guidelines for mitigation of impacts and how mitigation costs will be met; such

costs cannot and must not be externalised and passed on to affected communities, society at large, or the public purse. Those who benefit most from projects must be responsible for the proportionate share of the costs. ...When the ADB experienced an internal financial squeeze at the height of the Asian crisis, it chose to remedy this by making capital costlier for borrowing governments. We demand that the ADB shift the burden back from the borrowing to the donor countries.

The petition's arguments that the ADB take sole responsibility for costs incurred by destructive effects of globalization from above demonstrates how specific arguments for corporate responsibility to international citizenry are grounded in the contrasting value of global interdependence and solidarity.

The Bottom Line vs. The Helping Hand

The contrasting values of privileging the bottom line versus valuing sharing and helping others is one of the core conflicts in worldviews experienced historically in the aftermath of Hawai'i's illegal annexation (for the sake of American profits that could be earned through the cultivation of pineapple and sugar at the cost of Native Hawaiian cultural traditions and human and civil rights) as well as by anyone living in contemporary Hawai'i. The state (former sovereign nation) remains, in my view, at war with itself on this issue. A Native Hawaiian scholar expresses how these dual value systems create conflicted perspectives and cognitive dissonance in the daily lives of Native Hawaiians in particular in this way:

> Responsibility for others, allowing your thinking to be validated by others, and seeing yourself through the lens of "other" is sometimes antagonistic to a modern system of social mores. A few mentors spoke thus in bicultural terms. "Your uncles and aunts are your other parents and they have just as much responsibility in raising you and therefore your reaction to them and responsibility to them, and at the same time you're being inbred by western thought because you're American, you're growing up American at the same time, so you have these two ongoing, sometimes, conflict (sic)." (Keola Lake, 26 January 1997, qtd. in Meyer 136)

These contrasting values result in very different lifestyles, traditions around family obligations, attitudes toward how money and time is best spent, and cultural norms for speech, interaction, friendship, loyalty, and business. Thus that the globalization-from-below's demands for economic and social justice resonates well with Native Hawaiian value systems should come as no surprise. Both stand in stark contrast to the profit-driven assumptions behind globalization-from-above's privileging of global capital over human rights. In the petition, there are quite a few passages which demonstrate these rhetorical resistances to neoliberalism, making arguments for valuing people first (over corporate interests), for direct compensation to people who are negatively impacted by projects supported by the ADB, and for transparency and community participation. These passages argue strenuously that the financial costs and labor associated with these tasks are to be borne by corporate entities like the ADB and not by private charities or the government. They often outline quite precisely how the detrimental effects of irresponsible development should be addressed, revealing comprehensive knowledge of the ADB's inner workings, as well as the ability to imagine specific, concrete alternatives. Here is one representative example:

> The ADB should assess the compensation needs of all those people whose livelihoods have been negatively affected, particularly those displaced as a result of past ADB projects, using open, transparent and participatory processes. Following such assessments, the ADB should develop and implement adequate, just and timely compensation measures. The Bank Funds earmarked for compensation should be used for direct compensation and not for further studies and assessments, or to pay for consulting companies or experts. Funds for assessments and eventual compensation must be provided through project budgets and the ADB's own resources [. . .].

In this passage the resonating value of people over profit (to put a complex idea in its most simplest terms) is translated into the goals that characterize many social movements associated with globalization from below, such as transparency, community participation, economic justice, and corporate responsibility. These social goals are then embodied by specific social programs and rights that the petition works to rhetorically uphold as alternatives to the idea that "might makes right":

> We demand full and unconditional cancellation of the illegitimate debts of ADB's borrowing countries. The ADB must also immediately undertake a region-wide assessment of the debts owed to it by all borrowing countries. In particular, the assessment should focus on: a) the impacts of debt servicing on social and other essential services; b) the programmes and conditions under which the debts were contracted, as well as their legitimacy in terms of debt repayment.

Valuing people first is represented rhetorically in this passage and elsewhere throughout the petition as arguments for consumer and worker rights, social justice, and compassion for poor. Debt forgiveness is one significant retort to the "dominant" and "mainstream" expectation that the developing countries owe the developed countries something, particular after many of their independent means of economic sustenance have been demolished by forces which work to keep globalization from above in play. The economic injustice behind such an expectation is an argument the petition works as a way to call into question the self-described benign motivations behind the loaning of funds to developing countries by organizations like the ADB. This resonates with the

Native Hawaiian value of focusing on "the other" and of perceiving the self as connected to community, family, and ancestry in ways which call upon the individual to emphasize the needs of the community over his or her own desires. As Meyer puts it, "in this continuum with our *'ohana* [family], the focus is now on 'other' and how maintenance of relationships takes conscious and deliberate thought and action" (134).

Refusing to Play the Endgame

War, militarization, and the expansion of the American empire constitute what Neil Smith calls "the endgame of globalization." Opposition to the Iraq war from other developed countries was not inspired by a higher moral sense but rather by the resistance these countries had to seeing globalization become Americanization. The U.S. military is the world's eleventh largest economy, but, as we have witnessed during the recent financial crises, the U.S. economy is such a central pillar of global capitalist stability that allowing a crisis to unfold entirely was and remains unthinkable. And besides, the United States controls the organizations that would discipline them (Smith passim). In response to such overridingly powerful forces, we have seen how grassroots globalization from below and/or indigenous groups with alternative values and worldviews attempt to position themselves in protest. Through the strategic use of alternative rhetorical strategies, which value people's interdependence on land and one another over corporate profit, they reveal the hidden assumptions and motivations behind the "dominant," "mainstream" value systems and ideologies which keep globalization from above in place. As educators and researchers of rhetoric and as teachers of writing in college classrooms, we can use the tools of our trade to make the hidden assumptions behind globalization-from-above's premises explicit by teaching the analysis of rhetorical strategies employed both in favor and against this movement. I contend that this approach will result in 1) a richer, location-specific understanding of rhetorical practices that are often ignored or dismissed as "non-dominant," and that (2) as one consequence, this enriched understanding will help foster a pedagogical approach to the field of composition and rhetoric that acknowledges and appreciates a complex understanding of local and/or indigenous values, epistemology, and rhetorical opportunities, as expressed by the proponents of globalization from below.

In the opening of this chapter, I described Hawai'i as it is often portrayed and perceived by those who do not know it well—as isolated to the extreme. However, over time and through listening and growing to love Hawai'i's people and land, I have learned to see Hawai'i in a different light. As Manulani Meyer describes it, "we in Hawai'i are not living in the most 'isolated land mass in the universe' but rather, in one of the most interconnected lands in the world. Ocean connects us. Ocean is in us. We are Oceanic people" (147). Meyer adds that this "was a liberating idea that continues to inspire" her and that she is "indebted to the brilliant visionary and writer, Epeli Hauʻofa" for this understanding. She says: "*Mahalo*, Epeli," to which I respond "*Mahalo*, Manulani." May each of us be so fortunate as to be reminded in such a gracious way that "mainstream," "dominant" values are not always the necessary or correct ones. And that we need international solidarity and communication—globalization from below— and the voices of local and/or indigenous peoples to survive.

> Huli ka lima i luna, make ʻoe; huli ka lima i lalo, ola ʻoe [Turn the hands upward, you die; turn the hands downward (work) you live]. This is our famous saying all the time, all the time . . . from as far back as I know.
>
> (Abbie Napeahi, qtd. in Meyer 137)

Works Cited

Asian Development Bank Website. Accessed Sept. 10, 2010. <http://www.adb.org/>.

"Anti-globalization Movement." *Wikipedia: The Free Encyclopedia.* Accessed 15 September 2010. <http://en.wikipedia.org/wiki/Anti-globalization_movement>.

Bello, Walden, and Shalmali Guttal. "Honolulu Face-Off: Civil Society 1, Asian Development Bank 0." *Focus on Trade* 63, May 2001. Accessed Sept. 10, 2010. <http://www.nadir.org/nadir/initiativ/agp/free/bello/honolulu.htm>.

Brecher, Jeremy, Tim Costello, and Brendan Smith. *Globalization from Below: The Power of Solidarity.* Cambridge: South End P, 2000.

Chomsky, Noam. "Interviewed by Toni Gabric." *The Croatian Feral Tribune* 07 May 2002. Reproduced with permission. Accessed Sept 10, 2010. <http://www.architectureink.com/2002-06/chomsky4.htm>.

Di Alto, Stephanie. "Indigenous Peoples and Anti-Globalization Activism: Native Hawaiians and the Asian Development Bank." *International Studies Association*, San Diego, CA, March 22-25, 2006.

"Hawaiian Protesters Get in ADB's Face." *Hawai'i Indy Media.* 10 May 2001. Accessed Sept. 10, 2010. <http://www.nadir.org/nadir/initiativ/agp/free/adb/face.htm>.

Heen, Walter, Edward Richardson, Bumpy Kanahele, Hooipo Pa, Kunani Nihipali, and Paula Helfrich. "Gathering Places. Hawaii Comes of Age at ADB Meeting." *Hawaii Star-Bulletin.* Sunday, May 13, 2001.

"Indigenous Peoples." Asian Development Bank Website. Accessed Sept. 10, 2010. <http://www.adb.org/IndigenousPeoples/faq-01.asp>.

Jameson, Frederic. *Postmodernism, or, The Cultural Logic of Late Capitalism.* Verso, 1991.

Kent, Noel J. *Hawaii: Islands under the Influence.* New York and London: Monthly Review Press, 1983.

"Kanahele to Be Insider at ADB Meeting: Activist to Educate Delegates on Hawaiian Issues." KITV.com. May 2002. Accessed Sept. 10, 2010. <http://www.kitv.com/news/756313/detail.html>.

Mutume, Gumisai. "Next Stop For Anti-Globalization March—Hawaii." Inter Press Service. February 7, 2001. Accessed Sept. 10, 2010. <http://www.nadir.org/nadir/initiativ/agp/free/adb/ips.htm>.

Meyer, Manulani Aluli. "Our Own Liberation: Reflections on Hawaiian Epistemology." *The Contemporary Pacific* 13,1 (2001): 124- 48.

Nogelmeier, M. Puakea. *"Mai Paa i ka Leo: Historical Voice in Hawaiian Primary Materials, Looking Forward and Listening Back."* Unpublished dissertation. 1-44.

Schamel, Wynell, and Charles E. Schamel. "The 1897 Petition Against the Annexation of Hawai'i." *Social Education* 63, 7 (November/December 1999): 402-8.

Smith, Neil. *The Endgame of Globalization.* New York: Routledge, 2005

Starr, Amory. *Naming the Enemy: Anti-Corporate Movements Confront Globalization.* Sydney: Pluto P, 2000.

Trask, Haunani-Kay. *From a Native Daughter: Colonialism and Sovereignty in Hawai'i.* Revised Edition. Honolulu: University of Hawai'i Press, 1999.

Appendix

People's Challenge to the Asian Development Bank

May 9, 2001
Honolulu, Hawaii

The Asian Development Bank (ADB), which is holding its 34th Annual Meeting in Honolulu on May 7-11, 2001, is an institution that is now widely recognized as having imposed tremendous sufferings on the peoples of the Asia-Pacific. In the name of development, its projects and programs have destroyed the livelihoods of people, brought about the disintegration of local and indigenous communities, violated ancestral domains, undermined sovereign self-determination, promoted a sharp rise in inequality, deepened poverty, and destabilized the environment.

We, representatives of peoples, indigenous communities, and organizations throughout the region, have had enough of this destruction in the name of development. We have had enough of an arrogant institution that is one of the most non-transparent, undemocratic, and unaccountable organizations in existence.

We seek genuine dialogue with the ADB, demanding that it recognize the error of its ways and yield the space to promote alternative strategies of development that truly serve the people's interests.

In this spirit, we are presenting the following demands to President Tadao Chino:

I. Development must not be a process that creates refugees. The ADB creates refugees through physical displacement of peoples as well as alienating them from their communities, livelihoods and culture.

We demand an immediate halt to and independent review of all controversial/disputed ADB projects, especially those that directly threaten people's livelihoods and economic and social security like the Samut Prakarn Wastewater Management in Thailand and the Cordillera Highland Agricultural Resource Management Project in the Philippines. The ADB should not take any further action on these projects until critical issues are resolved.

a.) The ADB should acknowledge that ADB-financed projects have displaced peoples and created a new class of "development refugees."

b.) The ADB should assess the compensation needs of all those people whose livelihoods have been negatively affected, particularly those displaced as a result of past ADB projects, using open, transparent and participatory processes. Following such assessments, the ADB should develop and implement adequate, just and timely compensation measures. The Bank Funds earmarked for compensation should be used for direct compensation and not for further studies and assessments, or to pay for consulting companies or experts. Funds for assessments and eventual compensation must be provided through project budgets and the ADB's own resources.

Full direct compensation must be provided to all people negatively affected by ADB funded hydropower and other infrastructure projects in the Asia Pacific region. This must be done in a timely and transparent manner, in consultation with local peoples, and with ongoing monitoring and input from truly independent observers.

c.) The ADB must put into place appropriate mechanisms to monitor the environmental, social and economic impacts and costs of all projects and programs it supports in any manner or form. These mechanisms must include guidelines for mitigation of impacts and how mitigation costs will be met; such costs cannot and must not be externalised and passed on to affected communities, society at large, or the public purse. Those who benefit most from projects must be responsible for the proportionate share of the costs.

d.) The ADB must put into place transparent and universally accessible arbitration/grievance procedures through which the ADB can be held accountable for violation of its own guidelines. The ADB should put particular emphasis on this in both its public and private sector operations.

e.) The ADB should put justice high on its agenda. A rigorous mechanism for reparation for the negative impacts of past and existing projects should be set up.

f.) In solidarity with the people of Klong Dan, we demand that the Samut Prakarn project be immediately stopped, and that no further release of funds be made until the Inspection process is fully completed in a transparent and participatory manner.

g.) In solidarity with the advocates in Sri Lanka opposing the Sri Lanka Water Resource Management Project, we demand a halt to the project and a review of the Wildlife Management Project.

h.) The ADB should adopt and implement the fundamental principles and guidelines recommended by the World Commission on Dams, especially those regarding prior informed consent and the assessment of alternatives.

II. Current sectoral reform processes such as those in the agriculture sector in Pakistan and Thailand and in energy in the Philippines fail to fully capture the complex political-economic realities in these countries. Indiscriminate scaling down or abolition of agricultural and social subsidies exposes poor households with low access and endowments to start with to even greater insecurity.

We call for an independent evaluation and an immediate stop to all sectoral reform processes. The results of these evaluations must be used to re-work and restructure reforms, including content, sequencing and even alternative models.

III. We call for an immediate and independent review of the ADB's Private Sector Development (PSD) strategy with special focus on the impacts of this strategy on local populations, the public sector, national and sub-national government capacities and the overall business climate. The results of this review should feed directly into a fundamental rethinking and reworking of this strategy to serve local, sub-national and national economic priorities and needs, rather than those of external investors and foreign governments. During the period of the review and re-strategising, ongoing PSD initiatives should be slowed down and no new initiatives should be started. The review should also take into consideration political, social and economic realities such as distributional disparities that render markets uncompetitive and exclude the poor, as well as weak governance structures that render regulation ineffective and incapable of upholding consumer and worker rights.

IV. The ADB itself acknowledges that close to 70 percent of its loans to the developing countries will fail to produce lasting economic or social benefits in these countries. Yet the ADB insists that these debts be repaid, further contributing to the impoverishment in these countries.

We demand full and unconditional cancellation of the illegitimate debts of ADB's borrowing countries. The ADB must also immediately undertake a region-wide assessment of the debts owed to it by all borrowing countries. In particular, the assessment should focus on: a) the impacts of debt servicing on social and other essential services; b) the programmes and conditions under which the debts were contracted, as well as their legitimacy in terms of debt repayment.

When the ADB experienced an internal financial squeeze at the height of the Asian crisis, it chose to remedy this by making capital costlier for borrowing governments. We demand that the ADB shift the burden back from the borrowing to the donor countries.

V. We deplore the inconsistency with which the ADB requires good governance, transparency and accountability from borrowing governments while at the same time fails to impose the same strict standards on itself.

In its push for privatization, the ADB turns a blind eye to corrupt practices employed by borrowing governments such as the Philippines in the case of the power sector reform loan in order to meet conditions for the release of ADB loans.

Furthermore, we challenge the ADB to stop placing the entire blame for the failure of projects and programmes on governments and take institutional responsibility for the projects and programs it supports.

a.) The ADB should democratize decision-making within the highest levels, and function on the principle of one country, one vote, and not on the current practice based on the amount of subscribed capital.

b.) In general, the ADB should open to public scrutiny decision making and agreements between the ADB and host governments about projects and programmes. The ADB should review past and current decision making processes in light of their impacts on national sovereignty and where found wanting, these decision making processes must be changed to respond to national, rather than external interests.

c.) All of the ADB's review panels for projects, programmes, operations and governance must be equally balanced in their composition among affected peoples, civil society and independent experts. Further, affected peoples and civil society must have the right to select their own representatives on these panels.

d.) The ADB should locate all reviews and assessments of its projects, programmes, lending practices and decision-making processes within national and sub-national democratic processes such as parliaments, congresses and national assemblies. Directions for future policies and practices must emerge from public debates and discussions, and not through closed-door negotiations among elite groups of ADB management, national and government elites and technical "experts."

WE CALL ON THE ADB TO RESPECT THE RIGHTS OF PEOPLES OVER THEIR RESOURCES AND LIVES AND IMMEDIATELY IMPLEMENT THE AFOREMENTIONED DEMANDS.

ON MAY 9, WE MARCH IN SOLIDARITY WITH THE PEOPLES OF HAWAII WHO REJECT ANY FUTURE USE OF THEIR ISLANDS BY MULTILATERAL INSTITUTIONS LIKE THE ASIAN DEVELOPMENT BANK KNOWN FOR THEIR ANTI-PEOPLE AND ANTI-DEMOCRATIC POLICIES.

Endorsed by:
Northern Farmers Alliance, Thailand
Kanchanaburi Conservation Group, Thailand
Bor Nog Conservation Group, Thailand
Ban Krud Natural and Conservation Group, Thailand
Klong Dan Local Community Projection Group, Thailand
Isaan Framers Cooperative Federation, Thailand
Committee for the Solution of Farmer's Problems, Chiang Rai
Committee for the Solution of Farmer's Problems, Payao
Local Theatre Project, Thailand
Four Regional Alternative Agricultural Network, Thailand
Northern Farmer Network, Thailand
Kok-Ing-Nan River Network, Thailand
Mae Thood River Network, Lampang
Mae Mog River Network, Lampang
Mae Soi River Network, Lampang
Isaan Forest and Land Network, Thailand
Thai Network for People Living with HIV/AIDS, Thailand
Isaan River Network, Thailand
Chiang Mai Consumer Network, Thailand
Women Rights Network, Thailand
Chiang Rai-Payao Rural Women Network, Thailand
Labor Network, Thailand
Four Regional Slum Network, Thailand
Chiang Mai Community Network, Thailand
Media Center for People, Thailand
Eastern Farmer Network, Thailand
Southern Local Fisherman Federation, Thailand
Student Federation of Thailand
Committee for Natural and Environmental Conservation 16 Educational
        Institute, Thailand
Assembly of Isaan Farmer, Thailand
Assembly of Cassava Planter Thailand

Assembly of Indigenous People, Thailand
Assembly of the Poor, Thailand
Assembly of Moon River Basin, Thailand
Group for Save Wand River, Thailand
Nam Ping River Community Forest Network, Thailand
Love Muang Nan Group, Thailand
Assembly of Northern Community Forest, Thailand
NGO-Coordinating Committee for Development (NGO-COD), Thailand
Freedom from Debt Coalition, Philippines
Cordillera People's Alliance, Philippines
Focus on the Global South, Thailand
Focus on the Global South - India Programme
Fukuoka NGO Forum on the ADB, Japan
AID/WATCH, Australia
Creed Alliance, Pakistan
Global Justice Coalition, Australia
NGO Forum on the ADB (International Committee)
Non-Timber Forestry Project, Cambodia
Oxfam America
Oxfam Community Aid Abroad-Australia
International Rivers Network, USA
Asia Pacific Movement on Debt and Development (Jubilee South AP)
Environmental Foundation Ltd., Sri Lanka
ODA Reform Network, Japan
Mekong Watch, Japan
NGO Forum on Cambodia
PADETC, Lao PDR
ACTION AID, UK
Green Movement of Sri Lanka
Shelly Rao, Fiji
SUNGI Development Foundation, Pakistan
Youth for Unity and Voluntary Action (YUVA), India

World Wide Composition: Virtual Uncertainties

Chris M. Anson

> On one hand, globalization unfolds a process of standardization in which a globalized mass culture circulates the globe creating sameness and homogeneity everywhere. But globalized culture makes possible unique appropriations and developments all over the world, thus proliferating hybridity, difference, and heterogeneity. (Kellner "Theorizing Globalization")

Internationally, interest in the research and teaching of academic writing in higher education is burgeoning. New professional societies are emerging, some country-specific, others encompassing larger geographical areas. International conferences on writing are convening in the Middle East, Asia, Europe, Mexico, and South America (see CompFAQ). New international journals, books series, and other outlets for publication have appeared (such as the *Journal of Writing Research*), as well as professional listservs, blogs, and Internet forums. Encouraged by these expansions, national organizations such as the European Teachers of Academic Writing, the (now) International Writing Centers Association, and the (U.S.) Council of Writing Program Administrators are actively exploring ways to reach out to a more international community. The "internationalization" of composition is, as Donahue puts it, "a hot commodity."

There is little question that these activities are motivated by an interest in global communication, with the English language, the Internet, and North America as driving forces. As a general concept, globalization is typically defined as the worldwide interrelationships of economic, political, and technological activity, and it refers mainly to the interactions of corporations and other industrial institutions on an international scale, without geographical primacy (Kluver). To prepare learners for this global marketplace, higher-education administrators are recognizing the need to focus their institutional missions on enhancing students' abilities to communicate effectively, especially through the use of emergent digital technologies in the language that many linguists believe is becoming the world's lingua franca, English. A publication issued by the U.S.-based organization Achieve, for example, unequivocally places globalization, education, and technology on a metaphorical "front line in the battle for our economic future":

> The integration of the world economy through low-cost information and communications has an even more important implication than the dramatic expansion of both the volume of trade and what can be traded. Trade and technology are making all the nations of the world more alike. Together they can bring all of the world's companies the same resources—the same scientific research, the same capital, the same parts and components, the same business services, and the same skills. (Achieve 4)

From this perspective, the need for education in intercultural communication is undeniable. Brobman, for example, calls for an expanded conception of internationalization in technical writing, arguing that "the practical necessity of intercultural communication in a global marketplace necessitates internationalization" (427).

In the context of this internationalizing of interest in academic writing, the influence of North American composition research and pedagogy is a subject of considerable debate. Much international research on writing has demonstrated a certain degree of independence (as specific organizations or areas of research continue their work in various countries and regions). Related international movements, such as quality assessment of educational outcomes, have also led institutions and national oversight bodies to become more interested in the relationships among writing, learning, and academic performance (see Yorke). Yet a number of theorists have still expressed concern about the dominance of the American perspective, U.S. educational models, and instruction in English. Almost fifteen years ago, Muchiri and colleagues warned about the need to adapt North American composition principles to the specific educational settings of other countries, lest all eyes turned to the West for guidance. Likewise, from a linguistic perspective Zegers and Wilkinson favor a policy of plurilingualism in internationalized higher education, but based on their case study of Maastricht University, they worry that the dominance of English-language instruction will create students who are academically fluent mainly in English, and therefore can produce a limited set of professional genres associated with their Anglocentric studies.

Such warnings have done little to slow the fact that, as Schaub puts it, "the business of educating the world on the model of American universities is flourishing" (90). The almost universal, longstanding first-year writing curriculum that the American post-secondary model brings, along with over thirty years of its expanding attention to writing across the curriculum, have no doubt contributed to the spread of composition in other countries, and the presence of hundreds of American universities abroad has only helped to localize this emphasis. The dominance of published materials in the United States is also a factor, as Canagarajah has documented in Sri Lanka's adoption of American textbooks, curricula, faculty development materials, teaching methods, manuals, and testing kits (see also Phillipson). Some countries are even deliberately insourcing American education in place of sending their citizens to the United States to study, perhaps most dramatically demonstrated in the establishment of "Education City" in Doha, Qatar, where six American universities have installations on a 2,500-acre campus designed to become one of the most comprehensive and state-of-the-art educational institutions in the world (Qatar Foundation; see also Harman).

From an optimistic perspective, the internationalization of academic writing offers a productive exchange of ideas about teaching, learning, administration, and assessment. The practical outcomes of this worldwide expansion of interest in writing pedagogy and administration are many: increased international collaborations among teachers, peer-to-peer international tutoring and mentoring, global classrooms, content-focused collaborative student projects—as well as exposure to "layers upon layers of difference" and, ultimately, "multilingualism, divergence, and enduringly deep diversity" (Kalantzis and Cope). Yet although these and other practices promise exciting developments in the internationalization of education and richer intercultural educational experiences for learners worldwide, they are also not without risk. Just as globalization creates new opportunities for the expansion of writing pedagogy, the international community of writing scholars and teachers must approach this expansion with a spirit of collective critique and a concern for its sources, goals, distribution of power, and worldwide effects.

The purpose of this chapter is to demonstrate such a critique in the context of emerging opportunities for internationalized pedagogy in writing enabled by computer technology, such as the linking of classrooms between and among countries. After describing some roles that internationalism has played in pre-digital American post-secondary composition instruction, the first section considers how the Internet has enabled increased border-crossing in our pedagogies. These pedagogies challenge a "one-way" model of internationalization (in which American students read, learn, and write about other cultures and nations) in favor of a more collaborative, interactive model that involves cultural, social, and educational interrelationships between and among people in different nations. The second part of the chapter will then turn to the possible deleterious effects of increased international, technologically mediated pedagogies in writing, including instructional inequities, cultural dominance, the decline of teaching and learning in indigenous languages, and the specter of unfair labor practices.

The Role of Internationalization in Composition

The field of composition studies has a long tradition of interest in cultural issues, with the goal of helping students to reach deeper understandings about diversity of human experience and social and economic inequities (see George and Trimbur). Instructional innovation in this area began in the 1980s, eventually driving an entire sub-area of scholarship and the publication of a number multicultural anthologies for first-year composition courses (see Berlin; Fulkerson). Students write and read about cultural issues, or conduct mini-ethnographies as participant/observers in another cultural or subcultural context. The focus of such courses usually remains domestic, as suggested in Jay Jordan's review of the three popular multicultural readers recently adopted for composition courses. "Culture" is often synonymous with the complexities of human diversity in the United States, including immigrant populations, but international only through the lens of American social and political concerns, a problem that Schaub has associated with the "insularity" of American composition (87).

Before the rise of the Internet, composition's scattered international pedagogical orientations included theme-based courses, integrated classrooms, and study-abroad projects, all of which are still practiced. The first—courses "themed" to international issues—provide opportunities for students to research and/or write about international topics in specific papers and projects. For example, a second-semester themed composition course at Marshalltown Community College introduces students to international issues through three units on "cultural traditions," "power and dominance," and "the multinational society." Students collaboratively research various topics, make a presentation of their findings, and prepare a portfolio that includes a cover letter explaining "how their research expanded their knowledge of the culture or theme and how that knowledge affected their perceptions of their own culture" (Colbert). Similarly, an introductory composition course with the theme "Ourselves Among Others," organized under the auspices of the Midwest Institute for International/Intercultural Education (a self-funded consortium of two-year colleges), devotes half the course to topics such as "The International Family," "Work Here and Work There," and "The West and the World" (Tower).

As international as such courses can be in focus, for practical purposes they are not usually structured to create cross-cultural communication or collaboration; the engagement is with histories, autobiographical accounts, concepts, and ideas that come from texts, and for this reason the experience by its nature does not involve direct cultural contact. As Jordan points out, such courses may only weakly realize their intended outcomes:

> When [individualistic and isolationist] pedagogy occurs as part of a broader 'multiculturalism,' the potential exists for whatever political projects teachers and students envision for their composition classrooms to be short-circuited— for multicultural engagements to stop at the level of recognizing and even "tolerating" differences while leaving unquestioned the various structures that determine what those differences mean. (170; see also Jamieson, "Composition," and Grobman)

This lack of engagement is reduced in integrated classrooms, a second method for internationalizing composition pedagogy. In an integrated course, students from different parts of the world study, write, and interact with each other in the same physical spaces. Ibrahim and Penfield, for example, describe a course that brought together American students and students (in residence) from eleven other countries, resulting in gains "in respect for and understanding of different cultures that improved communication in speaking, writing, and relating that will benefit [the students] in future shared discourse communities." Similarly, at Iowa State University, several sections of first-year composition are taught each year as "cross-cultural" courses, meaning that half the students in each section are international students and the other half are students from the United States. These "50/50" courses are designed to "give special emphasis to cross-cultural and international issues" (Iowa State). A similar program at Purdue University found that "the mediated integration of US and international students in a cross-cultural composition course can be an effective way of addressing the needs of both NES and ESL students" (Matsuda and Silva). The international nature of such courses provides additional motivation to develop communication skills, partly through the diversity of their student audiences, while also fostering mutual understandings and respect.

Despite the appeal of such courses, they have not proliferated in composition instruction. Complex placement systems, the forced separation of ESL students from mainstream composition classrooms, and the lack of enough foreign students on some campuses to create much more than an experimental section militate against the systematic development of an internationalized writing curriculum based on integrated courses. And although such courses represent complex "contact zones" where diverse cultures, both American and international, "meet, clash, and grapple with each other" (Pratt 519), it is important to recognize that they are physically located on the native soil—and in the native educational context—of one student cohort.

Study-abroad programs represent a third though minor area of international influence in composition instruction, to the extent that students may fulfill a writing requirement at their home institution while living and learning in a foreign country. In such programs, written projects can focus on research related to the host country. For example, the Student Project for Amity Among Nations (SPAN), founded by students in 1947 at the University of Minnesota to encourage post-war understandings and good will, annually offers several study-abroad opportunities, each organized by a faculty mentor familiar with the host country. Students work for the academic year prior to the summer abroad setting up their research project, contacting interviewees, and planning their visit. During the trip, they write extensively, both for their project and in an experiential journal. The students devote the semester following the trip to writing up a substantial report of their research.

Most study-abroad experiences also include a strong component of *reflection*: interpreting and coming to understand the self in relation to the culture. As Taylor argues, travel-journal writing is an especially appropriate genre for such experiences because it encourages reflective observation and provides a way for teachers to assess the impact of the experience. The focus on written reflection—long the mainstay of service-learning initiatives (Anson "On Reflection")—only intensifies when students' travel abroad is linked to international service. But the favored genres remain personal, focusing inward on the self, as the writer interprets a new culture and reformulates her sense of identity in the midst of what can be a profoundly life-changing experience. This expressivist orientation may not effectively challenge students' ideologies or help them confront internal conflicts arising from their cultural experiences.

Even taken together, these three kinds of internationalization in composition—in subject matter, in integrated bricks-and-mortar classrooms, and in study-abroad and foreign service-learning programs—have represented a relatively small percentage of curricular experiences that fall under the banner of college composition. Although the situation is changing, a scan of syllabi, curricula, and textbooks from most universities shows that composition courses across the United States generally lack international orientations, touching on global issues sporadically through occasional readings or topics for students' papers and research (see Schaub).

In the past, interactive models of internationalized composition have also been limited logistically by available communicative media. A course in the 1950s involving pen pal exchanges might have yielded one or two letters between students, sent by ship or slow prop planes—hardly a very interactive experience. Today, however, new technologies enable more elaborate and extensive border-crossings in which students and teachers in different countries link up to produce individual and/or collaborative projects or use their interactions as the subject for writing. Several types of curricular innovations continue to expand and become more technologically sophisticated.

Global classrooms usually involve careful electronic coordination between teachers in two or more countries who integrate exchange-based and collaborative projects into their instruction, often creating international teams that investigate a topic and work together to produce a Web paper, site, or project. In communication instruction, global classrooms can focus on specific content or processes while providing an additional dimension of intercultural exchange and learning. The Global Classroom Project designed by TyAnna Herrington ("Where" and "Global"), for example, links students at Georgia Tech with students at universities in Russia and Sweden. Focusing on the analysis of cross-cultural communication, students investigate similarities and differences in news reporting across cultural divides, which allows them to analyze "cultural, historical, political, and other differences and similarities in [their] nation's characters." Other examples of global classroom projects include El Camino College's Global Studies course, which is linked to similar courses in three other countries through videoconferencing technology (Womack); and Eastern Carolina University's Global Understanding course, which allows students to learn about other cultures without traveling by pairing two cultures at a time for four weeks each on a round-robin basis through video conferencing and chat technology.

Global classrooms are increasingly popular in disciplines beyond composition that are "writing intensive" or involve significant amounts of written communication. For example, a project in the sciences at the University of New Mexico focuses on water and global environmental issues. Using Web programs and videoconferencing, it links students in the United States with those in Ecuador and Nepal to share analyses of their local rivers and streams (Nepal Study Center). Because interaction can now involve multiple media, including writing, data files, images, video, and sound, such cross-cultural experiences have important implications for communication-across-the-curriculum programs, including preparing students to participate in the international exchange of knowledge in their fields and making them aware of the relevance of their studies to global problems.

Intercultural classroom connections offer another variety of global classrooms but allow for less extensive collaboration, depending on the focus and nature of the relationships established between the two educational contexts. In such projects, students in one classroom use simple distance technologies, primarily email, chat programs, blogs, and forums, to carry on conversations with students in another country. One well-known facilitator of such exchanges is the Intercultural Email Classroom Connections (IECC) service, which provides free links between classrooms in different countries. Originally established in 1992 by three professors at St. Olaf College, IECC has facilitated exchanges between classrooms of 7,650 teachers in 82 countries (IECC). Many similar services and programs offer teachers and students opportunities for keypal (the electronic equivalent of pen pal) exchanges, especially in early stages of schooling. The e-Pals Network, for example, has over 111,000 linked classrooms involving six million students and teachers in over 191 countries (e-Pals).

Telementoring and *teletutoring* refer to online exchanges in which students receive individual help from experts or peers without meeting them in person (see Emery). Early literature defined these educational practices in terms of a relationship between a young(er) novice and an older mentor. These include "expert" services that are often answer-driven rather than highly interactive; "expert/novice" interactive programs in which a (usually older) mentor provides more sustained help and guidance to a (usually younger) tutee, often via email (see Friedman, Zibit, and Coote); and "telementor partnerships" in which an outside expert is paired with an entire class or group of learners, allowing for a greater range of interaction and the potential for more distributed expertise (see Reil). Recently, paired and peer mentoring and group interactions have increased in popularity. For example, peer-to-peer "teleapprenticeships" use networks to "create apprentice-like learning environments without requiring the participants to be in the same place at the same time . . . [and] allow novices to learn through participation in a remote community of practice" (Levin and Waugh, 40). Some corporations have also developed mentoring programs between employees and young learners as a public service. In the first three years of the Hewlett Packard Email Mentor Program, created in 1995, over 3,000 mentor relationships were established in the United States and five other countries between elementary students in science and math and HP employees. The program is now run by the International Telementor Center at Colorado State University (ITP; for a critique, see Lewis).

All three of these popular ways to connect students, teachers, and classrooms across international borders using digital technologies suggest new opportunities for writing oriented toward greater collaboration, internationalization, and constructivist models of learning. However, we know little about the effects of such collaborations on learners and on learning. Research on telementoring programs, for example, remains scant, and few studies have examined the interpersonal effects of online mentoring, a process that, when internationalized, becomes more complicated even as it holds out promise for greater global understanding and shared goals (Emery). More broadly, we have yet to explore the many social, cultural, linguistic, educational, and political issues associated with digitally-enabled border crossings, much less the complex dimensions of international cross-cultural collaborations in the arena of writing instruction. It is to some of these problematics that we will now turn.

International Networking in Composition: Proceeding with Caution

In a literature review titled "Crossing Frontiers: New Directions in Online Pedagogy and Research," Richard Kern and colleagues suggest that we are starting a second wave of thinking about digitally-mediated communication. Unlike our earlier focus on communication in individualized and networked classrooms, this wave concerns itself with long-distance collaborative projects and shifts the focus from language per se to cultural learning and literacy. Based on the selected studies, they conclude that the "affordances of this new medium problematize some of our earlier notions of interaction, culture, identity, and literacy" and compel us to "use the Internet not so much to teach the same thing in a different way, but rather to help students enter into a new realm of collaborative inquiry and construction of knowledge, viewing their expanding repertoire of identities and communication strategies as resources in the process" (12). As their review suggests, it is crucial that we more fully theorize international border-crossings in our pedagogy and investigate them from various theoretical perspectives. Five areas in particular should merit our concern.

1. Educational Capital and Underlying Goals

The history of international contact, from narratives of exploration and settlement to sophisticated trade agreements, is not rich in egalitarian, "win/win" accounts. Who gains from international virtual exchange? The history of service-learning shows a gradual evolution from an implicit emphasis on *noblesse oblige* to programs in which the "service" involves a more equal partnership between people who bring different talents, resources, and understandings together, eschewing a deficit model of the so-called clients of service (see Pearl; Scheibel, Bowley, and Jones). Similarly, work in cross-cultural exchange shows a theoretical movement away from a "foreign-cultural approach" in the 1980s, where the focus was on the "target country culture" without reference to the home culture or the relations between the two. In contrast, the more recent inter- and multicultural approach encourages an exploration of dominance, intercultural attitudes leading to the exchange of ideas, information, and interpersonal actions between persons of different groups or nations—a kind of dialectic (Risager). This dialectic includes, according to Kramsch, systematic reflection on both cultures that establishes a "sphere of interculturality" involving "commuting between worlds." Kramsch asks how learning about a culture can "become a process of cross-cultural education, which requires a Janus-faced perception of both the learner's own cultural context and the one being learned about"—in our case through telecultural connection. Such questions go to the heart of the social and educational goals behind intercultural partnerships, and the potential for disproportionate, misaligned, or too overly controlled outcomes and benefits to each partner.

Like all educational development, interest in the internationalization of composition emerges from ideologies of education and its perceived goals, both pragmatic and abstract. For example, one program might wish to foster greater global understandings in the wake of a particular international conflict, a second might be designed to support a "sustainable future" for the world by focusing on global problems of environmental degradation, social injustice, and social inequities, and a third could aim to "promote a western model of consumer/producer culture and supply the human cultural capital needed in a rapidly evolving global economy" (Farrell and Pappagianis 3). A critique of specific intercultural writing projects must begin with an understanding of their overt purposes and challenge them to consider the positions in which they place all participants as well as the consequences (local and global) of the exchange.

2. Social and Cultural Implications

What are the educational, social, and interpersonal consequences of virtually interacting with members of different cultures? Even technologies that allow online multimedia interaction and the sharing of text, photos, and video cannot entirely erase the effects of spatial dislocation, in spite of some degree of shared digital experience. If Zemelman and Daniels are correct in their hypothesis that "what students learn about writing depends more than anything else on the context in which they write"—that the "social context is the driving force behind literacy acquisition" (50)—then we must ask what sort of social context students are in when they experience difference virtually. Do students gain any greater cross-cultural understanding, empathy, and awareness of the kind that have been strongly documented in study-abroad programs[1] and touted as a rationale for increasing international focus in composition (Schaub)? Although digitally connected intercultural writing projects do not have the same goals, structures, or educational purposes as study-abroad programs, we have yet to fully research the possible gains (or losses) in intercultural understanding as a result of virtual interaction. And in some cases, as documented by Gillespie in her analysis of a collaborative online experiment between writing tutors in the United States and Germany, the lack of physical contact in electronic writing-related intercultural projects can lead to misunderstandings and frustration, us-and-them mentality arising from group solidarity in each physical setting, and even retrenchments in values or the reification of existing stereotypes.

In addition, the very electronic media that enable the cross-cultural communication often boasted in descriptions of digitally-enabled border crossings conceal, by the selectivity of users and their access to technology, some of each culture's realities, including social and economic inequities. This problem has its genesis in the material conditions of the conversants and in their selection and representation of information from their cultures. A wealthy Jamaican student, writing from his high-end computer in an elegant home on a hilltop above Kingston, may represent the issues facing his community and "Jamaican values" in ways that provide his e-pal in Anchorage, Alaska, with a distorted picture of his home country. The Alaskan, in turn, may ignore or misrepresent the history and current status of indigenous people in remote areas of her state or offer a rosy view of the future of oil drilling in the Alaska National Wildlife Refuge that falsely represents an American consensus on crucial environmental questions.

Without sufficient oversight of such international partnerships, such as preparing students to be thoroughly inquisitive and to use independent research to drive some of their interactions, these conversations may fail to realize the goals of cross-cultural awareness compared to being *in* the culture and at least vicariously experiencing more diverse perspectives. Disparities in students' existing views of each other's cultures, as well as existing national power dynamics, can also reinforce stereotypes and misunderstandings, subverting the goals of border crossing (such as when a student in Ghana learns nothing about the plight of immigrants and refugees in the United States from her American e-pal, who only strengthens the Ghanan student's milk-and-honey construction of a country that, like hers, faces important social, environmental, and political problems). Identity formation in digitally-enabled border crossing is also affected by what Hawisher and Selfe call the "conflicting forces growing out of the simultaneous move toward the global networked society and the need to stay rooted in particular cultures" (286). Such forces are illustrated in some cultures' valuing English over their own languages as the medium of interaction or Web searching while simultaneously worrying about the consequences of these choices to their own cultural identity or polylingualism. Chapters in Hawisher and Selfe's collection, each focusing on global literacies from the perspective of a specific culture, "indicate that individuals who use the Web are multiply defined (287)," or, as Castells puts it, their ethnic roots become "twisted, divided, reprocessed, mixed, differentially stigmatized or rewarded, according to a new logic of informationalization/globalization of cultures and economies that makes symbolic composites out of blurred identities" (59; qtd. in Hawisher and Selfe 287). As Lam points out, "rather than signifying Englishness, Americanness, or other exclusive cultural ideologies, the [English] language may well be used to represent Japanese popular culture or diasporic Chinese relations" (478). How students form and reform identities while interacting with each other with the added complexities of linked educational contexts (rather than self-sponsored social networking), and what these interactions yield to their learning, are yet to be extensively studied.

3. Discourse and Power

Plentiful research exists on the discursive practices and features of different cultures in composition (see, for example, Panetta). But Internet communication, with its multimodal features, its use of local and global communicative devices and Internet dialects, creates many new genres and socially constructed forms and conventions. It has been suggested that users of the Internet become acculturated to its norms and to a style of presentation of self and discourse that is still American and predominantly male (Payne, "English"; Spender)—that the "globalized, Western accent of the Internet requires cultural outsiders to online communities of practice to make non-trivial shifts in mindsets and identity"

(Chandler, Burnett, and Lopez).

A fruitful area for investigation arises from the question of whether the increasing international presence encouraged by cross-country and cross-cultural educational links will lessen or strengthen what's been described as "American cultural imperialism and the dominance of English" (Mason). Citing the work of Douglas Kellner, Darin Payne has questioned whether online exchange leads to "globalization from below"—the contestation and reconfiguration of ideology and power by those oppressed by dominant capitalist forces—or "globalization from above," the routine imposition of ideology, material culture, and sociopolitical identification that are the necessary grounds for the growth of global capitalism (Payne, "World"). A similar tension arises from "fast capitalism's" drive toward the normative versions of worldwide English and a desire among many language learners, especially outside the realm of schooling, to accept the "dissonances between and across standardized and peripheralized languages, englishes, and discourses" (Lu 45). This tension between linguistic normativity and multiply configured Englishes—what Skutnabb-Kangas, extending the work of Tsuda, calls the "diffusion of English" and "ecology of language" paradigms—has been well documented in Canagarajah's study of linguistic imperialism in Sri Lanka. There, "the maintenance of polyvocality with a clear awareness of [periphery subjects'] own socio-ideological location empowers them to withstand the totalitarian tendencies—of local nationalist regimes and Western multinational agencies—enforced through uniformity of thought and communication" (197; see also Phillipson). These and other issues concerning localized and nationalized versions of English call for a critical assessment of how students' chosen target language may diverge from the standard language in the English classroom and how their choice of target is simultaneously an act of investment and desire and a reaction to their marginal position in the English-speaking classroom and society (Ibrahim and Penfield; Prendergast).

4. Language Threat

Related to these questions of discursive and linguistic norming is a possible causal relationship between globalization of the Internet and the continued threat to hundreds of lesser-used languages around the world—or, more directly put, that "the English-dominated Internet [could] spell the death of other tongues" (Crystal, 1). Although indigenous people make up just 4% of the world's population, they speak a staggering 60% of the world's 6,000 languages (Romaine). Just as technology enables the storage, teaching, and dissemination of languages, it also *favors* certain languages (and even typography) over others in intercultural communication. And just as international educational collaboration can hardly be responsible for the death of a remote language in a community with no writing system or even consistent electricity to power a PC (if one were available), making computers available to such a community without considering the language(s) of the Internet may create new incentives for indigenous people to allow their languages to be subjugated and threatened. The "One Laptop Per Child" (OLPC) program, for example, is designed to "create educational opportunities for the world's poorest children by providing each child with a rugged, low-cost, low-power, connected laptop with content and software designed for collaborative, joyful, self-empowered learning." In areas without adequate electricity, the laptops can be solar-powered or powered by a crank, pedal, or pull-cord. While this project has laudable, worldwide educational goals, the capabilities of networked computers and their heavily market-laden content to "norm" the desires and aspirations of a culture must be considered alongside the linguistic code in which such massification occurs. In the educational contexts that are the focus here, we need to research the effects of globalized writing links and writing instruction on the relationship between dominant and shrinking languages. What class in the United States would be able to connect with students on the Independent Samoan island of Manono (where an American team recently installed a receiver to bring Internet connectivity to a small school there; see Wenmoth) in anything other than English, in spite of recent attempts to reestablish the Samoan language even on American Samoa (see Manase, Luaao, and Fiamalua)? To such a community, the message is clear: Interact in English or lose the opportunity of global partnerships.

The increasing popularity of digital exchanges also masks some of the disparities in who is linked to whom based on language preference. As Al-Jarf points out, only a few online forums currently involve Saudi students. Several English-language exchanges exist, including the 2,500-member Online Writing Collaboration Project developed at Indiana University of Pennsylvania by a Saudi graduate student in 2000, which links Saudi students to English-language speakers in different parts of the word (Al-Jarf, "Intercultural"). However, there exists only one online forum that links Saudi students to those who speak other languages (Al-Jarf "Using"). With increased digital access, some of these disparities are bound to disappear, but other factors, including geopolitical issues, may also perpetuate them (for one account, see Pandley). As Phillipson points out, the forces and resources behind the "diffusion of English" paradigm are massive. "Those who believe that all languages have value, and that use of one's mother tongue is a human right, need to be much more active in counteracting linguistic and professional imperialism, and creating favourable conditions for a viable, just Ecology of Languages" (197).

5. Labor Practices

The globalizing potential of technology also brings with it issues of labor in the realm of teaching and educational services. Large numbers of Internet collaborations, initiated first only for their educational benefits and created largely without remuneration, are paving the way for market-driven, profit-making services that take educational control and quality from the hands of educators and scholars of literacy and add to the pool of "disposable teachers" (Bousquet, Scott, and Parascondola). Outsourcing some aspects of writing instruction has already attracted the attention of educators and administrators in the United States. For example, over 1,000 institutions in the United States and abroad are utilizing an outside (for-profit) company, SmartThinking.com, for services such as grading essays from writing courses (SmartThinking.com; see also Jaschik). The company bills itself as "online tutoring and writing services that help students succeed." As such services become increasingly internationalized, they are providing certain advantages for rapidly developing, technologically entrepreneurial nations such as India and Malaysia. But a shadow falls on such a scenario when we consider how advantaged nations like the United States might further their own educational status and services through the exploitation of cheap overseas workers in the way that many U.S.-based companies now hire phone and Internet consultants in other countries to handle billing issues, provide advice about products, or offer troubleshooting services around the clock. By one estimate, the number of essays written by American students and sent to India for grading increased from 10,000 in 2008 to 30,000 in 2009 (Pathak). Already the exploited handservant of the academy, composition instruction could play a role in the proliferation of international academic sweat-shops which would make the typical American non-tenure-track writing position—with its substandard wages and lack of health and retirement benefits—look like a dream job. As Ohmann has warned, "the computer revolution . . . will indeed expand the minds and the freedom of the elite, meanwhile facilitating the degradation of labor and the stratification of the workforce that have been the hallmarks of monopoly capitalism from its onset" (683).

The history of composition is not a chronicle rich in international collaboration beyond a few important projects such as the International Association for the Evaluation of Educational Achievement's study of writing in over a dozen countries (Gorman, Purves, and Degenhart; Purves). But recent international activities, partnerships, conferences, and other exchanges hold promise for a new era in the study of academic writing, the exchange of instructional practices, and the partnering of classrooms for various writing-related purposes. We have only just begun a conversation on the internationalism of writing pedagogy from a scholarly perspective, founded on the principles of what Donahue calls "equal trade models of exchange" (231) and accompanied by continuous reflection on who benefits and who may be exploited by this work (Anson, "Take"). Among those areas urgently in need of such study is the use of technology to link writing students in different parts of the world. Without question, such technological uses bring with them the excitement of novel and theoretically principled initiatives. At the same time, they open doors to new forms of cultural dominance, control, and exploitation. The teaching of writing relative to the rapid expansion of English as a lingua franca must not fall prey to notions of the global, international, or world presence of English as "essentially a victory of what is perceived as a monocultural Western medium . . . [and] the English-using West's weapon in the clash of civilizations" (Kachru 447). As composition scholars and teachers worldwide, we must not let those doors go unguarded.

Note

1. For example, a major survey by IES Abroad, involving 3,400 respondents who engaged in study abroad between 1950 and 1999, found extraordinarily strong results documenting the major, lasting impact of the experience on self-confidence, increased maturity, and a changed worldview, including understanding one's own culture, seeking out more diverse friends, and interacting more positively with people from different cultures. These results also correlated with the amount of time spent abroad.

Works Cited

Achieve, Inc. and the National Governors Association. *America's High Schools: The Front Line in the Battle for our Economic Future.* Washington, D.C., 2005.

Al-Jarf, Reima. "Using Online Dialogue to Develop Cross-Cultural Understanding." *Iranian Journal of Linguistic Studies* 1 (2007): 15-28.

————. "Intercultural Communication: Saudi, Ukrainian and Russian Students Online." 37th National Educational Computing Conference (NECC). New Orleans, Louisiana. 22 June 2004.

Anson, Chris M. "Take Nothing for Granted: How International Collaborations Pressure Established Ideologies of Literacy Education and Research." Paper Presented at the Conference on College Composition and Communication. New Orleans, LA. 3 Apr. 2008.

————. "On Reflection: The Role of Journals and Logs in Service-Learning Courses." *Composition, Community, and the Academy: Theory and Practice.* Ed. Linda Adler-Kassner, Robert Crooks, and Ann Watters. Washington, D.C.: American Association for Higher Education, 1998. 167-80.

Berlin, James. "Composition Studies and Cultural Studies: Collapsing Boundaries." *Into the Field: Sites of Composition Studies.* Ed. Anne Ruggles Gere. New York: Modern Language Association, 1993.

Bousquet, Marc, Tony Scott, and Leo Parascondola, eds. *Tenured Bosses and Disposable Teachers: Writing Instruction in the Managed University.* Carbondale: Southern Illinois UP, 2004.

Brobman, Laurie. "Beyond Internationalization: Multicultural Education in the Professional Writing Contact Zone." *Journal of Business and Technical Communication* 13,4 (1999): 427-48.

Canagarajah, A. Suresh. *Resisting Linguistic Imperialism in English Teaching.* Oxford UP, 1999.

Castells, Manuel. *The Power of Identity.* Malden, MA: Blackwell, 1997.

Chandler, Sally W., Joshua Burnett, and Jacklyn Lopez. "On the Bright Side of the Screen: Material-World Interactions Surrounding the Socialization of Outsiders to Digital Spaces." *Computers and Composition* 24,3 (2007): 346-64.

Colbert, P. J. "A Thematic Approach to Internationalizing English II." Marshalltown   Community   College. <http://puma.kvcc.edu/midwest/modules/writing/WRI020PC.htm>.

CompFAQ,   International   Writing   Studies   Wiki. <http://comppile.tamucc.edu/wiki/CompFAQsInternational/Home>.

Crystal, David. *Language and the Internet.* Cambridge: Cambridge UP, 2001.

Donahue, Christiane. "Internationalization and Composition Studies: Reorienting the Discourse." *College Composition and Communication* 61,2 (2009):

212-43.

Eastern Carolina University, Global Studies Course. <http://www.ecu.edu/cs-acad/globalinitiatives/course.cfm>.

Emery, Katherine A. "Online Mentoring: A Review of Literature and Programs." *Friends for Youth Mentoring Services*, 1999. <http://www.homestead.com/prosites-ffy/files/onlinementoring.htm>.

ePals Global Community. <http://www.epals.com>.

Farrell, R. V., and George Pappagianis. "Education, Globalization, and Sustainable Futures: Struggles over Educational Aims and Purposes in a Period of Environmental and Ecological Challenge." Annual Meeting of the Comparative and International Education Society, Orlando, FL. 7 Mar. 2002. ERIC Document Reproduction Service No. ED470963.

Friedman, Audrie, Melanie Zibit, and Meca Coote. "Telementoring as a Collaborative Agent for Change." *Journal of Technology, Learning, and Assessment* 3,1 (2004): 3-41.

Fulkerson, Richard. "Composition at the End of the Twenty-First Century." *College Composition and Communication* 56,4 (2005): 654-87.

George, Diana, and John Trimbur. "Cultural Studies and Composition." *A Guide to Composition Pedagogies*. Ed. Gary Tate, Amy Rupiper, and Kurt Schick. New York: Oxford UP, 2001. 71-91.

Gillespie, Paula. "Writing across Borders." International Writing Centers Association Conference, Minneapolis, MN. 20 Oct. 2005.

Gorman, T. P., Alan Purves, and R. E. Degenhart. *The IEA Study of Written Composition I: The International Writing Tasks and Scoring Scales.* Oxford: Pergamon Press, 1988.

Grobman, Laurie. "'Just Multiculturalism': Teaching Writing as Critical and Ethical Practice." *Journal of Advanced Composition* 22 (2002): 815–45.

Harman, Danna. "American Education Thriving . . . in Qatar." *Christian Science Monitor,* Feb. 22, 2007. <http://www.csmonitor.com/2007/0222/p01s02-wome.html>.

Hawisher, Gail E., and Cynthia L. Selfe. "Conclusion: Inventing Postmodern Identities: Hybrid and Transgressive Literacy Practices on the Web." *Global Literacies and the World-Wide Web*. Ed. Gail E. Hawisher and Cynthia E. Selfe. New York: Routledge, 2000. 277-89.

Herrington, TyAnna. "Where in the World Is the Global Classroom Project?" *If Classrooms Matter: Progressive Visions of Educational Environments*. Ed. Jeffrey Di Leo and Walter Jacobs. New York: Routledge, 2004.

————. "The Gobal Classroom Project: Syllabus." Georgia Technological Institute. <http://www.lcc.gatech.edu/~herrington/classes/gcpf06/index.html>.

Ibrahim, Nizar, and Susan Penfield. "Dynamic Diversity: New Dimensions in Mixed Composition Classes." *ELT Journal* 59 (2005): 217-25.

IECC Home Page. <http://www.iecc.org>.

IES Abroad. "Benefits of Studying Abroad."
     <https://www.iesabroad.org/IES/Students/alumniSurveyResultsStudents.ht
     ml>.
Iowa State University, Department of English. "Special First-Year Composition
     Courses." <http://engl.iastate.edu/resources/fc/special-isucomm-foundation-
     courses>.
ITP: International Telementor Program. <http://www.telementor.org>.
Jamieson, Sandra. "Composition Readers and the Construction of Identity."
     Writing in Multicultural Settings. Ed. Carol Severino, Juan C. Guerra, and
     Johnnella E. Butler. New York: MLA, 1997. 150-71.
Jaschik, Scott. "Outsourced Grading." *Inside Higher Ed,* 22 Sept. 2005.
     <http://insidehighered.com/news/2005/09/22/outsource>.
Jordan, Jay. "Rereading the Multicultural Reader: Toward More 'Infectious'
     Practices in Multicultural Composition." *College English* 68,2 (2005): 168-
     85.
Kachru, Braj B. "World Englishes and Culture Wars." *The Handbook of World
     Englishes*. Ed. Braj B. Kachru, Yamuna Kachru, and Cecil L. Nelson.
     Malden, MA: Wiley-Blackwell, 2009. 446-71.
Kalantzis, Mary, and Bill Cope. "On Globalisation and Diversity." *Computers
     and Composition* 23,4 (2006): 402-11.
Kellner, Douglas. "Theorizing Globalization." *Sociological Theory* 20,3 (2002):
     285-305.   Available   online   at
     <http://www.gseis.ucla.edu/faculty/kellner/essays.html>.
Kern, Richard, Paige Ware, and Mark Warschauer. "Crossing Frontiers: New
     Directions in Online Pedagogy and Research." *Annual Review of Applied
     Linguistics* 24 (2004): 243-60.
Kluver, Randy. "Globalization, Informatization, and Intercultural Communica-
     tion." *American Communication Journal* 13,3 (2000). Available online at
     <http://acjournal.org/holdings/vol3/Iss3/spec1/kluver.htm>.
Kramsch, Claire. *Context and Culture in Language Teaching*. New York: Ox-
     ford UP, 1993.
Lam, Wan Shun Eva. "A Case Study of a Teenager Writing on the Internet."
     TESOL Quarterly 34,3 (2000): 457-82.
Levin, James, and Michael Waugh. "Teaching Teleapprenticeships: Electronic
     Network-Based Educational Frameworks for Improving Teacher Educa-
     tion." *Interactive Learning Environments* 6,2 (1998): 39-58.
Lewis, Chance W. "Telementoring: A Teacher's Perspective of the Effective-
     ness of the International Telementor Program." *Journal of Interactive
     Online   Learning   1,1   (2002).
     <http://www.ncolr.org/jiol/issues/getfile.cfm?volID=1&IssueID=2&Article
     ID=67>.
Lu, Min-Zhan. "An Essay on the Work of Composition: Composing English
     against the Order of Fast Capitalism." *College Composition and Communi-*

cation 56,1 (2004): 16-50.

Mason, Robin. "Distance Education across National Borders." World Bank Global Distance Education Net. <http://www1.worldbank.org/disted/Policy/Global/coll-03.html>.

Matsuda, Paul Kei, and Tony Silva. "Cross-Cultural Composition: Mediated Integration of US and International Students." *Composition Studies* 27,1 (1999): 15-30.

Manase, Bernadette, Elisapeta Luaao, and Mataio Fiamalua. "American Samoa Language Arts and Culture Program." *Stabilizing Indigenous Languages.* Ed. Gina Cantoni. Flagstaff: Center for Excellence in Education, Northern Arizona University, 1996. <http://www.ncela.gwu.edu/pubs/stabilize/index.htm>.

Muchiri, Mary N., Nshindi G. Mulamba, Greg Myers, and Deoscorous B. Ndoloi. "Importing Composition: Teaching and Researching Academic Writing beyond North America." *College Composition and Communication* 46,2 (1995): 175-98.

Nepal Study Center. "Creating a Virtual International Environmental Research Institute: Developing Communities of Learners to Sustain Healthy Rivers." University of New Mexico. <http://nepalstudycenter.unm.edu/internationallinkages.htm>.

Ohmann, Richard. "Literacy, Technology, and Monopoly Capital." *College English* 47 (1985): 675-89.

OLPC: One Laptop Per Child Program. http://laptop.org/en/index.shtml.

Panetta, Clayann Gilliam (Ed.). *Contrastive Rhetoric Revisited and Redefined.* Mahwah, NJ: Erlbaum, 2001.

Pandley, Iswari P. "Literate Lives across the Digital Divide." *Computers and Composition* 23,2 (2006): 246-57.

Pathak, Kalpana. "Indian Professors Clear Outsourcing Test." *Business Standard,* December 11, 2009. <http://www.business-standard.com/india/news/indian-professors-clear-outsourcing-test/379226>.

Payne, Darin. "The World Wide Agora: Negotiating Citizenship and Ownership of Response Online." *Trauma and the Teaching of Writing.* Ed. Shane Borrowman. Albany: SUNY Press, 2005. 11-28.

———. "English Studies in Levittown: Rhetorics of Space and Technology in Course-Management Software." *College English* 67,5 (2005): 483-507.

Pearl, A. "Democratic Education as an Alternative to Deficit Thinking." *The Evolution of Deficit Thinking.* Ed. R. Valencia. London: Falmer Press, 1997. 160-210.

Phillipson, Robert. "English for Globalization or for the World's People?" *International Review of Education* 47.3/4 (2001): 185-200.

Pratt, Mary Louise. "Arts of the Contact Zone." *Profession* 91 (1991): 33-40.

Prendergast, Catherine. *Buying into English: Language and Investment in the New Capitalist World.* Pittsburgh: University of Pittsburgh Press, 2008.

Purves, Alan C. (Ed.). *The IEA Study of Written Composition II: Education and Performance in Fourteen Countries.* Oxford: Pergamon Press, 1992.

Qatar   Foundation.   "Education   City." <http://www.qstp.org.qa/output/page301.asp>.

Reil, Margaret. "Tele-Mentoring Over the Net: The Real Power of the Internet Is the Energy Generated by Human Interaction." *iEarn Learning Circles.* <http://www.iearn.org/circles/mentors.html>.

Risager, Karen. "Language Teaching and the Process of European Integration." *Language Learning in Intercultural Perspective.* Ed. Michael Byram and Michael Fleming. Cambridge: Cambridge UP, 1998. 242-54.

Romaine, Suzanne. *Vanishing Voices: The Extinction of the World's Languages.* Oxford: Oxford UP, 2000.

Schaub, Mark. "Beyond These Shores: An Argument for Internationalizing Composition." *Pedagogy* 3,1 (2003): 85-98.

Scheibel, Jim, Erin M. Bowley, and Steven Jones. *The Promise of Partnerships: Tapping into the College as a Community Asset.* Providence, RI: Campus Compact, 2005.

Skutnabb-Kangas, Tove. *Linguistic Genocide in Education—or Worldwide Diversity and Human Rights?* Mahwah, NJ: Erlbaum, 2000.

Smarthinking. <http://www.smarthinking.com>.

SPAN: Student Project for Amity Among Nations. Minneapolis: University of Minnesota. <http://www.umabroad.umn.edu/PROGRAMS/span/index.html>.

Spender, Dale. *Nattering on the Net: Women, Power and Cyberspace.* Toronto: Garmond, 1995.

Taylor, Nancy. "The Travel Journal: An Assessment Tool for Overseas Study." *Occasional Papers on International Educational Exchange* 27 (1991). ERIC Document Reproduction Service ED 331 046.

Tower, David. "International Module: Ourselves Among Others." Kalamazoo Valley   Community   College. <http://orgs.kvcc.edu/midwest/Modules/?MOD=English>.

Tsuda, Yukio. "The Diffusion of English: Its Impact on Culture and Communication." *Keio Communication Review* 16 (1994): 49-61.

Wenmoth, Derek. "Derek's Blog: Musings on the Use and Impact of Technology in Education, and of the Future of Education in General." <http://blog.coreed.net/derek/2006/08/bringing_remote_schools_in_sam.html>.

Womack, Mari. "The Global Classroom." *Anthropology News,* Sept. 2008. <http://www.anthrosource.net/doi/abs/10.1111/an.2008.49.6.36>.

Yorke, Mantz. "Assuring Quality and Standards in Globalised Higher Education." *Quality Assurance in Education* 7,1 (1999): 14-24.

Zegers, Vera, and Robert Wilkinson. "Squaring the Pyramid: Internationalization, Plurilingualism, and the University." Conference on Bi- and Multilingual Universities, Helskinki, Finland, 3 Sept. 2005. <http://www.palmenia.helsinki.fi/congress/bilingual2005/presentations/zege rs.pdf>.

Zemelman, Steven, and Harvey Daniels. *A Community of Writers*. Portsmouth: Heinemann-Boynton/Cook, 1988.

Index

About the Editors

Darin Payne is Associate Professor of Rhetoric and Composition at The University of Hawai'i, where he teaches graduate and undergraduate courses in writing, rhetoric, and new media. He has published in a variety of journals including *College English; JAC: A Journal of Composition Theory; Rhetoric Review; Works and Days; Kairos: A Journal of Rhetoric, Technology, and Pedagogy; The Journal of Electronic Publishing*; and *Teaching English in the Two Year College*. His work has also appeared in anthologies by Oxford UP, SUNY P, and Erlbaum. In 2005 Darin was awarded the College of Languages, Literatures, and Linguistics Excellence in Teaching Award, and in 2002 the Arts and Sciences Faculty Award. In 2009 he was a finalist for the university's Distinguished Graduate Mentoring Award. He is presently serving as the English Department's Undergraduate Program Director.

Daphne Desser is Associate Professor at the University of Hawai'i. She is currently serving as the Director of Rhetoric and Composition.

About the Contributors

Chris Anson is University Distinguished Professor of English and Director of the Campus Writing and Speaking Program at North Carolina State University, where he helps faculty in nine colleges to use writing and speaking in the service of students' learning and improved communication. A scholar of writing, language, and literacy, he has published 15 books and over 90 essays and journal articles, and he has spoken or run faculty-development workshops across the United States and in 18 other countries.

Rebecca Dingo is author of *Networking Arguments: Rhetoric, Transnational Feminism, and Public Policy* and co-editor with J. Blake Scott of *The Megarhetorics of Globalization*. She is a jointly appointed assistant professor in English and Women's and Gender Studies at the University of Missouri.

Bruce Horner, formerly a WPA at the University of Wisconsin-Milwaukee, is Endowed Chair in Rhetoric and Composition at the University of Louisville, where he teaches courses in composition, composition theory and pedagogy, and literacy studies. His recent books include *Cross-Language Relations in Composition*, co-edited with Min-Zhan Lu and Paul Kei Matsuda, and *Writing Conventions*, co-authored with Min-Zhan Lu. His recent work explores translingual approaches to writing theory and pedagogy.

Lachlan Paterson is a graduate of Te Tumu, the University of Otāgo's School of Māori, Pacific, and Indigenous Studies. In 2006 he published *Colonial Discourses: Niupepa Māori 1855-1863*, which explored the messages disseminated in mid-nineteenth century Māori-language newspapers. After several years at Massey University, Lachy returned to Te Tumu, where he teaches both Māori history and Māori language. He is currently investigating the lives and interactions of twentieth-century women missionaries of the Presbyterian Māori Mission.

Eileen Schell is Associate Professor of Writing and Rhetoric and Chair and Director of the Writing Program at Syracuse University. She is the author of *Gypsy Academics and Mother-teachers: Gender, Contingent Labor, and Writing Instruction* (Heinemann, 1997) and co-author of *Rural Literacies* (SIUP, 2007) with Kim Donehower and Charlotte Hogg. Her recent co-edited collection is *Rhetorica in Motion: Feminist Rhetorical Methods and Methodologies* (Pittsburgh, 2010). Schell teaches undergraduate and graduate courses in writing and rhetoric and leads community writing groups for military veterans and senior citizens.

Sharon McKenzie Stevens is an independent scholar living in Ashhurst, New Zealand. She is a two-time teaching award recipient; author of *A Place for Dialogue: Language, Land Use, and Politics in Southern Arizona* (University of Iowa Press 2007); and co-editor of *Active Voices: Composing a Rhetoric of Social Movements* (SUNY Press 2009). She is also founding chairperson of RECAP: The Society for Resilience and Engagement of the Community of Ashhurst and Pohangina, Inc., a Transition Town organization active in Ashhurst and the Pohangina Valley region. Nāu te rourou, nāku te rourou, ka ora te manuwhiri.

Donna Strickland is the author of *The Managerial Unconscious in the History of Composition Studies*. She directs the Composition Program at the University of Missouri, where she is Associate Professor of English.

L. Hill Taylor, Jr. teaches in the first-year writing program at North Carolina State University and also holds an adjunct appointment at Duke University. Dr. Taylor's writing has included analyses related to rhetorical strategies used by Latino/a, Indian, African, and African-American students to make meaning and create space in "real" and virtual environments and the construction of composition theory based on diverse and globalized positionalities. His current book project focuses on "bright green" environmental discourses and indigenous environmental knowledge.